Complete Spiritual Doctrine
of
ST. THERESE OF LISIEUX

Complete Spiritual Doctrine
of
St. Therese of Lisieux

By REV. FRANCOIS JAMART, O. C. D.

Translated by

REV. WALTER VAN DE PUTTE, C. S. SP.

ALBA · HOUSE   NEW · YORK

'SOCIETY OF ST. PAUL, 2187 VICTORY BLVD., STATEN ISLAND, NEW YORK 10314

NIHIL OBSTAT
Very Rev. Gall Higgins, O.F.M., Cap.
Censor Librorum

IMPRIMATUR
✠Francis Cardinal Spellman
Achbishop of New York

June 5, 1961

First printing 1961
Second Printing 1963
Third Printing 1977

Library of Congress Catalog Card Number 61-8203
ISBN: 0-8189-0347-3

Contents

Introduction

MUCH has been written about St. Therese of Lisieux. This is not surprising when we consider the mission she received from God and the importance of her message. The Sovereign Pontiffs themselves have taken delight in emphasizing the value of her teaching.

Pius XI called Therese "a word of God," a "master of the spiritual life" sent by God to point out to us "a sure way of salvation," an "easy way to bring us to perfection and the fullness of love." Completing the judgments of his predecessors, Pius XII declared that "this Way, conceived under the inspiration of the Holy Ghost, is suitable for learned men, for those who, like the apostles, are responsible for souls, as well as for the lowly and the unlearned."

It has been said truthfully that "since the first Pentecost there has never been seen in the Church such a ratification of one person and of that person's ideas." (Father Combes).

Therese's message consisted in recalling that God is merciful Love, a love that stoops down in order to draw us to Himself. "The proper characteristic of love," she wrote, "is that it stoops down . . . it must stoop down even to nothingness and transform that nothingness into fire." [1] It was Therese's mission to teach us "a way of confidence and love," a little way very short and direct leading us to love God as Therese loved Him.[2] She called this "the way of spiritual childhood." [3] Some have held the opinion that Therese's mission was rather that of calling back sinners to God's merciful Love. To prove it they have quoted words which express her ardent desire for the salvation of sinners. Most certainly she showed deep compassion for sinners. She tells us that from

Christmas, 1880, God made her a "fisher of souls." Again, in 1887, moved by the sight of the divine Crucified and the blood flowing from His pierced hands, she resolved to remain at the foot of the Cross, to catch His Blood and pour it over souls.[4] Ten years later she declared that she wanted to sit "at the table of sinners and eat with them the bread of sorrow." [5] She even offered to suffer in order to obtain the grace of faith for unbelievers. The cruel sufferings that marked the end of her life seem to indicate that God had accepted that offering.[6] This apostolate she desired to continue after her death, even promising that, in heaven, "she would not rest as long as there were souls to be saved." [7]

Nevertheless, however much Therese was devoted to sinners, her zeal was not principally directed to them. This we learn from what she said after she had resolved to stand by the Cross that she might distribute the redemptive Blood of the Savior: "At that time, I was not yet drawn by the souls of priests." [8] She had not yet understood her vocation as a Carmelite; but this was revealed to her during her trip to Italy; [9] and, once in Carmel, she learned that the special object of the Reformed Order of St. Teresa of Avila was to pray for priests. In fact, when she was interrogated prior to her profession, and asked her reason for entering Carmel, she replied: "I have come to save souls and especially to pray for priests." [10] This resolution she later confirmed several times. "Our mission as Carmelites," she wrote, "consists in forming workers who will save millions of souls; we shall be their mothers." [11] "What a beautiful vocation is ours, to preserve the salt by which souls are preserved. This is the vocation of Carmel, since the unique end of our prayers and sacrifices is to become the apostle of apostles, praying for them." [12] This vocation she was to continue to fulfill in heaven, "helping priests and missionaries." [13]

Those words show us her zeal for the salvation of sinners, her interest in the sanctification of priests; they do not reveal the full meaning of her mission. This mission was not confined to those two categories of persons. It was as Catholic and universal as the Church, extending to all souls. Our Saint made this known in terms that leave no doubt on the subject.

Speaking to Mother Agnes, two months before her death, she said: "I feel that my mission is just beginning, my mission of making others love the good Lord as I love Him and giving to souls my Little Way." And when Mother Agnes asked her to explain, she added: "It is the Way of Spiritual Childhood," "the Way of confidence and total abandonment to God." [14]

It was in order to secure the continuance of that mission that she asked that her written notes or manuscript should be published for "this will do much good and souls will come to realize that everything comes from the good Lord." [15] She guaranteed that it expressed the truth and she even promised that she would return after her death to warn us "if she had misled us by (teaching us) her Little Way."

According to the testimony of her own sisters and her fellow religious: "Therese's message consists essentially in the Way of Childhood." This is affirmed by Mother Agnes who, according to Therese, knew her thoughts intimately; by Sister Genevieve, "her other self" and by the other Carmelites of her convent.

This was also the judgment of Benedict XV, Pius XI and Pius XII. On the various occasions on which these Supreme Pontiffs proposed Saint Therese of the Child Jesus as a model for our imitation, they recommended that we should follow "the Way of Spiritual Childhood."

This same point is emphasized in a letter which Msgr. dell'Acqua wrote to Father François de Sainte Marie when the latter presented to the Holy Father the autobiographical manuscript of the Saint: "The Holy Father," he writes, "hopes that your work will give a more accurate and deeper knowledge of the Way of Spiritual Childhood which it was St.

Therese's mission to recall to us." Father Combes rightly declared that "all are agreed that the Little Way constitutes the essence of her doctrine and message;" "Therese perceived that doctrine with the certainty of a divine revelation."

It is our privilege to deliver that message of her "Little Way" in the present work. We have made extensive use of exact quotations because every word of our Saint sheds new light on her message and brings out a fresh nuance of her thought. Readers, we feel sure, desire to know the *complete* thought of this modern Saint who wrote *for moderns*.

Therese is known as "the Little Flower" and some associate her with roses without thorns. She herself wished men to know how much she suffered in her life. Hence, we include a chapter on that subject. The quotations cited in the present work have been taken from the authentic manuscripts of the Saint.

We are grateful to the Carmelite nuns of Lisieux for their kind assurance that our work "represents the pure doctrine of Therese—without any deviation."

Acknowledgment

The translator is deeply grateful to the many who have assisted him in his work. He is especially indebted to Professor Patrick Flood who, from the very beginning, acted as an ever stimulating goad; to Father Herbert Farrell, C.S.Sp. for his advice; to Sr. M. St. Bernard of Maryknoll, to Mother Marie Therese of Jesus Crucified, O.C.D. and Mrs. Antoinette de B. Edrop, for their careful corrections and excellent suggestions; to Miss Margaret O'Rourke for her charitable assistance in typing the copy for the printer; to the Society of St. Paul, to whose geneorsity we owe the printing of this translation.

This has been a labor of love on the part of zealous lay

apostles and representatives of various Orders and Congregations. May this "summa" of Christian spirituality inspire many readers with the ardent desire for a life that is guided by its principles.

Duquesne University   WALTER VAN DE PUTTE, C.S.SP.

CHAPTER I

Spiritual Childhood: The Way of Holiness

THE message of Jesus to the world, the "good news" brought by the Gospel, is the revelation of God's ineffable love for man.

It is not true that the Old Testament took no cognizance of this love, but it is true that this love does not shine forth there as it does in the New. That is why the Evangelists and the Apostles in their Letters, being unaccustomed to conceive God as so loving, speak about it with such admiration. St. John even designates love as being the proper characteristic of God: "God *IS CHARITY.*" (I John, 4:16).

This love of God for man is manifested above all in the Incarnation: "God so loved the world that He gave us His only-begotten Son." (John, 3:16). Not only did He give Him to us, but for our sake He delivered Him to a cruel Passion and to the death of a criminal on a Cross. St. John and St. Paul repeatedly echo Christ's words in their Epistles: "In this is the love (of God) . . . that He sent His Son a propitiation for our sins." (I John, 4:10). "Christ loved me," says St. Paul, "and died for us when we were sinners." (Eph., 5:2; Rom., 4:8).

Christ's death was destined to reconcile us with God and to make us recover the divine life we had lost. The Father, by sacrificing His Son, wished to make Him the Head of a Mystical Body of which we were to be members. Having become our Head, Jesus would infuse His life in us in order that, living in Him and through Him, we might be henceforth children of

God. This, of course, meant adopted, but nonetheless true children of God, animated by the Spirit of Christ with a truly filial piety towards our heavenly Father. "Behold," exclaims St. John, "what manner of love the Father has bestowed upon us, that we should be called children of God and *SUCH WE ARE.*" (I John, 3:1).

Further, in order to maintain and nourish the supernatural life in us; in order to unite us to Himself and transform us into true members of His Mystical Body, our Lord, on the eve of His death, gave us His body and blood as our food, under the sacramental species of bread and wine. Love could do no more. Now, such a charity demands that we love God with a boundless love.

God is our Creator; from Him we receive our nature and for Him alone we are made; hence we should love Him with all the powers of our being. But we also become God's children, engendered by Him through grace. Because of that adoption we should love Him all the more. As children of God, living by the life of Christ, animated by His love, we must love God as Christ loves His Father. Love that does not reproduce the sentiments of Jesus is not worthy of God.

But in order to love after the manner of Christ, it is not enough to love God alone, even though our heart be given totally to Him; we must also love our neighbor. The love of God is perfect only when it extends to all who are loved by God, to all who are His children. Our love for Christ is true only when it embraces all those who are incorporated in Him. Jesus has given His love to us and He wants us to love our brethren as He has loved us. This is His new commandment, that is like the first, and without which we cannot be united either to Him or to the Father.

We see then that the whole law can be reduced to *CHARITY*: "Love is the fullness of the law." Unfortunately, our self-love which seeks to satisfy itself in all things, prevents us from loving God and our neighbor with all the devotion that is their due. That is why Jesus demanded of all who came to Him that they should "deny themselves"; why He declared that in order to walk after Him and go to the Father, it is necessary to humble our pride and become once more like little children. The whole of the spiritual life is thus reduced to two elements: love of God and detachment from ourselves.

In order to be a saint, it is then necessary to forget ourselves, to love God with our whole soul and to love our neighbor for His sake. Animated by faith and love, we must cling to Christ and endeavor to reproduce His life in our own. He who imitates Christ necessarily renounces himself and strips himself of inordinate self-love.

The spirituality of the early Christians was inspired by those principles. They approached God in all simplicity by remaining united to Christ. They avoided everything that might impede that union or distract them from Jesus. They trained their minds and hearts after the model of the divine Master: "Let this mind be in you which was also in Christ Jesus." (Philip., 2:5).

PRIMITIVE SPIRITUALITY GRADUALLY BECAME MORE COMPLEX

At a later time it was judged that this goal would be more easily attained with the help of spiritual treatises. Methods of prayer were developed and spiritual formation was synthesized as a means of helping those who could not receive personal guidance. This was very useful but, as a result of it, there developed a multiplicity of ascetical rules and practices which tended to obscure the heart of the matter: that interior disposition of confident love for God, which should be the basis of our relations with Him.

People got the impression that a complex and rigorous course of asceticism was necessary for any one who aimed at perfection. The example of many saints seemed to confirm them in this erroneous view. Most saints had indeed lived a life full of austerity and hard penances, macerations of all sorts, vigils, humiliations, the contempt of men, etc. Holiness thus came to be looked upon as the portion of a few privileged souls. Again, those penitential saints were often favored by extraordinary graces: visions, revelations, miracles, prophecies. . . . Those facts seemed to put the pursuit of sanctity beyond the reach of the ordinary man.

THERESE'S MESSAGE

But now, in our own day, there appeared a Carmelite nun, who was young in years and apparently had no authority to speak, and yet she insisted on teaching "a Little Way very straight and short, a Little Way entirely new" which would lead men to perfection. Whereas others had declared that sanctity was something that was hard to attain, she said that it is easy. She maintained that in order to reach it, it was not necessary to engage in manifold practices, to perform rigorous penances, to receive extraordinary graces. What was needed was simply that we acknowledge our "nothingness" and approach God with love and confidence. "Sanctity," she proclaimed, "is an interior disposition which makes us humble and little in God's arms, conscious of our weakness and trusting even to audacity in the goodnes of our Father." [1] She was thus inviting a return to evangelical simplicity.

In view of the wrong notions that had previously been held, it was not surprising that this doctrine of Therese would arouse suspicion. What authority had this nun who had died after only a few years spent in a monastery? Was her teaching to be accepted in preference to that of the masters in the spiritual life and learned theologians? But there were others who, carefully examining Therese's words, recognized in them an echo of the Gospel and of the voice of God.

Opposition to her teaching soon died away. The Little Way to sanctity gained the approval of the highest authorities in the spiritual life and was confirmed by the teaching of the Church. Then there broke out a "hurricane of glory," issuing from the highest teaching authority of the Church, and it became clear to the world that this Saint had indeed sent forth to men a new heavenly message, "omen novum" to use the words of Pius XI (May 18, 1925).

HISTORY OF THIS MESSAGE

Therese's message became public property with the appearance of her autobiography, *The Story of a Soul.*

At first Therese had not thought of putting her own story into writing. It was her sister Marie who asked the Prioress, Mother Agnes, to have Therese write her memories of childhood and youth. This was done and thus were written the first eight chapters of what is now called *The Story of a Soul.* Begun in the early part of 1895, they were given to Mother Agnes, January 20, 1896.

Later on, Sr. Marie asked Therese to confide to her "the thoughts of her heart" and what she called her "little doctrine." The result is now incorporated in Chapter XI of that same *Story.* These pages were written between the 13th and 16th of September, 1896. They are rightly dated as of the 8th of this month because it was during her retreat in preparation for the anniversary of her profession (which she had made on September 8, 1890) that our Saint received the light that clarified her doctrine.

On June 3, 1897, at the request of Mother Agnes, Mother Marie de Gonzaga ordered Therese to add the description of her religious life. The last pages of this manuscript, written between the 8th and the 10th of July, were in pencil because the Saint was no longer able to hold the pen. They are now Chapters IX and X of *The Story of a Soul.*[2]

We note the late date of these manuscripts because this adds to their value. They contain, as it were, the fruit of her mature reflections and sustained observation. For Therese was endowed with a keen and exceptionally precocious intelligence, and with a remarkable power of psychological insight and observation. She herself remarks that, as a child, without seeming to do so, she paid attention to everything that was said and done around her.[3] Later, this inclination made her observe a great number of things, led her to study others and gain a deep knowledge of her own mind and heart.[4]

When she was still very young, her sisters realized that she had very sound judgment. She declared, herself, that in her childhood she had appraised things in the same manner in which she judged them at a later date.[5] The trials of her early life also helped to mature her spirit.[6]

Finally, Therese drew profit from her reading and the Carmelite instruction she received during her religious life. She did not indulge in that sort of spiritual gluttony that makes some "pious" persons devour a great quantity of sweetly devotional books. Her spiritual reading list can be reduced to Holy Scripture, the Imitation of Christ, Father Surin's *Foundations of the Spiritual Life,* Father Arminjon's *The End of the Present World and the Mysteries of the Future Life,* and the works of St. Teresa of Jesus and of St. John of the Cross.

Her cheif source of enlightenment, however, was the Holy Ghost Himself. He had been her Guide from her childhood and had favored her with mystical graces at an early age. It was in truth the Holy Spirit who, through the Sacred Scriptures, revealed to her what became "Therese's doctrine"; and Jesus, speaking to her heart in mental prayer, made known to her the secrets of His love.

This Theresian doctrine developed gradually, and in the measure of its growth Therese taught it to her novices. That is why, when she was asked to write her life and describe her experiences, she had no difficulty in expressing them.

However, the three manuscripts, which are now united

in the one volume called *The Story of a Soul,* were not originally destined for the public. The first, recounting the memories of her early years was intended only for her family, and that was also the intention of her sisters. This explains the freedom and simplicity with which they are written and why they contain details that might seem childish.

The second, addressed to Sr. Marie of the Sacred Heart, was written for this Sister alone. The third was supposed to help those who would write the death notice of Therese and this was the only part that was expected to become publicly known.

However, because many souls might draw profit from Therese's doctrine, it had been considered opportune to make her writings known to a wider public.

As early as June, 1897, Mother Agnes was thinking of publishing the manuscript which describes the Saint's life. She spoke to Therese about it and the latter had no objection. She merely asked "her little Mother," as she called her, to revise it and they did so together. Finally, Therese herself very definitely desired such a publication: "The manuscript should be published without delay after my death. If you commit the imprudence of speaking of it to anyone except our Mother, the devil will set a thousand traps in order to prevent its publication, which, however, is very important." [7] God had made her understand that her doctrine was destined for all souls and that a special mission had been entrusted to her from on high. [8]

HAS THERESE'S DOCTRINE ANY AUTHORITATIVE VALUE?

Therese's own testimony. The value of her doctrine and the authenticity of her mission are vouched for by a three-fold testimony: that of the Saint herself, that of the Sovereign Pontiffs and God's own testimony.

Therese frequently testified in favor of her teaching and

her mission. A few weeks before her death, she told Mother Agnes: "This notebook (that is, her manuscript) truly mirrors my soul. Dear Mother, these pages will do much good. By them souls will know better the gentleness of the good Lord." [9] "Do you think, then, that this MS will do much good to souls?" "Yes, it will be a means of which the good Lord will make use to answer my prayers." [10] Therese felt sure that her doctrine came from God. "They will recognize," she told Mother Agnes, "that all that I have written comes from the good Lord Himself."

She announced to her novices: "If I lead you into error with my Little Way of Love, be not afraid that I shall permit you to follow it for any length of time. I would soon re-appear after my death and tell you to take another road. But if I do not return, believe me when I tell you that we never have too much confidence in the good Lord who is so powerful and merciful. We obtain from Him as much as we hope for." [12]

Therese has not returned to correct her teaching. But on the night between the 15th and 16th of January, 1910, she appeared to the Mother Prioress of the Carmel of Gallipoli and proclaimed to her: "My Way is sure!" [13] On September 25, 1897, a few days before her death, she again confirmed it to Mother Agnes: "I now feel sure that all I have said and written is true." [14]

However, her writings would not be the only means she would use to help souls. She would herself intervene directly and personally. She first announced that she would send down a shower of roses.[51] A few weeks later, being asked: "So you will look down on us from above?" she replied: "No, I will come down." [16] And almost immediately afterwards she added: "I cannot reflect much on the happiness that is in store for me. Only one expectation causes my heart to throb and that is, the love I shall receive and the love I shall give. I think of all the good that I would like to do after my death: to help priests, missionaries and the whole Church." [17]

But the fundamental text in which she most clearly and categorically expresses the role she expected to play is found in the words: "I feel that my mission is about to begin, my mission of making souls love the good Lord as I love Him, of giving my Little Way to souls! If my wishes are granted, my heaven will be spent on earth until the end of the world. Yes, I want to spend my heaven in doing good on earth.[18] I shall not be able to rest until the end of the world, and as long as there are still souls to be saved; but, when the Angel shall have said 'time is no more' then will I rest. I shall then be able to rejoice because the number of the elect will be complete and all shall have entered into joy and repose. My heart leaps with gladness at this thought." [19]

The following day, returning to the same thought, she declared: "God would not give me the desire of doing good on earth, if He did not intend to fulfill it. He would rather give me the desire of finding my repose in Him." [20] Soon after this, when someone read to her a passage that dealt with eternal beatitude, she remarked: "This is not the thing that attracts me, but love. To love, to be loved, and to return to earth to make Love loved." [21]

She frequently repeated these same thoughts, adding that she felt certain that God would grant her petition.[22] For instance, she told Mother Agnes: "I know now that all my expectations shall be fulfilled. . . . Yes, the Lord will perform marvels for me which will infinitely surpass my immense desires." [23]

Such an assurance can only have its source in God. She gave a reason which in others might be considered an impertinence: "In Heaven, the good Lord will do all that I want, because on earth I never did my own will." [24]

She had also an intuition of the affection that would be given to her personally because of her doctrine and the favors she would obtain for others: "I know very well that everyone will love me." [25] On the other hand, she knew that her mission would meet with difficulties, that the importance attached to her doctrine would invite contradictions: "But God's will shall be accomplished in spite of the jealousy of men." [26] Finally, one day when Mother Agnes seemed to grieve at the thought that she would soon be separated from her beloved Therese, the latter murmured with an indefinable smile on her lips: "After my death you will go to the mail box and there you will find consolations." And to a sister who spoke to her on the same subject, she said: "Don't worry; Mother Agnes will not have time to think of her sorrow, for, until the end of her life, she will be so busy with me that she will not be able to do all that she will be asked to do." [27]

But here is something stronger than all we have said up to now: About six weeks before her death, turning towards Mother Agnes and her sisters, Therese said: "You do know that you are taking care of a little Saint?" [28] A few days later rose petals, which she had strewn on her crucifix, having fallen on the ground, she remarked: "Gather up those petals; later on people may be glad to have them; do not lose any of them." [29]

Words like these seem contrary to the most elementary humility and can only be explained by the clear view that God gave her of her union with Him and of her own holiness. We are certain that this is so and find corroboration of it in her affirmation, a few hours before her death, that she had understood humility of heart and had never sought anything but the truth. It is perfectly clear, therefore, that she had spoken the words just quoted in the light of divine truth.[30]

"God," says St. John of the Cross, "shows to souls that have reached perfect love and are close to their entrance into the kingdom, their own beauty and the gifts and virtues the Lord has given them. Because in these souls all is changed to love and thanksgiving, without their being touched by presumption or vanity, they are free of corruptive leavening."[31]

In the discourse which Benedict XV pronounced after the

Decree on the heroicity of the virtues of Therese (August 14, 1921) he referred to the apparently proud predictions of our Saint. He confirmed that "St. Therese, who was very humble during her life, would not have been able to express herself, at the hour of her death, in terms that were seemingly contrary to humility, except under the influence of a divine inspiration . . . and God's special will to exalt the merits of spiritual childhood."

TESTIMONIES OF SUPREME PONTIFFS

Therese's providential mission has other foundations than her own intuitions. The truth of her doctrine is guaranteed by the voice of others.

The various Popes who have occupied the throne of Peter since her death have confirmed her teaching with the authority of the Vicar of Christ. First of all, they have given praise to Therese herself. Pius X proclaimed her "the greatest Saint of modern times"; Pius XI refers to her as "the beloved child of the whole world, an exquisite miniature of perfect holiness, a master of the spiritual life." [32] This great Pope even speaks of her as "the star of his pontificate."

They did more than canonize the Saint herself. They canonized her "Little Way." Benedict XV affirmed that "Therese, who was a disciple of a Religious Order in which the glory of the Doctorate adorns the weaker sex, has so much knowledge herself that she was able to point out to others the way of salvation." The same Pope saw in her doctrine "the secret of sanctity for the faithful throughout the whole world," adding: "This *Secret* must not remain hidden from anyone." It is not "reserved for innocent souls in whom evil has not destroyed the graces of childhood; it is also suitable for those who have lost their childhood innocence." [33]

Pius XI went even farther. He declared that St. Therese is

"a WORD OF GOD" descended from heaven to reveal "spiritual childhood to us by means of her writings and to point out to others a sure way of salvation." [34] According to the same Pontiff, that young nun, from the depths of her cloister, presents to us "an example which all the world can and should follow." She "opens up an easy road" that we may ascend even to perfection and the fullness of love.[35] He prophesied that the practice of this doctrine would bring about a "profound renewal of Catholic life in its entirety and the regeneration of society." [36]

Finally, Pius XII, completing, as it were, the judgments of his predecessors, said that Therese's Way, conceived under the inspiration of the Holy Ghost is suitable for the children of God who have reached adult years; it is suitable for learned men as it is for the lowly and the unlettered; [37] it is even very practical for those who, like the apostles, bear a great responsibility for souls. Such testimonies need no commentary. With perfect clarity they confirm the providential mission of St. Therese and canonize her doctrine.

God Himself Confirms Therese's Mission

Finally, we are permitted to make the statement that God Himself has confirmed Therese's mission and her Way. Few human beings knew our Saint at the time of her death. But as soon as the manuscript which contains the "story of her soul" was published, her fame spread in a "hurricane of glory." Men began to admire her, to love and invoke her. From all parts of the world people clamored for a copy of her book. Everywhere, souls desired to follow her in her Little Way. Therese, on her part, caused a "shower of roses" to fall from heaven. She sowed miracles and transformed the hearts of men. Hence, her Cause of Canonization was quickly introduced and the Process progressed with unusual rapidity.

Opened at Bayeux in 1910, it ended with Therese's beatification by Pius XI on April 29, 1923. Two years later, on May 17, 1925, the same Pope canonized her.

Since that time she has grown in popularity. Men of all races invoke her and there is no place on earth where the Gospel has been preached in which Therese is not known. Her manuscript has been translated into about forty languages or dialects and has been distributed in millions of copies. And most surprising of all, today theologians and masters of the spiritual life study and ponder her writings, become disciples in her school. They are convinced that this young nun has traced for us an authentic way of holiness, has brought us a vital message that is eminently suitable for people of our time.

Pius XII did not fear to compare the spiritual genius and influence of St. Therese of Lisieux with the genius and activity of a St. Augustine, a St. Francis of Assisi and a St. Thomas Aquinas.[38]

OPPORTUNITIES AND IMPORTANCE OF THERESE'S DOCTRINE

God has greatly glorified this humble Carmelite. He has permitted her to pour out and distribute her favors far and wide and, no doubt, this is in recompense for her heroic virtues and eminent sanctity. But this by itself does not explain the spiritual radiation, the torrent of graces which, under God, have issued from her.

Other saints have passed through this life and have been flaming torches of knowledge and sublime models because of their shining virtues and heroic deeds, but how many can we name who have exercised the sanctifying influence of our Saint? If God has desired that Therese's sanctity should shine with such brilliancy before the eyes of men; if He has given her such an extraordinary hold on people, it must be that, besides showing them her virtues, He wished to confirm and, as it were, proclaim as His own, the spiritual doctrine of this Saint.

The facts we have mentioned are, so to speak, God's signature, underwriting her manuscript and assuring the truth of her "Little Way" so that souls may be prompted to follow it. They proclaim that St. Therese was sent by God to open a new way of spirituality, a way of littleness, love and confidence. In times like ours when man is filled with the thought of his own importance, when he thinks he can by his own efforts build a better world and attain happiness by his own powers, there is an evident opportuneness in Therese's doctrine.

She reminds us that we are but weakness and powerlessness, that we are unable to accomplish anything without God's assistance. On the other hand, simplifying the way that leads to holiness, she reduces perfection to its essential elements, separates it from all those external manifestations which led souls to believe that holiness is beyond our powers and that it depends on extraordinary graces. St. Therese thus made holiness accessible to all. Now, if God in this manner facilitates our access to holiness, it must be also because He wants a greater number to reach that goal. If He makes the road more simple it is because He wishes all souls to follow it.

The words of the Vicar of Christ leave no doubt on that subject. They formally proclaim that the doctrine of spiritual childhood is suitable to all souls without any exception; that there is no soul which cannot and which ought not to follow it; that, according to the testimony of our Lord, it is even necessary for our sanctification.[39]

It follows that, unless God gave to anyone a special direction, there is no one who can neglect it with impunity. St. Therese of the Child Jesus is the master of the spiritual life for men of today, the doctor of a new era of spirituality.

What, then, is this way of Spiritual Childhood?

Many authors have dealt with the doctrine of St. Therese of Lisieux. Not all have properly grasped its meaning. "We have often noticed," declares the Carmel of Lisieux, "that every one tries to adapt the Theresian doctrine to his own views of the ascetical and mystical life, and thereby takes away its originality." [40]

The question which has often been asked, is what constitutes the fundamental characteristic of Therese's doctrine. Here again the answers differ according to the mentality of the writer or according to what impressed him most. Some affirm that that fundamental note is simplicity—others, confidence—for others again, it is love or a sum of several virtues taken together.

Now, the true characteristic of the Theresian doctrine is not found in this or that particular virtue, nor in any sum of virtues. Other saints or spiritual writers have insisted on humility, or love or on simpliicty.

When we carefully look for the dominant character of Therese's doctrine, we find that it does not consist in any particular virtue but in a special attitude of mind. Everything is based on and flows from an attitude of spiritual childhood. It is this which gives unity to her teaching and imparts to it that simplicity which is so striking.

Again, we could mention other authors who have spoken of spiritual childhood but none have made it the basis for the spiritual life for the reason and in the way Therese has done it. Let there be no doubt about this, for she said so explicitly to Mother Agnes "Mother, (my Way), is the way of spiritual childhood." [41]

The Meaning of the Way of Spiritual Childhood

Therese has fully explained this on two different occasions. One day, Mother Agnes asked her what was the exact nature of the Way she desired to teach to souls after her death. She replied: "It is the way of spiritual childhood, the way of confidence and abandonment to God. I want to teach them the little means which have proved so perfectly success-ful for myself. I want to tell them that there is only one thing for us to do here below: to throw at Jesus' feet the flowers of little sacrifices, to win Him through our caresses. That is the way in which I have taken hold of Him, and that is why I shall get such a good welcome." [42]

A few days later, having been asked what she meant by remaining a little child, she replied: "It means that we acknowledge our nothingness; that we expect everything from the good Lord, as a child expects everything from its father; it means to worry about nothing, not to build upon fortune; it means to remain little, seeking only to gather flowers, the flowers of sacrifice, and to offer them to the good Lord for His pleasure. It also means not to attribute to ourselves the virtues we practice, not to believe that we are capable of any-thing, but to acknowledge that it is the good Lord who has placed that treasure in the hand of His little child that He may use it when He needs it, but it remains always God's own treasure. Finally, it means that we must not be discouraged by our faults, for children fall frequently." [43]

In these two texts are expressed all the fundamental char-acteristics of childhood.

First, there is *LITTLENESS OR HUMILITY*, which acknowledges its nothingness and attributes nothing to itself. The little child is naturally weak and powerless. He cannot do anything by his own strength. He depends on his father and mother for everything. He can scarcely put one foot before the other or, if he wants to climb the stairs, he is unable to raise his foot or make the first step. He recognizes this and confesses it.

Next, there is *POVERTY*. The child owns nothing. He

has only what is given to him. He depends on his parents for everything.

Then, there is *CONFIDENCE*. The child knows his father and mother. If he has nothing, he knows that the parents are there to help him, feed him, give him all he needs in order to exist and act; hence, he does not fail to have recourse to them and is not anxious about anything.

There is also *LOVE*. However small and poor a child may be, he already possesses one thing in a charming way, and that is love. He has a heart cut to his size, but it is very much alive and very tender. He loves his mother effusively and sometimes, above all, his father. He hugs them because he loves them. He *ABANDONS* himself to them.

Finally, the child is *SIMPLE*. Everything in him is simple; his thoughts as well as his words; his actions also. A little one is capable only of little things.

These, then, are the qualities of childhood which Therese transposed into the supernatural order. They characterize her Way of Childhood, and these we must reproduce in our relations with God. Pius XI confirmed this, saying that spiritual childhood consists "in feeling and acting under the impulse of virtue, as a child feels and acts by nature." (Homily at the Mass of Canonization).[44]

However, all the qualities we have mentioned are not equally characteristic of the "Little Way." Hence, when we are asked which ones, among these virtues designate the essential characteristic of the Little Way, we must reply: on the one hand, humility, spiritual poverty and confidence are its fundamental dispositions; on the other, love is its soul. Nevertheless, what is truly predominant in her Way is confidence, a confidence that is fearless, boundless and unwavering. It is this which makes Therese's Way seem unique in the history of spirituality.

She declared this herself. After saying that her "way" was spiritual childhood,[45] she added that it is in a special manner "the way of confidence and abandonment." This was also the interpretation given to it by her sisters.

THE SOURCES OF THERESE'S LITTLE WAY

The question has been asked where Therese has discovered her doctrine, and the answer has generally been that she had found it in the Gospel. It has also been maintained that she was inspired by St. Paul, St. John of the Cross and other spiritual masters.

It is certain that Therese was inspired by Holy Scripture, particularly the Gospel. It is in Holy Scripture that she discovered her Little Way; it was the Word of God that revealed to her the infinitely merciful love of God and Jesus Christ. All her teaching is evidently permeated by the spirit of the Gospel.[46]

There are also certain points in her doctrine that resemble the teaching of other saints. This is natural, since they drew their thoughts from the same source, which is the Word of God, and were taught by the same Spirit; hence, the saints express themselves in identical or similar fashion. This resemblance is particularly evident when we compare Therese with the saints of Carmel. She had received the traditional Carmelite training. She had read at least in part the works of St. Theresa of Jesus, and especially those of St. John of the Cross, who was her favorite author; hence, we find echoes in her teaching of the doctrine of these masters. Therese is a true Carmelite.

Through her contact with St. John of the Cross, she deepened the foundations of her "Little Way," namely, humility, poverty of spirit, detachment from creatures, the necessity of approaching God with pure faith, love and confidence.

Nevertheless, what she had found in others she did not simply take over, but thought it out in her own personal way and with the light received from the Holy Ghost. "Her knowledge," declared Benedict XV, "came to her from the secrets which God reveals to children." The "Little Way" which she lived and taught is truly her own doctrine and not that of any other.

Having been asked one day who had taught her this doctrine, she replied: "Jesus alone. No book, no theologian taught it to me, and ye: I feel in the depths of my heart that I possess the truth." [48]

Her Way, according to her own testimony, is also a reproduction of the life of the Holy Family as it was lived in Nazareth. Although the Gospel is extremely reticent regarding that life, we may justly believe that it was not marked by extraordinary macerations of the flesh nor by brilliant deeds such as are met with in the lives of the saints.

The life of Jesus, Mary, and Joseph, was quite ordinary. It consisted merely in performing well the daily tasks, in the practice of the common virtues, a perfect abandonment to the will and wishes of God. It was above all animated by great love. This, at least, is the way Therese conceived it.[49] And it is that kind of life which she desired to live herself and to teach to others.

How did Therese Discover her Little Way of Spiritual Childhood

It was in June, 1897, that she told the story of her discovery.

From her childhood, Therese had desired to become a saint. That desire had grown with the years and she strove for it with her customary zeal.[50] But she soon realized that, in spite of her good will, her efforts were insufficient. She was all the more impressed by the feeling of her own inadequacy because sanctity, as it was pictured in the lives of the saints, looked like a summit of a high mountain lost in the clouds, and quite beyond the reach of ordinary people.

On the other hand, however, she could not persuade herself that God would inspire aims impossible to attain. Hence, she thought, in spite of her littleness she could still aspire to holiness.[51] But how was this to be achieved? It is not possible to add anything to one's stature. She had to accept herself as she was and suffer her imperfections. She then recalled that in certain houses an elevator or lift replaces the stairs and does this quite efficiently. Hence, in her desire to get to heaven, Therese began looking for some very straight and short road, a new way, an elevator that would lift her up even to God, for she was too small to climb the steep staircase of perfection.

In her search for this way, she turned to Holy Scripture. God had already been speaking to her for a long time through Sacred Writ.

One day she casually opened a collection of texts of the Old Testament which had been made by her sister Celine and found this passage of Proverbs: "Whoever is a little one let him come to me." (Prov. IX, 4).

The answer was pertinent. In order to attain holiness we must be little. It is even necessary to grow in littleness. But since on account of our littleness we are unable to attain it by our own powers, it is necessary to have recourse to God.

However, the solution remained incomplete. What would God do for the little one who came to Him? She opened the Scriptural notebook once more and God replied through the mouth of Isaias (66:12): "You shall be carried at the breasts, and upon the knees they shall caress you."

This time the answer was conclusive. God through Christ (the divine "elevator") would raise the little one even unto Himself and make her a saint.[52]

Hence, in order to be a saint, we must go to God by way

of humility, confidence and abandonment: by way of spiritual childhood.

He who enters that road and delivers himself to Christ is carried away by Him to the heart of God who sanctifies us.

This way of spiritual childhood, Therese called a "little way very straight, very short—entirely new." [53]

The Way is STRAIGHT, for it has removed spiritual complexities which were like so many detours in our march towards God.

The Way is SHORT, for being straight it simplifies the spiritual life, reducing it especially to humility and confident love.

The Way is NEW, in comparison with the systems which were then in vogue, but also because she insists more than anyone had done before on merciful Love. Jesus, speaking about charity had said in a similar manner that He gave us a new commandment, although that commandment had already been given. But He had raised it to a higher perfection.

It will be noted that Therese's Way is not based, as it has been maintained, on the passage of St. Matthew: "Unless you become like little children, you shall not enter into the kingdom of heaven." (Matthew, 18:3). The latter text does not even appear in full in The Story of a Soul; and, after all, it does not contain a complete answer to the question which Therese had asked herself. For those words require a detachment and a return to a state of humility and littleness which Therese had already reached. It is, therefore, on the texts of Proverbs and Isaias quoted above that her Way is founded. They give us the true meaning of the Theresian doctrine and at the same time express its profound theological foundation.

Therese never intended to systematize her thoughts and intuitions nor the elements of her spirituality in the scattered texts of her writings and in her conversations.

We find the first allusion to spiritual childhood in a letter she wrote to Celine on July 18, 1893. Her "Little Way" developed progressively around the year 1895. On July 17, 1897, Therese, for the first time, explicitly stated that her "Little Way" was one of spiritual childhood, and she defined its principal elements.[54] These latter were developed somewhat later when she added Chapters IX and XI to her *Story of a Soul*. A further insight into her teaching on the central point, is given by her conversations in August 1897 with Mother Agnes, and some letters she wrote to Mother Agnes and to Celine; to Father Roulland and Father Bellière.

THE WAY OF CHILDHOOD AND THE FATHERHOOD OF GOD

Some have said that the foundation of the Theresian doctrine lies in the fatherhood of God. It is very true that Therese considers God most specially as a Father. She had learned this from the Gospel. But in God she saw above all the "Father of infinite mercy," merciful Love. It was to that love that she attributed the mystery of her vocation, of her entire life and above all of the privileges that Jesus bestowed on her soul.[55]

Later, considering that every soul has for its mission to glorify some divine perfection, she declared that she had honored God especially in His infinite mercy. It was through that mercy that she contemplated all the other attributes of God.[56]

Finally, it was to merciful Love that she offered herself as a victim. Everything, therefore, seems to confirm the truth that the Theresian spirituality has for its foundation the merciful love of the heavenly Father, just as it is also founded on the merciful love of Jesus. Indeed, she addressed herself more often to Christ than to the Father, since Jesus is indeed "the 'Elevator' which must raise us to heaven."

CHAPTER II

Humility — Littleness

THE first characteristic of a child and that which first strikes us is its littleness. In the supernatural order we must likewise first of all recognize our littleness. This is the disposition that characterizes our true condition and puts us in our right place before God. To be little spiritually means to be humble. Littleness, however, implies a certain simplicity, an effective note of sweet self-effacement.[1]

To a sister who asked Therese what she meant by remaining a little child before God, she answered: "It means that we acknowledge our nothingness, await everything from the good Lord, refuse to attribute to ourselves the virtues we practice, but believe that we are incapable of doing anything that is good." [2] This, in fact, is what humility is: to acknowledge that we possess nothing ourselves and that everything comes to us from God; to admit that we cannot accomplish anything of ourselves but expect everything from Him; to refer to Him the little good we discover in ourselves or happen to do; to see ourselves, in other words, as we are: weak, powerless, poor and wretched.

It is primarily because humility puts us in our right place, in our true condition, that Therese makes humility the basis of her Way: "It seems to me that humility is truth. I don't know whether I am humble, but I know I see the truth in all things."

To that first reason she added another, and one that is truly Theresian. It is the fact, namely, that "it is proper to divine love to lower itself; hence, the lower we are, the more we attract God;"[3] on the contrary, when we lift ourselves up we go counter to that movement of love.

Finally, Therese practiced humility out of love, to prove her love:

"To ravish Thee, quite little I shall remain;
My self forgetting, I'll charm Thy loving Heart." [4]

However, according to her, humility must not consist in the mere acceptance of our state of dependence and incapacity. *We must love to see ourselves as we truly are.* We must bear the imperfections that are inherent in our nature; be happy to see ever more clearly how wretched is our condition; we must even will to become ever more little.[5]

To discover those deficiencies in ourselves does not mean that we have created them. They were in us but we had failed to notice them. Our discovery of them has only given us a better understanding of our true condition. Now, the better we know ourselves, accepting to see ourselves as we truly are, and the more truthful we are with ourselves, the more pleasing shall we be to God; and we shall also be more ready for the workings in us of God's merciful Love.

Therese took delight in being hidden, unknown and counted as nothing. She took pleasure in being despised: [6]

"I want to hide in this world;
I want to be the last in all things,
For You, my Jesus." [7]

She desired to be "but a small grain of sand, most obscure," well-hidden from all eyes; a grain of sand which is always in its right place, that is, under the feet of everybody, reduced to nothing, to which no one gives a thought and whose existence is as it were unknown; a grain of sand which desires nothing but to be forgotten, and does not even wish to be despised or insulted—this would be too glorious for a grain of sand; for it has to be seen in order to be despised. No, it desires only to be forgotten!

"Nevertheless, it desires to be seen by Jesus," for if Jesus were to neglect it, it would not receive anything any more, and it is so very much in need of Him. On the other hand, it is not to be feared that being looked on by Jesus will cause it to be lifted up in its own eyes. Nevertheless, "one glance of Jesus, just one, suffices. That is enough for a little grain of sand."

Having made this one exception, Therese continues vigorously: "Yes, I desire to be forgotten and not only by creatures but by myself; I would like to be so reduced to nothing that I would no longer have any desires. . . . The glory of my Jesus, that is all. For my honor, I abandon it to Him, and if He seems to forget me, well! He is free to do so, for I no longer belong to myself but to Him." And she adds with a holy mischievousness: "He will tire more quickly of making me wait than I shall tire of waiting for Him." [8]

We cannot but admire so much understanding, such a love of humility and this at such an early age, for she was then only fifteen. Rarely have more profound thoughts been expressed on this virtue.

Did Therese herself discover this idea that to be forgotten is something higher than to be despised and receive insults, or did she learn it from others? It does not matter. In any case, she marked it with her own stamp. In the passage we have quoted certain expressions may, at first sight, seem excessive, but if we try to understand them in the sense in which Therese herself understood them, we shall find them quite normal. When, for example, she says that she would desire to be so totally reduced to nothing that she no longer has any desire, it is clear that she does not exclude all desires, for such a thing would be inhuman. She wants especially to exclude desires which would cause her to attract the notice of others, to put herself forward in any way, to seek any special attention that would flatter human pride.

The last sentence of Therese merits special attention. It emphasizes the note of confidence and abandonment, which is characteristic of Theresian spirituality. She knows that for those who forget themselves and seek Him alone, the love of Jesus is so great that, although He may sometimes seem to have forgotten them, He cannot do so for very long. He will return to them before they tire of waiting for Him. Hence, *far from grieving at the knowledge of her own persistent imperfection, Therese took a genuine delight in it.*[9]

She even expected to find new imperfections in herself every day.[10] She declared that those lights that revealed to her her littleness and nothingness, did her more good than the lights of faith.[11] Hence, she considered that the greatest thing the Almighty had done in her was to reveal to her her nothingness and her incapacity for doing any good.[12]

Such reflections might seem strange. For it is faith that puts us in contact with God and is the principle of the supernatural life as well as the source of love. And yet we have to recognize that Therese is right, for what would be the advantage of having the lights of faith if, through lack of humility, we did not place ourselves before God with the dispositions that are necessary before He can communicate Himself to our soul. God gives grace to the humble, and to them alone.

Therese accepted her imperfections and wretchedness with a good heart. When she felt stirrings of her nature or yielded involuntarily to imperfections, far from being astonished, she took delight in it and drew benefit from it: "I know the means for being always happy and drawing profit from my miseries. Jesus seems to encourage me on this road. . . . He teaches me to profit from everything, both from the good and the evil that I find in myself." [13]

In fact, as long as we have good will, our faults can serve to instruct us and help us to make progress. For they make us distrust ourselves and look for means to correct our imperfections. If, after committing a fault, we accept the humiliation that follows from it, this merits for us an increase of love. This is the way saints react. They are no more exempt from weakness than we are. Far from grieving on their account, they accept themselves as they are and make use of their imperfections to raise themselves nearer to God. Those falls must appear the more natural to us because, in the way of perfection, we remain children. It is inevitable, therefore, that we should make false steps. The little one who learns to walk unavoidably falls from time to time.[14]

"I have many weaknesses, said Therese, "but I am never astonished because of them. I am not always as prompt as I should like to be in rising above the insignificant things of this world. For example I might be inclined to worry about some silly thing I have said or done. I then recollect myself for a moment and say: 'Alas, I am still at the point from which I started.' But I say this *with great peace and without sadness. It is truly sweet to feel weak and little.*" [15]

How much these reflections of St. Therese differ from what are possibly our own habitual sentiments and ways of acting.

Again Therese wrote: "We would like never to fall. What an illusion! What does it matter, my Jesus, if I fall at every moment? I come to recognize by it how weak I am and that is gain for me. You see by that how little I am able to do and You will be more likely to carry me in your arms. If You do not do so, it is because You like to see me prostrate on the ground. Well, then, I am not going to worry, but I will always stretch out my suppliant arms towards You with great love. I cannot believe that You would abandon me." [16]

Elsewhere she writes: "If I am humble, I am entitled, without offending the good Lord, to do small foolish things until I die. Look at little children. They constantly break things, tear them up, fall, and all the while, in spite of that, they love their parents very much. Well, when I fall in this way, like a child, it makes me realize my nothingness and my weakness all the better and I say to myself: 'What would become of me? What would I be able to accomplish if I were to rely on my own powers alone?' " [17]

This becomes even clearer when we realize that these so-called powers are sometimes paralyzed by physical conditions or by external causes. Therese knew this better than anybody. "It is a great trial," she told a novice, "to see only the dark side of things, but that does not entirely depend on yourself. Do what you can to detach your heart from earthly cares and especially from creatures, and then feel certain that Jesus will do the rest." [18]

Hence, when she tells us elsewhere that, "when we commit a fault, we should not blame it on a physical cause, such as illness or the weather, but attribute it to our own imperfection," we must understand her correctly. She is not denying that the body and external conditions influence our minds and our moral conduct. This would contradict reason and psychological experience. It would also be contrary to Holy Scripture which states that "the corruptible body is a load upon the soul, and the earthly habitation presses down the mind that muses upon many things." (Wis., 9:15).

While our Saint does not deny that our responsibility is lessened by such causes, she does affirm that God always grants the graces that are necessary to overcome all obstacles when we have recourse to Him. Furthermore, she warns us that if we take refuge behind physical infirmities, to excuse ourselves for our imperfections and our falls, we run the risk of overlooking our personal responsibility for them. She wants us rather to recognize that responsibility and to confess that, when we have fallen, it is because we did not have a recourse to prayer as we should have had, or because we have been wanting in generosity. We are then closer to the truth and that is wholly to our advantage.

Therefore, when we fall "as children," that is, through weakness and not through lack of good will, our imperfections and faults do not offend Jesus, however numerous they may be, even if they are repeated until the end of our life; neither do they prevent us from loving our Divine Lord greatly.[19] Hence, they should not disturb nor sadden us. We should, on the contrary, accept them calmly, or, as St. Therese often repeated, we should accept them with "mildness and great peace." [20] When we accept with mildness the humiliation of having manifested our imperfection, the grace of God returns immediately."

Our faults make us realize how weak we are, the extreme need we have of God, and the danger we run to trust ourselves. In this way our faults keep us humble, make us seek our support in Christ and thus they strengthen our love.[21] "It is only when His children ignore their constant lapses and make a habit of them and fail to ask His pardon that Christ grieves over them; but He is full of joy at the sight of those who love Him and, after each fault, ask His pardon and cast themselves in His arms. He then recalls only their desires of perfection."

She concludes this section very fittingly with the words: "Ah! How little we know of the goodness and merciful love of Jesus!" [22]

Therese even desired that others should know her imperfections. One day, when she was suffering greatly from fever, she was asked to come quickly and help in a heavy task of painting that had to be done at once. For a moment her features betrayed an interior struggle which Mother Agnes noticed. Soon afterwards Therese wrote to her: "Your little daughter shed tears a little while ago, tears of repentance but, even more, of gratitude and love. Yes, this evening I gave you an exhibition of my virtue, of my treasures of patience! And to think that I preach so nicely to others! I am glad that you witnessed my imperfection. I am much more pleased because

I have been imperfect than I would be if, sustained by grace, I had been a model of virtue." [23]

She went even farther than that. Like St. Paul, *she gloried in her weakness, in her infirmities:* "You are mistaken, my dear friend," she wrote to her cousin, "if you imagine that your little Therese walks with ardor in the path of virtue. She is feeble, very feeble. She feels that weakness every day; but Jesus is pleased to teach her the science of glorying in her infirmities. That is a great grace and I pray Jesus to teach it also to you, for there alone are found peace and repose of heart." [24]

She inculcated her novices with the same principles. In her instructions in the novitiate, she constantly returned to the subject of humility.[25] To those who were afraid of being judged imperfect, she declared: "That they find you imperfect is precisely what you need. That is a real blessing, for you can then practice humility which consists not only in thinking and saying that you are full of faults, but in rejoicing because others think and say the same thing about you." [26]

It might be objected that there is danger in such an attitude, for if it is proper to accept ourselves as imperfect at the beginning of our spiritual life, *we might have to regret that we are still in that imperfect condition after many years* and especially at the end of our life. Therese, however, had no such fear and she wished to have humility practiced to that very point. She knew that the more we advance on the road to perfection, the further away we seem from its end. Hence, she was satisfied when she recognized her own imperfection. "She even found delight in it." "My peace," she sang, "consists in remaining small; hence, when I fall on the road

> "I can quickly rise again
> And Jesus takes me by the hand." [27]

One day—it was during her last illness—some object had

been brought to her that was more of a nature to distract her than to help her recollection. She refused it; but, after a moment's reflection, she corrected herself and said to the sister: "I beg your pardon; I acted from a natural impluse." And a little later, she added: "How happy I am to see that I am imperfect and that I am in need of God's mercy at the hour of my death!" [28] These are admirable words, for how many are willing to accept their imperfection with so much serenity at that supreme moment? They are not even willing to accept it during the course of their life.

Therese notes this with regret: "In order to belong to Jesus we must be little, but there are few souls who aspire to remain in that littleness." [29] And elsewhere: "In order to enjoy the merciful love of Jesus, it is necessary to humiliate ourselves, to acknowledge our nothingness, and this is a thing which many are unwilling to do." [30] Little to a certain point, they are dissatisfied with dragging on in that condition, constantly meeting the same difficulties and struggles, relapsing into the same faults or imperfections, and remaining always poor and powerless.

They imagine that it would be more profitable for their soul if they were not hindered by their wretchedness, and if, on the contrary, they could tend Godwards with even, regular steps and with a free and detached heart. Indeed, it is painful to be constantly confronted with our miseries. But, if God considers it right to leave them with us, is it right for us to complain? Does He not know better than we do what things are profitable to our soul?

These repeated falls, moreover, are often necessary to make us know ourselves better, to convince us of our need of divine help, and teach us humility of heart.

We know, of course, that "we cannot do anything without God." (John, 15:5). We repeat this, thinking that we have understood the meaning of these sacred words, but we belie this truth in our conduct, sometimes without being aware of it. But God cannot act efficaciously in our soul and bring it to perfection unless it is perfectly humble and quite convinced that everything comes from Him. That is why He permits us to fall repeatedly until we realize our extreme wretchedness and our absolute need of divine help. Such divine conduct is but wisdom and mercy.

On the other hand, as long as those falls displease us, they cannot do us harm. If, on their occasion, we turn to God with a confidence that is proportionate to our misery, they will be a source of progress for us.

We ought then to understand that it *is precisely our weakness that will serve to give us strength.* "It is my weakness that gives me confidence," Therese likes to repeat, recalling St. Paul (II Cor., 12:20).[31] It is because God sees our weakness, our incapacity and wretchedness, and especially because He wants us to acknowledge and love our littleness and misery that He comes to our assistance. "God wants humility of heart." [32] If we were stronger, we would not need His help. But when He sees that we are convinced of our nothingness, that we love our wretchedness and appeal to Him, He stoops towards us and "gives with divine generosity." [33]

Some might object, *"Why must we love this state of imperfection?"* Is it not enough that we acknowledge and accept it? No! It is not enough to acknowledge the truth. We must also love it. We have a perfect grasp of truth only when we love to see ourselves as we truly are in God's sight. Moreover, we do not love the state of imperfection for its own sake. We love it because it disposes us for God's merciful action in our soul. "The thing that pleases Jesus when He beholds my soul," wrote Therese, "is that I love my littleness and my poverty and have a blind hope in His mercy." [34]

God wants us to acknowledge that we receive everything from His mercy. He glories in fashioning saints from the clay of poor creatures like us. "The God of strength loves to show His power by making use of nothing." [35] He desires, says St.

Paul (Eph., 2:7) to show "in the ages to come the overflowing riches of His grace in kindness towards us in Christ Jesus."

Let us, then, accept our wretched condition. "Let us humbly take our place among the imperfect. Let us consider ourselves little and in need of God's support at every instant. As
soon as He sees that we are truly convinced of our nothingness, He extends His hand to us. If we are still trying to do
something great, even under the pretext of zeal, our good
Lord Jesus leaves us alone." [36]

In order to make us bear our misery with greater facility,
Therese, with the true spirit of Carmel, counselled that *we
keep our eyes fixed principally on Jesus and refrain from looking fixedly at our imperfections.* "When we see that we are
wretched, we no longer wish to look at ourselves but we gaze
at our only Beloved." [37] "We have merely to love Him, without looking at ourselves, without examining our faults too
much." [38] "If you are nothing, do not forget that Jesus is *All.*
Hence, lose your little nothingness in His infinite All and
think only of that All, who alone is lovable." [39]

Here, then, is a truly efficacious remedy and it has the
additional advantage of lifting up our soul while disengaging
it. It is a Carmelite recipe, for Therese repeats the teaching
of St. John of the Cross, who urges us to leave everything
behind and to turn lovingly towards God when we meet with
difficulties and temptations. Saint Teresa of Jesus likewise
gave the advice that one should rather contemplate God's
infinite greatness than fix one's eyes on one's wretchedness.

However, although the passive acceptance of our littleness coupled with confidence in God's help is very efficacious,
it does not suffice. To limit the Theresian doctrine to that
would be to deform it.

*Therese demands over and above that, that we effectively
practice humility.* This is a point that she insists on repeatedly.
In the prayer she composed to obtain that virtue, she
expresses her firm intention of submitting herself to all her

sisters, of placing herself in the lowest rank amongst them; and she asks to be humiliated [40] every time she fails in this respect. She strove unceasingly to carry out her resolution by embracing gladly the humiliations that came her way.[41] She received with joy the hurtful remarks that were sometimes addressed to her and greeted with a friendly smile sisters who spoke in that way. When others judged her unfavorably, she accepted it in silence: "Why should we defend ourselves," she declared, "when we are misunderstood and misjudged? Let us leave that aside. Let us not say anything. It is so sweet to let others judge us in any way they like. O blessed silence, which gives so much peace to the soul!"

To a sister who had told her that she preferred to be corrected when she was wrong rather than when she was blameless, Therese replied: "I prefer to be accused unjustly, for then I have nothing to reproach myself with, and joyfully offer this to the good Lord. Then I humble myself at the thought that I am indeed capable of doing the thing of which I have been accused." [42]

She even took delight in the humiliations she sometimes suffered from postulants and novices. "Jesus," she writes, "sometimes allows others to serve me a good salad with plenty of vinegar and spices and in which nothing is wanting except oil. . . . With a simplicity that delights me, my novices tell me about the struggles I occasion and the things in me that are displeasing to them. . . . Truly, here is more than joy. This is a delicious banquet which fills me with delight."

"One day when I had been particularly eager to suffer humiliation, a novice took it upon herself to satisfy me so well that I was reminded of Semei cursing David. Thinking that this came from the Lord, my soul relished with delight that bitter food which was served to me in such abundance." [43]

Two months before her death, a reflexion expressed by a sister during recreation was reported to her. She had said:

"I don't know why they talk about Sister Therese of the Child Jesus as if she were a saint. It is true she had practiced virtue, but it is not a virtue she acquired through humiliations and sufferings." "And I," confessed Therese, "when I recall how much I have suffered from my early years! O how profitable it is to learn what others think of me when I am about to die!"

Nevertheless, as we have said before, she thought that if she were seeking humiliations and contempt, she might draw attention to herself and receive the esteem of others. Hence, she preferred to be forgotten and aimed specially at being ignored. She found her happiness in a hidden life, in being unknown even to her sisters, and in forgetting herself.[45] In this she was right; for forgetfulness demands more than humility; it implies self-denial in all its aspects.

It is clear, then, that humility, the humble acceptance of our imperfections, is the basis of the Way of Spiritual Childhood. Our Saint even seems at times to give it too exclusive a place in the pursuit of perfection, as when she declares that it is "the only means to make rapid progress in love," and "the only way by which saints are made." [46] "To humble ourselves, to suffer our imperfections with patience, this is true sanctity, the source of peace." [47]

One day she was asked how she had succeeded in attaining that unalterable peace which filled her soul: "I have practiced self-forgetfulness," she answered. "I have tried not to seek myself in anything." [48]

Since humility is so important, it is evident that no one is excused from practicing it. It is necessary to all, irrespective of their dignity or age.[49] "It is possible to remain little even when we are charged with the most formidable functions and ... even when we are in extreme old age." If we want to grow in love we must grow in humility and the measure of our humility will be that of our progress.

This shows us that one of the greatest graces which God

had bestowed on Therese was that profound understanding of humility and the firm establishment of that virtue in her which made her confess that "she had understood humility of heart" and "seemed humble according to what she saw in herself." [50]

We may add that one of the great benefits that she conferred on us is the teaching *that a loving consideration of our misery is the firm foundation from which we can ascend towards God.*

CHAPTER III

Spiritual Poverty

THE small child is not only weak; it is also poor. Not only can it do nothing, but it possesses nothing. It has only what its parents give it. Therese, with the keen spiritual feeling that characterizes her, applies these observations to her own Little Way of Spiritual Childhood: "In order to remain a little child, we must expect everything from our good Lord, as a child expects everything from his father, without worrying about anything." [1]

Nevertheless, a child grows up and a time comes when his father wants him to earn his living and become self-sufficient. Therese, on the contrary, judged herself incapable of earning her living, that is, of developing in herself the life of grace; neither did she want to grow up. She desired "to remain always little and poor, in order to expect everything from God." She realized that such a spirit of poverty and humility makes us lean on God rather than on ourselves and is the best means of attracting His powerful help.

Therese has most clearly expressed her mind on that subject in what is now Chapter XI of *The Story of a Soul*. It was to Sr. Mary of the Sacred Heart (her own sister) that she wrote this admirable letter. In it she reveals her own longing to fulfill all vocations and undergo the torments of all the martyrs. This only discouraged her poor Sister Mary because she found no such desires of martyrdom in her own heart and she sadly concluded that her love was not genuine.

Therese told her consolingly that "desires of martyrdom are *NOTHING*." They are only a consolation which Jesus sometimes grants to weak souls, because He wishes to animate their generosity and enable them to bear sufferings with patience. He does not give them to souls that are sufficiently strong to remain steadfast and loyal to Him, in spite of their natural repugnance for suffering. By withholding such consolations, Jesus gives them "a privileged grace," the gift of fortitude that is suited to their circumstances and to their state of soul. Therese cited the example of the divine Savior Himself who emptied the cup of His Passion to the last drop in spite of the sorrow that flooded His soul.

Therese seems to minimize the value of such desires. They are, actually, a sign of a soul's generosity and this was true in her own case; but by lessening their importance, she hoped to console her sister who did not have such experiences. Also, she wanted to make her understand that what pleases God in us is not the fact that we have such desires, but that we love our poverty. These desires are an effect of grace and, yet, they might lead us to displeasing God if we dwelt on them with self-complacency.

This thought she develops in a masterly page which is one of the richest jewels of her spirituality: "Dear Sister: How can you say that my desires are a proof of my love? I know only too well it is not that at all which pleases the good Lord when He looks in my soul. The thing that pleases Him is that I love my littleness and poverty and have a blind hope in His mercy. . . . O my beloved sister, understand well that in order to love Jesus and be His victim of love, the weaker we are and the more completely without desires or virtues, the more we shall be disposed to receive the benefits of His consuming and transforming love working within us. It is enough to have the one desire of being a victim, provided we are content to remain always poor and powerless."

We now have her complete thought. We know her secret. We possess the means of truly loving Jesus and being transformed in Him. It consists, on the one hand, in loving our littleness, our weakness. On the other hand, we must have complete trust in God's mercy and desire to be His victim of love. No matter how wide is the extent of our littleness, or of our indigence, nor how deep the abyss of our misery, they cannot be an obstacle to God's action. On the contrary, we shall be ready for that action in proportion to our need. The greater our weakness, our poverty and our misery, the readier we are for His mercy. Hence, we ought the more eagerly to accept our littleness and our misery; for the work of divine mercy consists precisely in filling up the void of our wretchedness. God's love is satisfied only "when God stoops down to our nothingness and transforms that nothingness into fire." [2]

Unfortunately, most souls impede the operation of His merciful love because, not only do they refuse to accept their poverty and weakness, but more especially they do not even realize how poor and weak they are. This Therese records with sorrow: "To consent to remain always poor and powerless, there lies the difficulty! Actually, where can we find one who is truly poor? Is not he alone truly poor who is so humble-minded that he believes himself to be nothing? Oh! let us then remain far away from all that is vain-glorious! Let us love our littleness, our lack of sensitivity. We shall then be poor in spirit and Jesus will come for us, however far we may be from Him, and will set us afire with His love. How I wish that I could make you understand what I feel. . . . It is confidence and confidence alone that should lead us to Love." [3]

A few days before her death, she developed the same thought: "I cannot lean on anything, nor can I count on anything I have done to build up my confidence in God. But the consciousness of my poverty has served as a true light for me. I knew that I had never been able, during my life, to pay any of the debts I owed to God but that I could make of that very knowledge a source of spiritual wealth and power. Then I made this prayer: 'O my God, pay the debt yourself, but do it in a way that only God can do, so that it may be infinitely better than if I myself had fulfilled my obligations.' And I recalled with great consolation these words of the Canticle of St. John of the Cross: 'Pay my debts' . . . So great a favor could never be repaid by men, but our very incapacity fills our soul with peace, for we know how completely we depend on God alone." [4]

We see, then, that to be poor and to accept our poverty gives us, so to speak, the right to ask God to discharge our debts towards Him and to do it as only He can. After all, is not this what we do when we offer to the Father the infinite merits of Jesus, His dearly beloved Son?

In the same letter, which is often quoted as expressing most perfectly the Theresian doctrine, there is a sentence which was not fully copied in extracts of letters that were formerly published, because it was feared that it might be misinterpreted.

Therese wrote that "the weaker we are and the more we are without desires or virtues, the more are we receptive of the operations of God's love in us."

What is meant by "without virtues"? It is clear that a Christian soul, speaking absolutely, cannot exist without virtues. We receive virtues in baptism, together with grace. A soul, however, can be said to be without virtues if she has not exercised nor developed them; in such case, she possesses them only in germ, somewhat as she received them. Now if such a soul, acknowledging her poverty and desiring to improve herself, has recourse to God with a confidence equal to her poverty, she places herself in the dispositions that are most suitable for the operations of merciful Love. Again, a soul could consider herself without virtues if, despite the fact that she applies herself to their practice with good will, she still judges that she has not progressed in them as she should have done and cannot recognize their presence in herself. If such a soul, accepting her poverty, puts her confidence in God, she will quickly experience God's action in herself.

Both these interpretations are in harmony with the context. We believe, nevertheless, that the first is the more obvious and corresponds best with the thought of the Saint. The more a soul is defective in the practice of virtue, the more God's mercy shines in fulfilling all her needs.

As far as the expression "without desires" is concerned, it is evident that this must not be taken literally, for Therese admits her own desire of being a victim of love. These words, then, should be understood in reference to the desire for martyrdom or other similar desires. The desire of loving God above all things and doing His will is the only one that perfectly corresponds to His love and, hence, it suffices, since it comprises all the others. However, we must carefully avoid giving a wrong interpretation to this part of Theresian spirituality. The passage which we have explained has the value of an axiom and, yet, it should not lead us to lean exclusively on divine mercy, laying claim to it because of our misery. God in His infinite mercy is inclined to help our poverty, but that does not dispense us from action. On the contrary, this divine inclination that we recognize in Him should prompt us to correspond with the advances of His mercy. God requires our cooperation.

Therese knew this better than anyone. Hence, while remaining poor, she never let pass an opportunity to show her love of God and she neglected no act of virtue. But she never counted on her works to insure her progress. She wanted to owe everything to the divine liberality alone. She expected everything from God. "Behold," she said, "if we abandon ourselves, and place our confidence in God, while making every small effort and hoping everything from His mercy, we shall be rewarded as much as the greatest saints." [5] And elsewhere: "I feel always the same audacious confidence that I will become a great saint, for I do not count on my own merits since I have none, but I hope in Him who is virtue and sanctity itself. It is He and He alone who, being satisfied with my feeble efforts, will raise me to Himself and, covering me with His infinite merits, will make me a saint." [6]

Therese's affirmation that we can be "rewarded as much as the greatest Saints" might seem an overstatement, as indeed it would be if we took it in too literal a sense. For all souls cannot expect to reach the degree of sanctity of the saints whom God has specially chosen to fulfill a very special role in the Church. Hence, that is not the meaning that Therese wished to convey.

Every saint is called to attain his particular degree of glory and is rewarded according to his merits. It is, nonetheless, true that those who base their spiritual lives on humility and poverty, animated by confidence in God, enhance considerably their personal merits and achieve a degree of sanctity akin to that of the great saints.

Therese, then, relies above all on the efficacy of grace. She even wanted to depend only on the grace necessary for each moment. After all, it is only at the moment when we receive those graces that they are effective in our souls. "I am very poor," she told a novice; "it is the good Lord who provides me from moment to moment with the amount of help I need to practice virtue."[7] "I have noticed many times that Jesus does not want to give me a store of provisions (for future needs). He feeds me at every instant with an ever new kind of food. I find it in me without knowing how it got there. I simply believe that it is Jesus Himself who is hidden at the bottom of my poor little heart and acts in me in such a way that I recognize, at each moment, what He wants me to do at that particular time."[8]

Her spirit of poverty went so far *that she did not even aim at gaining personal merits for the enrichment of her own soul.*

Therese knew, of course, that every action properly performed is meritorious in the sight of God, but she did not want to reserve these merits for herself. She wanted to remain poor and to owe her grace and her happiness solely to the merits of Christ and to God's mercy. She offered to God, for the salvation of other souls, every reward for the virtues she practiced.

"When I reflect," she wrote, "on the words of the good Lord 'I come quickly and my reward is with me to render to each one according to his works' (Apoc., 22:6-12), I say to myself that He will be very embarrassed with me, for I have no works. He will then be unable to render to me according to my works. Well! I have confidence that He will render to me according to His own works!" And in her offering to Merciful Love, she exclaims: "After this earthly exile, I hope to enjoy You in the Fatherland, but I do not want to acquire merits for Heaven. I want to labor solely out of love, having no other purpose than that of consoling Your Sacred Heart and saving souls which will love You eternally. In the evening of this life, I shall appear before You with empty hands for, O Lord, I do not ask You to count my works. I want to be clothed with Your justice and receive from Your own love the eternal possession of Yourself."

This sounds like an echo of St. Paul's words: "For His sake I have suffered the loss of all things and I regard everything as refuse that I may gain Christ and be found in Him, having no longer a justice of my own . . . but the justice through faith in Christ." (Philip., 3:9).

On another occasion, speaking of the use she made of her spiritual wealth, she said: "I shall always be as poor as this. I don't know how to save up. All that I earn is immediately spent as the price of souls and for Holy Church and also to shower roses upon all, both just and sinners. I have not yet found one moment when I could say to myself, 'Now I am going to work for myself. . . .' [10] Don't hoard anything. Give away your spiritual goods as quickly as you earn them." These she considered as something that ought to be invested to serve God's interests in the best way possible.

The same spirit of spiritual poverty made her labor and

urge others *to labor for God, without being concerned about receiving rewards for their efforts;* to be content never to know their progress; to accept trouble and to feel only repugnance, in spite of their deeds and prayers. "Offer to the good Lord," she said, "the sacrifice of never gathering any fruit; that is, of always feeling repugnance for suffering and humiliation. Offer Him the sacrifice of seeing all the flowers of your desires and good will fall to the ground without producing anything. In the twinkling of an eye, at the moment of your death, He will know how to bring forth rich, ripe fruit on the tree of your life."

When her questioner objected that she herself would always be found imperfect, Therese answered: "The fact that people recognize your imperfection, well, that is as it should be; it is your gain. That people consider you to be wanting in virtue does not rob you of anything nor does it make you poorer. They (your critics) are the losers; they lose interior joy, for there is nothing sweeter than to think well of one's neighbor. As far as I am concerned, I experience great joy not only when others recognize my imperfection but, above all, when I realize myself that I am imperfect." [11] And to her cousin she wrote: "You must not wish to see the fruit of your efforts. Jesus takes pleasure in keeping for Himself alone those nothings which console Him." [12]

We are sometimes inclined to think that if we were aware of our progress this would encourage our efforts and stimulate our generosity. There is a certain amount of truth in this opinion. It is better for us, however, not to recognize our progress: "You do not need to know what the good Lord is doing in you," said Therese; "you are too little." [13] And to her sister Celine she wrote: "Jesus teaches His Therese to draw profit from everything, from the good as well as from the evil she finds in herself. He teaches her how to speculate in the bank of His love or, rather, He transacts that business Himself, without telling her how He does it, for that is His affair and not that of Therese. Her sole concern is to leave everything in His hands without keeping anything in reserve, without even asking the pleasure of knowing what profits her bank is making." [14] For God acts more efficaciously in a soul that is ignorant of such things and keeps her thoughts fixed on Him alone. Even if God should withdraw from a soul the special favors He had previously given, let her remember that they were but loans and let her refrain from complaining when God takes them back again. "Jesus may take back everything that He has given me," she sang, and, addressing the Blessed Virgin in her poem, she added: "Tell Him never to hesitate in acting thus with me."

Our spirit of poverty and detachment must be such that our souls remain trustful and at ease even if God despoils us of all special favors, or seems indeed to withdraw completely from us and to leave us helpless. Being, then, without any support except our faith in God alone, we are able to rely absolutely on Him: "Our sole good consists in loving God with all our heart and being poor in spirit while we are in this world," [16] for "there is no joy like that of being truly poor in spirit." [17]

CHAPTER IV

Confidence

IT is not sufficient that we acknowledge our littleness and incapacity, that we recognize our poverty and our wretchedness and even that we love to see ourselves in this condition. This loving acceptance of truth has, no doubt, the priceless advantage of putting and keeping us in our proper place; and it also counteracts the tendency to excessive confidence in ourselves. But, over and above this, an understanding of our own insufficiency makes it all the more imperative that we should count on the help of God to sustain us in our efforts towards perfection.

The child, in his weakness and poverty, runs to his father for help. So it must be also in the spiritual life. The child of God knows that he has a Father in heaven. He approaches God with confidence and expects Him to assist him so that he who is weak and powerless may accomplish what he is unable to do by his own powers. Even a partial knowledge of the heart of his heavenly Father should give him a boundless confidence in Him, for, if God is a Father, He must possess the qualities that are proper to paternal love, such as tenderness, devotion, watchfulness. Since He is God, these attributes are infinite. He is infinitely wise and infinitely powerful; He knows all things; He can do all things, and His attributes are at the service of His merciful love. It follows that the confidence of a child of God knows no limits.

Moreover, God has proved to us that He is infinite mercy. The Father gave us His Son, His only-begotten One, and permitted Him to suffer the most cruel torments. This Son, on His part, "annihilated Himself," clothing Himself with our human misery. He immolated Himself on the Cross. He gives Himself to us as our food, that we may be transformed in Him and be incorporated into His Mystical Body.

Like a "Hound of Heaven," the love of God is in constant pursuit of our souls. The Father constantly enfolds us in His infinite tenderness. Jesus never ceases to love us. He is always ready to pour out His graces on us, to enlighten, console, sustain and transform us, and that finally leads us to partake of His glory and blessedness.

Therese at an early age received an understanding of the infinite mercy of the heavenly Father and she grasped it ever more clearly as she progressed in her intimate knowledge of God. It was through the prism of that mercy that she contemplated and adored the other perfections of God. Seen with those lights, each of God's attributes appeared radiant with love and inspired confidence.[1]

However, God's mercy is not the only source of our confidence. The Father gave us His Son "and with Him all good things." [2] We can, therefore, rely on the merits of Jesus Christ. They belong to us and we can present them to the Father as ours.

Resting on such a foundation, how can we entertain doubts about God's providence? On the contrary, are we not compelled to an extremity of confidence? Indeed, this is increasingly evident as we recall that all we could possibly ask of Him is nothing in comparison with what God has already given or promised us. It is true that God is also infinite justice, but the rigors of His justice are softened by a blending with mercy and love. "Justice itself," said Therese, "and justice even more than any other divine perfection, seems to me to be clothed in love." [3] If justice demands that God exact from us what is His due and that He make us expiate our faults, it also takes into consideration our human wretchedness. It takes account of our ignorance, our weakness and all the circumstances which lessen the guilt of the sinner. God knows better than any other, the clay from which we were fashioned and the burdens that oppress our will and impede our freedom.

"That justice which frightens so many souls," wrote Therese, is for me a source of joy and confidence. To be just means more than to be severe in punishing the guilty. It takes account of right intentions and wishes to reward virtue. I expect as much from the justice of our good Lord as from His mercy." [4] "It is because He is just that He is compassionate and full of mildness, slow to punish and rich in mercy. For God knows our weakness. He remembers that we are but dust. As a father is tender towards his children, so is the Lord compassionate towards us." [5]

Hence, whether we contemplate God's mercy, which makes Him always will our good and inclines Him to have pity on us, or whether we consider His justice, we have all the reasons in the world for putting the most complete trust in God.

Therese was so permeated by the virtue of confidence that, according to Mother Agnes, "it constituted the special mark of her soul." [6] "My Way," she herself wrote, "is one that is full of confidence and love." [7] She tried to impress this on all who addressed themselves to her, affirming that "we never have too much confidence in the good Lord who is so powerful and merciful" and that "we obtain from Him as much as we hope to receive from Him." [8]

She maintained that "a lack of confidence offends Jesus and wounds His Heart." [9] Finally, as far as she herself was concerned, "to put limits to our desires and our hopes means that we reject the infinite goodness of God." [10]

In admirable pages which she wrote at the request of Sister Mary of the Sacred Heart, she describes in a charming way that is not without depth, to what extent we should have confidence in Love. She pictures herself as a little bird, covered only with a light down but which, with the eyes and heart of an eagle, dares to gaze at the sun of Love and eagerly desires to fly to Him. Unfortunately, the bird can scarcely raise its wings, but this does not sadden it. With daring abandonment, it remains in its place, keeping its eyes constantly fixed on the sun in spite of clouds, wind and rain. If, at times, dark clouds hide the sun, the bird remains unperturbed, for it knows that its sun continues to shine (though it cannot be seen.) Moreover, if lashed by storms and blinded by temptations, it seems even to have lost faith in a hereafter, it nevertheless remains in the small place and continues to look in the direction of the light that the eyes can no longer see. This is, then, an occasion for pushing its confidence to its extreme limit, and in this it finds perfect joy.

But it is also possible that the little bird, being unable to rise, forgets its sun, gets lost in earthly trifles and allows its wings to get drenched. Even then, it must not yield to discouragement. It should not hide, to weep over its wretchedness and then die of remorse. It must, on the contrary, turn again towards its sun, dry its wings in the rays of its well beloved star and talk with him of its own infidelities, "for, in its audacious trust in Him, it believes that it will more fully attract the love of One who did not come to call the just but sinners."

If, in spite of all this, its expectations remain unfulfilled, if the star remains hidden . . . the little creature consents to stay in its place, shivering from the cold, but rejoicing in the suffering it deserves.

Finally, it might happen that the bird, being unable to see the star, since it is completely veiled, ends, in spite of itself, by closing its eyes and yielding to sleep. That does not matter. When it awakens and realizes what has happened, far from sorrowing, it has but to take up again its loving service and remain in a state of interior peace. And Therese concludes: "O Jesus, how happy is your little bird to be so feeble and so little! What would become of it, if it were great? It would never have the audacity to act in that childlike manner towards You!"

Therese also thought that this audacity of hers came from the fact that Jesus had overwhelmed her with love. Hence, she immediately cried out: "O Jesus, let me tell You, in my boundless gratitude, that Your love becomes truly folly. In the presence of such folly, how could I prevent my heart from trying to fly to You? How could I set limits to my confidence? What a pity that I am not able to reveal Your ineffable condescension to all little souls. . . . I feel certain that if—though this is impossible—You found one soul that is more feeble and insignificant than mine, You would inundate it with even greater favors, provided that this soul would abandon itself with absolute confidence to Your infinite mercy." [11]

Therese was convinced that every human soul can attain to sanctity, provided it be humble and confident.

Having read the life of Joan of Arc, she first wished to imitate the latter's glorious exploits, but God made her understand that her own glory would consist, instead, in becoming a great Saint. "This desire," she writes, "may seem presumptuous in one who is as weak and imperfect as I am, yet, I always feel the same audacious confidence that I will one day be a Saint. I do not rely on my own merits, for I have none; but I hope in Him who is Virtue and Holiness itself. It is He alone who, being satisfied with my feeble efforts, will raise me to Himself and, covering me with His infinite merits, will make a saint of me. . . ." [12] If all souls that are weak and powerless felt as I do, who am the smallest of all, none would despair of reaching the summit of the mountain of love, for Jesus does not demand great actions, but only abandonment and gratitude." [13]

What about those who have long delayed in returning God's love?

According to Therese, that is no reason for giving way to discouragement and fear: "There are souls for whom God's mercy exercises endless patience and to whom He gives His light only by degrees." [14]

Are mortal sins, even numerous grievous faults, an obstacle to confidence in God?

Therese replies: "I know for certain that even if I had on my conscience all the sins that can be committed, I would go and cast myself in the arms of Jesus with a heart torn by repentance, for I know how much He cherishes the prodigal child that returns to Him. It is not because the good Lord, in His providential mercy, has preserved my soul from mortal sin, that I ascend to Him on the wings of confidence and love. . . ." [15] Her confidence was based not on the virtues she had practiced in life, but on the merciful love of God.

But ought we not to be discouraged when our spiritual life has failed to develop as we should have desired?

Still less have we reason for losing confidence in God when, in spite of our efforts, we repeatedly fall into the same faults and experience dryness of spirit. Discouragement springs from self-love, from a refusal to acknowledge our true condition of soul. It shows that we are rebellious against our own littleness and spiritual poverty. "The sorrow which casts us down," said Therese, "is the hurt to our self-love." [16] She also declared that "to brood gloomily over our own imperfection paralyzes our soul." [17] We do more harm to ourselves by yielding to discouragement than by falling through weakness, for we deprive ourselves of the resilience we need to rise again after our falls.

It shows us, too, how defective is our trust in God, for to a great extent God comes to our help in proportion to our consent to remain little and to rely on Him; "He measures His gifts," said Therese, "according to the amount of confidence He finds in us." [18] Hence, if we refuse to accept our lowly state, if our trust in Him should fail, it is to be feared that God may limit the assistance He gives to our souls.

Even in her early childhood, Therese had trained herself

to an attitude of absolute trust in God in all circumstances. She had already grasped what others take long years to learn, that discouragement is wasteful, not gainful for the soul. On the evening of her First Communion she wrote in her diary: "I shall never be discouraged," a resolution to which she firmly adhered throughout life. Her childlike confidence in God was never weakened by external happenings, by her own imperfections nor even by her faults. On the contrary, she learned from such occurrences to recognize the weakness of her own nature and to judge the defects of others with greater understanding and charity: "The memory of my faults humbles me; it causes me never to rely on my own strength, which is but weakness, but especially it teaches me a further lesson of the mercy and love of God." "When, with childlike confidence, we cast our faults into the devouring furnace of Love, how can they fail to be consumed forever?" [20]

"I am not always faithful," she writes elsewhere, "I often fail to make one of those little sacrifices which give so much peace to the soul; but I do not get discouraged. Instead, I abandon myself in the arms of Jesus: I endure the trial of having less peace at that moment and try to be more watchful the next time. . . . O my dear Mother, how sweet is the way of love! We can fall, of course; we can commit many infidelities, but," she adds, "quoting St. John of the Cross, 'love knows how to draw profit from everything and it quickly consumes whatever might have displeased Jesus.' All, then, that remains at the bottom of our hearts is a humble and profound peace." [21]

"A glance of love cast towards Jesus and the knowledge of our profound misery makes reparation for everything." "We have only to beg pardon and all is repaired by that act of love. Jesus opens His Heart to us. He forgets our infidelities and does not want to recall them. He will do even more: He will love us even better than before we committed that fault." [22] "I entrust my infidelities to Jesus for, in my audacious abandonment to Him, I believe that I shall in this way gain greater power over His Heart and attract more fully the love of Him who came not to call the just but the sinners." [23] In these lines she unfolds before our eyes the boundless mercy of the Heart of Christ.

Our Saint has written delightful passages on this subject and from amongst them we choose the following examples:

"I assure you," she told her sister, "that the good Lord is much kinder than you can imagine. He is satisfied with a glance, with a sigh of love. . . . In regard to myself, I find it easy to practice perfection, because I have learned that the way to Jesus is through His Heart. Consider a small child who has vexed his mother by a display of bad temper or disobedience. If the child hides in a corner through fear of punishment, he feels that his mother will not forgive him. But if instead, he extends his little arms towards her and with a smile cries out: 'Love, kiss me, mamma, I will not do it again,' will not his mother press the little one to her heart with tenderness, and forget what the child has done? And yet, though she knows very well that her dear little one will misbehave again at the first opportunity, that means nothing if the child appeals to her heart. He will never be punished. . . ." [24]

In the same vein she says, with a naive sense of humor, "Our Lord has one great weakness. He is blind and He really knows nothing about arithmetic. He does not know how to add, but to blind Him and prevent Him from adding the smallest sum . . . you must take Him by His Heart. This is His weak spot." [25]

"To take Jesus by His Heart" seems to be an adequate expression of her thought, for she uses it repeatedly. Moreover, she confesses candidly that she herself exploited that stratagem: "It is this way that I took hold of the good Lord and that is why I shall be well received by Him." [26]

She preserved that same confidence and unalterable peace during the long period of dryness which made her incapable of praying and practicing any virtue. "Even if the fire of love seemed to have gone out, I would keep on throwing fuel in it and Jesus would take care to light it up again." [27] And when that state of dryness continued, she gracefully commented: "Jesus will tire sooner of making me wait than I shall tire of waiting for Him." [28]

Finally, at a certain moment she had almost a presentiment that this dryness would remain with her until her last breath. But that did not discourage her: "No doubt, Jesus is not going to wake up before my great retreat in eternity but, instead of grieving on this account, I feel great joy." [29]

> "Yes, let Him hide!
> Quite gladly I will wait for Him
> Till that great Day that has no setting sun
> And darksome faith must die." [30]

Following Therese's example, let us make our confidence commensurate with the greatness of the Divine Being and proportionate to the abyss of tenderness of the Heart of God! We must refuse to confine it to the limits of our poor conceptions. We must remember that God takes pleasure in giving to His children whatever they need, whatever may make them happy. He is glorified when He distributes to them His gifts without measure. Jesus is never annoyed when we ask for things that are in harmony with His designs. If He has often given us preventive graces, when we had failed to pray, with much more readiness will He listen to our petitions.

Considering that children commonly importune their parents with the audacity peculiar to childhood and that, on their part, "parents frequently act foolishly and show weakness in giving in to their children," Therese believed [31] that

God, too, had His weaknesses towards those who approach Him with the dispositions of a child: "When we hope for something from the good Lord that He did not intend to give us, He is so powerful and rich that He owes it to His glory not to disappoint us and He grants us our desires . . . but we must tell Him: 'I know very well that I shall never be worthy of this favor. I merely extend my hand to You, like a small beggar child, and I am sure that you will fully satisfy me.' " [32]

It is possible that God will not hear us immediately. Sometimes He makes us wait. He knows better than we do ourselves what is good for us and what is the right moment to help us. Moreover, He does not have to take an account of the element of time to do His work in our soul. "Jesus does not take time into consideration, for time does not exist in heaven. He has merely to consider love." That is why "one glance, one moment of His Heart can cause His flower to open out for all eternity." [33]

It is unfortunate that many souls are lacking in confidence. Such an attitude is not in conformity with the infinite mercy of God or the intercessory value of Christ's infinite merits. Such a lack of confidence in souls of this type is often induced by too much consideration of their unworthiness and the poverty of their works.

Let us, then, understand the truth that our accomplishments, however excellent they may be, are not the true basis of our confidence. This should depend entirely on the merciful love of the Father, on faith in Jesus Christ.

Therese had not studied theology but was enlightened by that wisdom which God generously pours into souls that are "little" and "simple." She, thus, knew better than many theologians and theorists of the spiritual life what are the respective roles of God and man in the work of our perfection, and the conditions that must be fulfilled to insure its success. For her, rapid progress in the way of love depends on remaining very little and placing our confidence in God: "It is Jesus who does everything in me; I do nothing, except remain little and weak." [34]

She was merely re-stating in her own words what St. Paul taught long ago: "When I am weak, then I am strong;" [35] "our sufficiency is from God;" [36] and it is through the grace of Christ that we are saved. (II Cor., 12:10; 3-5)."By grace you have been saved . . . and that not from yourselves, for it is the gift of God; not as the outcome of works, lest anyone may boast." [37] (Eph., 2:8).

That does not mean that Therese considered good works useless, for this is contrary to revealed truth. She desired that men should make every effort to correct their faults, to acquire virtues and attain sanctity: "Let us struggle without respite. Let us go on, however much we are tired of the struggle. Where would our merit be if we fought only when we feel courageous? It does not matter that you have no courage, provided you act as if you had courage."

Nevertheless, she professed that it is not from our works we must expect our progress. The reason we work is to prove to God that we have good will. "Be like a little child," she counselled a novice. Practice all the virtues and so always lift up your little foot to mount the ladder of holiness; but do not imagine that you will be able to ascend even the first step. No! the good Lord does not demand more from you than good will. From the top of the stairs, He looks at you with love. Very soon, won over by your useless efforts, He will come down and take you in His arms. He will carry you up. But if you stop lifting your little foot, He will leave you a long time on the ground." [38]

"We must do all that lies in our power," she also affirmed; "we must give without counting the cost; we must constantly renounce ourselves. In one word, we must prove our love by all the good works we can perform; but, since all that we can do is very little, it is of the greatest importance that we put our confidence in Him who alone sanctifies those works and that we recognize that we are indeed useless servants, hoping that the good Lord will give us through grace all that we desire." [39]

She confirmed this teaching by an example from the Gospels. The Apostles had been fishing in the sea of Galilee. They had labored the whole night and all their labors had been fruitless; but, trusting in Christ's words, they then cast their nets and immediately caught a great quantity of fish. "Jesus wanted to show them that it is He alone who can make our efforts fruitful." [40]

These expressions are clear and explicit and leave no room for doubt. There are those who insist upon voluntary efforts as if everything depended on them. Therese, on the contrary, affirms that, however necessary they may be, they do not suffice for spiritual progress. It is God who is the principal agent: "If I had accomplished all the works of St. Paul, I would still consider myself an unprofitable servant. . . ."[41] It was precisely this which constituted the great fault of St. Peter: he relied too much on his own strength and loyalty. God allowed this so that we might see how little men can do without His help. He desired to teach us that we must rely on Him alone." [42]

On this subject she claimed to have personal experience. She had struggled fruitlessly for many years to correct her excessive sensitiveness. Finally Jesus, taking account of her efforts and touched by her prayer, cured her in one instant.[43]

Therese's explicit teaching is, perhaps, more decisive still. Towards the end of her life, some one said to her: "You must have struggled very much to reach your degree of perfection." She replied with an indefinable tone of voice: "It is not that at all." She explained herself then in those memorable words which, as it were, summarize her doctrine: "Sanctity does not consist in this or that practice. It consists in a disposition of the heart which makes us humble and little in God's arms, conscious of our weakness and confident even to audacity in the goodness of our Father." [44]

When we understand these illuminating words which speak with such depth about confidence, we cannot doubt that St. Therese of the Child Jesus had as her mission to reveal to us the mercy and tenderness of the Heart of our heavenly Father and to inspire us with boundless confidence in Him. She had the soul of a simple and loving child. She had penetrated into divine secrets and she understood that God stoops down to a soul in proportion to its poverty and to the extent that this soul, recognizing its incapacity, has greater confidence in Him.

Let us, then, cultivate in ourselves the soul of a little child, a heart that is simple and full of confidence in the good Lord, repeating with St. Paul: "I know in whom I have believed." [45] However great our wretchedness, or however useless our efforts may seem; however numerous our repeated faults, we must never despair of reaching our goal. Let us accept our lot of always feeling our imperfections, and of feeling them even to the end of our days.

What God expects from us is love and confidence and good will. Therese wrote a few months before her death: "I try to make my life one act of love and I do not worry any more about my littleness. On the contrary, I rejoice in being little. I dare hope that my exile will be short: but this is not because I am ready for heaven. I feel that I shall never be ready if the Lord Himself does not deign to transform me. He can do this in an instant. After all the graces with which He has overwhelmed me, I also expect Him to grant me that of His infinite mercy." [46]

We should constantly remember that the essential thing for us is that we reach perfection at the moment planned by God. He is able to bring us to it in an instant, even at the moment of our death. If we abandon ourselves to God, place our confidence in Him, make our own small efforts but expect everything from His mercy, He will give us, at that moment, all that is still lacking in our perfection. According to St. Therese, He can make us attain to the very summit of the mountain of love: [48] "The most holy souls are perfect only in heaven."

CHAPTER V

Love of God

ONCE we realize that God is merciful Love, we go to Him with confidence. In its turn, "confidence leads to love." [1] Now, love is the soul of the Way of Spiritual Childhood, just as it is the foundation and guiding principle of the spiritual life and is the only means by which the soul can rise to full perfection. For without love, we will not have either the fidelity or the generosity that are required to bring our efforts to a successful end.

Carmel has always affirmed the primacy of love, especially through those two outstanding witnesses, St. Teresa of Avila and St. John of the Cross. It was only natural, then, that St. Therese of Lisieux should have imbibed the spirit of her Order. She had particularly admired St. John of the Cross, the Father of the Carmelite Reform, whose works were always at her elbow. There she had read that "love alone can repay love" and that "it is all important that we fill our lives with acts of love, in order that our soul may be quickly consumed and arrive with short delay at the vision of God." [2]

Such thoughts must inevitably have had a motivating influence on a soul as loving as hers, for from her tenderest years Therese had thirsted for the contemplation of God. In fact, as soon as she became acquainted with these passages, she began to repeat them to herself in order to stimulate her love.

Nevertheless, it would be wrong to attribute Therese's love to those sources alone, for she had also a deep appreciation of the Gospels. In them she saw God manifesting Himself as essential Love; she saw clearly that "God is love" (I John, 4:16).[3] There also she learned the extent of God's love for us and concluded that His love is a merciful love that delights in stooping down to our miseries in order to deliver us from them. God, thus, bends down to our nothingness, to transform it into a fiery love for Himself.[4] Having gained this insight, Therese, like St. John, devoted herself wholeheartedly to the task of making her life a complete act of love. At a later date she wrote that God had chosen her particularly in order that she might glorify His infinite mercy.[5]

This faith in God's merciful Love is truly the root principle of the entire Theresian spirituality. From it springs its fundamental characteristics. It developed in the soul of Therese that ardent love which animated her throughout life. It inspired her with the noble desire of offering herself as a victim to merciful Love, in order to receive torrents of that divine love—which so many reject—and to love God *WITH HIS OWN LOVE.*

Strongly characteristic of childhood, love is the feeling that predominates one's early years. The child loves its parents tenderly and gives expression to his affection in many charming ways. This was an additional reason for giving love a prominent place in the Way of Spiritual Childhood.

In numerous texts Therese brings out the important role of love: "I understand so very well that it is only through love that we can render ourselves pleasing to the good Lord, that love is the one thing I long for. The science of love is the only science I desire." [6] She told her cousin Marie Guérin: "I know of no other means to reach perfection than by love. To love: how perfectly our hearts are made for this! Sometimes I look for another word to use, but, in this land of exile, no other word so well expresses the vibrations of our soul. Hence, we must keep to that one word: love." [7] "Regarding self," she told her sister Leonie, "I find it very easy to practice perfection, for I realize that we have merely to take Jesus by His

Heart." [8] Finally, she declared to Celine: "Merit does not consist in doing or giving much. It consists in loving much." [9]

Love was both the driving force and objective of all her actions. Just as she looked at all the attributes of God through the prism of His merciful love, so did she endeavor to do everything out of love and for love, "to give pleasure to the good Lord," to "Jesus," [10] to "give Him joy, that He might be loved." [11] "How easy it is to please Jesus, to ravish His Heart," she wrote to Celine. "We have merely to love Him, while, at the same time, forgetting ourselves." [12] And to Leonie: "If you wish to be a saint, it is easy . . . aim only at pleasing Jesus, at uniting yourself intimately with Him." [13]

Although every virtue has its own proper motive, Therese motivated all her virtuous acts by love. She affirmed that she had learned this method from Jesus Himself: "Directors make people advance in perfection by performing a great number of acts of virtue, and they are right. But my Director, who is Jesus Himself, teaches me to do everything through love." [14]

She knew, of course, that saints ordinarily work for the glory of God but, she said, "I am a little soul and I labor solely for His pleasure. I would be happy to suffer the greatest pains, were it only to make Him smile even once." [15]

She put all the energy she possessed in the service of love, as is evident from her own words in the poem *A Lily Among Thorns:*

"When my youthful heart was afire
    with the flame we call love,
You came and claimed it for Yourself.

And You alone, O Jesus, could satisfy my soul,
For boundless was my need of loving You." [16]

The keen obligation St. Therese felt of giving Jesus all her love was intensely sharpened because He had not only preserved her from any grievous sin, but even from any fully voluntary fault. As she said, He had remitted all her faults in advance. In that preservation from faults she saw the proof of God's unique love for her, of Jesus' desire "that she should love Him unto folly." [17]

For her part, seeing that God is so little loved even by those who have consecrated themselves to Him, and "knowing that Jesus is thirsting more than ever for love," she desired to make up for it, to make compensation to God for the ingratitude of men, to make her life one great act of love, to love Jesus "more than He had ever been loved before." [18]

In reality, her life was a continual act of love: "While growing up," (she is speaking about the time when she was about five years old) I loved the good Lord more and more. I often gave my heart to Him. I did my best to please Jesus in all my actions and was very careful never to offend Him." [19]

The perfection of her smallest actions, her love of suffering, her ardent zeal for souls, as well as her profound recollection which kept her united to Christ in all circumstances, mark the extent of her love. This, usually, was not a mere sensible feeling, though sometimes, under the influence of an emotion, she had transports of love which she was unable to control. She had had experiences of this kind even before her entrance into Carmel in 1887.[20] She was similarly favored on several occasions after becoming a Carmelite.

While finishing the manuscript written for Mother Mary Gonzaga, she was seized with one of these transports of love, and it was this which inspired her to write one of the most beautiful pages we possess: "You know, O my God," she exclaims, "that I have never desired to love anyone but You, and that I seek no other glory. Your love went before me in my childhood. It has grown with me and now, it is an abyss of which I cannot sound the depth. Love attracts love. Mine leaps towards You. I would like to fill the abyss which attracts it, but, alas! it is not even a drop of dew lost in the ocean! In order to love You as You love me, I must borrow your own love. . . . O my Jesus, it seems to me that You could not fill any soul with more love than you have given to me. . . . No, here below, I cannot conceive a greater immensity of love than that which it has pleased You to bestow gratuitously on me without any merit on my part." [21]

On another occasion, while walking in the garden supported by Mother Agnes, she stopped to look at a small white hen which covered her chicks with her wings, her eyes filled with tears and Mother Agnes said to her: "You are crying!"—"I cannot answer you at this moment," she replied, "I am too greatly moved."

Having returned to the infirmary she explained: "I wept because I remembered that the good Lord used that comparison in the Gospel to make us believe in His love. That is the way He has acted towards me throughout my life. He has hidden me entirely under His wings. A moment ago I was unable to control myself. My heart was overflowing with gratitude and love. It is a good thing that the good Lord hides Himself from my sight and only rarely and, as it were, through bars,[22] shows me the effects of His mercy."[23]

How well those words reveal her intense love!

She said that her loving desires were for her "the greatest of martyrdoms." It was in order to satisfy that desire of love that she wanted to keep her eyes always fixed on the divine Word, her "Eagle whom she adored," and to remain under the fascination of His gaze. She begged Him to dive down on His prey and carry it off to the Furnace of love, to plunge her into that Furnace for all eternity.[24] She added, however, that she did not see very well what more she would have after her death than what she already had. "I know," she said, "that I shall see the good Lord, but as far as being with Him, I already am totally with Him here on earth." [25] Hence, she declared that if she were not to attain some day to those higher regions of love to which her soul aspired, she would, nevertheless, have tasted more sweetness here below in her martyrdom and folly, than she would enjoy amidst the delights of her heavenly Fatherland.[26]

Therese's love for God and our Lord had all the qualities which a human soul could hope for. She loved with a love that was most exclusive and complete. It was most disinterested, generous, tender and delicate.

1.   THERESE'S EXCLUSIVE LOVE

First of all, it is certain that no other love ever touched her heart, and that Jesus possessed it entirely. She was still very young when she felt a great desire of never loving anyone but the good Lord, to find no joy except in Him.[27] Jesus was "her first, her only friend, the one and only one whom she loved; He was her All." [28]

> "Jesus," she sang, "You alone can satiate my heart.
> There's nothing here below that can beguile me.
> You are my only love." [29]

This singleness of her love for Christ was chiefly the fruit of her first Communions, and it continued to grow even stronger as time went on. "When Jesus shall have transported me to the blessed shore of Carmel," she wrote a few days before her entrance, "I will give myself entirely to Him, for I want to live for Him alone."[30]

However, when she had entered the cloister, her heart, thirsting for affection, felt very lonely and friendless. Instinctively, she turned to her Mother Prioress (Mother Marie de Gonzaga), but, sensing the danger that she might become too much attached to her Superior, she immediately repressed her feeling, for she knew that Jesus wanted her for Himself alone: "He knows well that if He gave me but a shadow of happiness, I would attach myself to it with all the energy and all the powers of my heart."

During her retreat before receiving the habit, she reaffirmed her resolution: "Since I cannot find any creature that satisfies my heart. I want to give everything to Jesus. I will not give even one atom of my love to creatures." [31]

On the day of her profession, in order that that disposition might be the soul of her holocaust, she placed over her heart the following prayer: "O Jesus! May I never seek nor find anyone but You alone! May creatures mean nothing to me and may I mean nothing to them, but may You, Jesus, be everything!" [32]

She was wont afterwards to renew this resolution to love Christ only with a vehement fervor that revealed how strongly and completely it bound her to Him. "Let us not leave anything in our heart except Jesus," she wrote to Celine.[33] And to Mother Agnes: "You know the One whom I love and whom alone I want to please." "Jesus alone; no one but Him. The grain of sand is so small. If it wished to put anyone beside Him in its heart, there would be no room for Jesus." [34]

2. THERESE'S DISINTERESTED LOVE

The most perfect selflessness marked Therese's love for God, for she loved Him solely for what He is in Himself: Perfection and Infinite Charity. This divine Charity suffused her soul with love of gratitude for all God has done for us in preparing us for eternal happiness with Himself by giving His only begotten Son to become one of us.[35] She loved Jesus for Himself and for His excessive love which made Him sacrifice Himself unto death for sinners. Never did she love in order to receive. She never even thought of serving God "in order to merit heaven or obtain graces." "I do not want to give," she said, "in order to receive. I am not a self-seeker. It is God that I love and not myself." [36]

This does not mean that she was indifferent to the acquisition of merits. To Mother Agnes who had asked her, "Do you want to acquire merits?" she answered: "Yes, but not for myself; for souls, for the needs of the Church." [37]

Neither does it mean that she was not interested in eternal beatitude. She wished to reach the degree of glory which God had destined for her.[38] From her infancy she had longed for that happiness, and the desire had constantly increased. Her letters express this on every page. It was this hope which, to a great extent, sustained her in her sufferings, especially during the cruel trial of her father's illness. Despite these facts, she did not labor and suffer in view of reward. "My dear Celine," she wrote, "you understand that it is not to win a crown or to gain merit for myself; it is to give pleasure to Jesus;" for "it is not glory, even heavenly glory that my heart seeks. . . . My glory will be the splendor reflected on me from the brow of my mother the Church. What I seek is love. I want nothing else but to love You, O Jesus." [40]

In this connection, she confessed that it was with a certain repugnance that she sang at Sext on Sundays, in a faulty Latin translation, the words in which the Psalmist declares that He fulfills the divine law in view of recompense (propter retributionem). While singing these words, Therese protested interiorly: "O my Jesus, You know well that it is not for the reward that I serve You, but solely because I love You and in order to save souls." [41]

Nevertheless, the thought of eternal happiness prompted her to love even more: "Reflecting that eternal reward has no proportion to our small sacrifices in this life," she wrote, "I wanted to love Jesus passionately . . . give Him a thousand marks of love, as long as I was able to do so." [42]

She had the same disinterestedness regarding the favors or consolations which God ordinarily grants to souls that

serve Him generously: "Jesus does not want us to serve Him
for His gifts; it is He Himself who must be our reward." [43]
"I do not desire sensible affection, a love that I feel, but only
a love that is felt by Jesus. Oh! to love Him and cause Him
to be loved!" [44] She even said that she was happy not to be
consoled, and commended others to be detached from such
favors, so that they might be attached to Jesus alone.

With keen psychological insight she recognized that self-
love often insinuates itself into sensible affection, especially
when it is accompanied by consolations. "You do not feel your
love for your Spouse," she writes to Celine. "You would like to
have your heart be a flame that rises towards Him without
a trace of smoke. . . . But notice that the smoke that surrounds
you is intended only for you. It has for its purpose to hide
from your eyes your love for Jesus. The flame is seen by Him
alone. In this way, He has it all for Himself, for when He
lets us catch a glimpse of it, self-love soon comes along like
an evil wind that extinguishes everything." [45] This thought
Therese summarized thus: "Our love for Jesus is truly great
when we do not feel its sweetness. It then becomes a martyrdom. . . . [46] When, on the contrary, we begin to seek ourselves,
true love dies away.[47] Unfortunately, many serve Jesus when
He consoles them, but few are willing to keep Him company
when He is asleep." [48]

She went so far in her desire to love God for Himself alone
that she would have been glad to have God remain unaware
of her good actions: "I love Him so much that I would like
to give Him pleasure without His knowing that it is I. When
He knows that I am giving Him pleasure and sees it, He is,
as it were, obliged to return love for it. I would not like to
give Him that much trouble." [49]

She knew, of course, that such a thing is impossible, but
this was her way of expressing the distinterestedness of
her love.

3. THERESE'S GENEROUS LOVE

As can easily be deduced from her selflessness, Therese's love is also marked by a very great generosity. Very early in life, almost as it were by instinct, she had understood that love is proved by deeds and is nourished by sacrifice. Hence, she was always careful never to refuse anything to Jesus, but to give without stint, never neglecting anything that could please Him. "We do not bargain when we love." [50] "Jesus," she writes, "teaches me not to refuse Him anything and to be pleased when He gives me an opportunity for proving to Him that I love Him. This I do peacefully, with complete abandonment." [51]

However, such are we that we are not always equally well-disposed. Especially is this true when our Lord seems to deprive us of His presence and to leave us to ourselves. "Life is often burdensome," she confessed to Celine. "What a bitterness, but also what sweetness! Yes, life is painful. It is hard to begin a day of labor. . . . If only we could feel Jesus! We would do everything for Him . . . but no! He seems to be miles away. We are alone with ourselves. Oh, what annoying company we are to ourselves when Jesus is not present . . . but . . . He is not far away. He is right there, quite near and looking at us. Indeed, He is there begging us to offer Him our sorrow . . . He hides, but we feel that He is present." [52] Hence, "the grain of sand determines to set to work without joy or courage or energy. This good-will, then, eases and energizes His undertaking. He wants to labor through love." [53]

Elsewhere she says: "What great grace is ours when, in the morning, we seem to be filled with lassitude and to lack both courage and strength to practice virtue! Then is the ideal moment to put the axe to the root of the tree, though our effort may lag for a few moments and we may neglect to gather our treasures. This is the critical moment, for we may be tempted to give up everything. However, we can repair everything and even gain in grace through an act of love, though it be unaccompanied by any sensible feeling. Jesus smiles. He helps us without appearing to do so and the tears He sheds over the wicked are wiped away by our poor, feeble efforts, by our small gift of love. Love can accomplish all things. Things that are 'most impossible' become easy where love is at work." [54]

She herself proved the truth of these words. She gave to God all He asked. "To love," she wrote, "means giving everything and giving ourselves." [55] "I love Him so much that I am always satisfied with anything He sends me." "I love all that He does." [56] Hence, at the end of her life, she was able to testify in her favor that since the age of three she had never refused anything to God. [57]

Jesus repeatedly proclaimed that men prove their love for Him by fulfilling the divine will. That is why believing souls try to conform to that rule. For them to live in union with God's will is to live in God. Therese lived such a life; she loved to say that "her only desire, her only joy on earth, was to do God's will."

"Perfection," she also declared, "consists in doing the will of God, in being what He wants us to be." She proved this admirably during her religious life. If, in every state of life, we must recognize God's will in the orders of our lawful superiors, this is even more true of religious life where everything is regulated by obedience and tends by means of it to lead us to perfection.

Therese had understood this. On the day of her profession, she asked God the grace of fulfilling her promises to perfection. It was her intention to live the Carmelite life as it had been planned by her Mother, St. Teresa of Avila. In this she saw an infallible means of living "in truth." This, to her, was the straight way that leads to God.

"How great and numerous the anxieties from which we

free ourselves," she said, "when we take the vow of obedience! How happy are simple religious! Their only compass is the will of their superiors; hence, they are always certain of being on the right path. They need not fear to be mistaken even when it seems certain that the superiors are mistaken. But when we stop looking at that infallible compass, when we leave the path pointed out to us, under the pretext of doing the will of God, and because He does not seem to enlighten properly those who, nevertheless, represent Him, we immediately get lost in arid roads where the waters of grace are soon dried up." [58]

Even when we are treated with severity, we must see in it a permission of God. "I know well, my mother, that you deal with me as with a soul that is weak, as with a spoiled child. Hence, I have no difficulty in bearing the burden of obedience, but, it seems to me, from what I feel in the depths of my heart, that I would not change my conduct and that my love for you would not weaken if you preferred to handle me with severity, for I would still see that it is the will of Jesus that you should act thus for the greater good of my soul." [59]

She instilled her novices with the same love of obedience to the rule: "Even if all were to fail in the observance of the rule," she said, "that would not be a reason for justifying ourselves," and, repeating the words of her holy Mother, St. Teresa, she added that "everyone should act as if the perfection of the Order depended on her personal conduct."

Religious life, considered in itself, usually gives no opportunity for anything but ordinary actions; hence, Therese had no opportunity of undertaking work of any importance. Moreover, she considered herself to be "but a very small soul which can offer only very small things to God." [60]

But very small things can have very great value; for the latter depends on the love with which they are done: "Our Lord considers not so much the greatness of our actions nor the difficulty that accompanies them. He has no need of our works but craves only our love." [61]

And so a soul that desires to correspond to the love of God, endeavors to mark all her actions, even the most indifferent, with that divine stamp, and it is this that gives them their inestimable value.

Therese applied herself to the observance of the Rule with all the care which works done for God deserve, and with all the love of which she was capable. Obedience guided her at every moment and her fidelity was absolute.

Mother Agnes testified at the Apostolic Process that she did not remember having ever seen her sister disobey even once, not even in the smallest matters. Sister Marie of the Trinity, likewise, affirmed: "I lived always with her and, yet, I never saw her commit the smallest imperfection. I always saw her behave in the way that she believed to be the more perfect. As Therese corrected me when I committed a fault, I would have liked to find some imperfection in her in order to be able to excuse myself, but I never did." [63]

One of her novices confessed that she avoided Therese because she found her too perfect. Others have affirmed that they never heard her take part in useless conversation or waste a minute of her time. They never noticed in her one moment of bad humor, nor "a lack of charity." On no occasion did they find her "being in the least unfaithful to the smallest point of the Rule." [64] Not only did she obey the orders of her Superiors, but she did what she guessed were their wishes, and an advice, once given to her, remained in force, as far as she herself was concerned, until the end of her life.[65]

"When I wanted to recall the text of one of our rules," a novice declared, "I had merely to watch the way Sister Therese acted." [66]

She had even acquired the habit of obeying each one of her sisters.[67] She was most punctual. As soon as the bell sounded, she interrupted the conversation or stopped writing, leaving a word unfinished. One day, seeing her older sister continue to write down some important counsel after the bell had sounded, she said: "It is much better to lose that and to perform an act of regularity. If only we knew the value of regularity!" [68]

We can now understand why, a short time before her death, Therese was able to say that, if she had to live her life over again, she would act as she had done. How many of us will be able to make such a declaration at that supreme moment?

All work that is undertaken for God should be done with special care and attention. Unfortunately, that does not always happen, even in religious life. Therese had more than one occasion to observe this and she deplored the fact that "many perform their actions in a careless or nonchalant way; few fulfill their duties as perfectly as possible."

Religious life, however, implies more than regular observances. It is often seasoned with renunciations and sacrifices. Therese learned this from her own experience but she accepted everything in a spirit of perfect submission to the divine will: "Allow Jesus to take and give whatever He wills," she said, "perfection consists in doing His will." [69] It even happens that God, judging a soul to be capable of showing Him a greater love, sends her trials which give her an opportunity for such love. "The greatest honor He can do to a soul is not to give her much, but to ask much from her." [70]

It was thus that God acted towards Therese. He tried her severely in both body and soul, and, during the last months of her life especially, she suffered a true martyrdom.

We might expect that being exhausted by illness and hovering between life and death, she would have felt a great longing for heaven and exulted at the thought that she was soon to possess God, who had been the object of all her desires; but she showed nothing of the kind.

In her, the very strongest aspirations were subordinated to the divine will. The desire of pleasing God was so deeply anchored in Therese's soul that she no longer desired anything for herself. "The only thing that satisfies me," she said, "is doing the will of God. . . . What pleases me most is what God loves and what He chooses for me." [71]

She did not ask that prayers should be offered to give her relief in her sufferings: "I have asked the good Lord not to hear the prayers which would put an obstacle in the way of His designs in my regard." [72]

She did not prefer to die rather than to live; or, if at times she expressed some satisfaction because she felt death was near, it was only because God was calling her. "I am glad to die," she wrote, "not because I shall be freed from suffering here below; on the contrary, suffering is the only thing which seems desirable to me in this valley of tears. But I am glad to die because I know well that such is the will of God." [73] And a little later: "The thought of heavenly bliss gives me no joy. . . . It is only the thought of accomplishing God's will which constitutes all my joy." [74] The latter consideration was completed, as she expresses it elsewhere, by the hope of loving God as much as she had desired it, and "of causing Him to be loved by a multitude of souls." [75]

4.   HER LOVE WAS TENDER AND THOUGHTFUL

Finally, Therese's love was tender and thoughtful. It was this delicacy that made her hide her sufferings, for fear that God would see them and suffer on their account.[76] This, of course, is pious exaggeration, for Therese knew that God does not change and that He is unable to experience pain. But those sentiments express in a childlike way the extreme sensitivity of her soul.

The same delicacy prevented her from invoking God directly to obtain temporal graces from Him. She did not want Him, as she expressed it naively, "to experience the regret of having to refuse those that were not in conformity with His will." [77] She transmitted such petitions through the hands of the Blessed Virgin; for since Mary knows God's designs, she would present to Him only those prayers that were agreeable to Him.

It has been said that her love was a filial love, the love of a child for his Father in heaven. It is certain that Therese loved God in a filial manner. She had towards God, considered as a father, that confident love "which has no fears, which goes to sleep and forgets itself as it lies on the Heart of its God, like a child in its father's arms." [78] "She loved God, as a child loves his father," said Sister Genevieve, "and used the most unexpected ways to express her affection." [97]

She also loved Jesus in a very particular way. As soon as we begin to read her writings, we notice that it is above all Jesus that she desired to please. The part which Jesus had in her love was such that, according to her sisters' testimony, her interior life was "centered in Jesus." [80]

She dealt with Him with that familiarity which seems natural to those who remember that our God has "loved us to excess." She herself told us that she loved to "take hold of Jesus through His Heart," and to "caress Him."

> "To You alone, O Jesus, I must cling;
> And running to Your arms, dear Lord,
> There let me hide;
> Loving with childlike tenderness."

On several occasions she urged her correspondents to act likewise.[81] If any one had objected that such conduct showed a lack of respect and exaggerated sentimentalism, Therese would, no doubt, have answered that a most tender love and even familiarity are quite compatible with the greatest reverence. For Jesus called us brothers and friends.

He surrounds us with loving care; He even anticipates the desires of those who are totally devoted to Him. Hence, He allows us to approach Him in a familiar, intimate way. God has revealed Himself as Love; "God is Charity." Jesus, by His example, has revealed that one loves truly only when one pushes love to its extreme consequences, "because of the excessive charity with which He loved us." Hence, we cannot claim that we love God unless we love Him to that same degree and give ourselves entirely to Him. Therese's message, which is entirely based on love, reminds us of this truth in an admirable manner. Her life was a living illustration of it. We owe an immense debt of love to God, for "He has loved us first" and from all eternity "in perpetual charity." We are debtors towards Jesus Christ because of His life and His death. To so much love we should have responded by an unwavering fidelity. May we, henceforth, apply ourselves to the task of rendering to God love for love!

Love is, at the same time, the root principle, the food and the end of all spiritual life. Without it we cannot forget ourselves nor give ourselves to God. Without it, we will lack fidelity and generosity. This is what Therese meant when, on the eve of her death, she told Sister Genevieve: "It is love alone that counts."

CHAPTER VI

Love of our Neighbor

THE precept of charity has not God alone for its object. It extends also to our neighbor. Moreover, when we truly love our neighbor by that very fact we love God also, for we were all made after His image and likeness, and God is, above all, present in us by His grace.

But there is another reason for loving our neighbor and that is our incorporation in Christ. For all who are members of Christ's Mystical Body are one in Christ; Christ is in them and all are in Christ. When they are in the state of grace, His life circulates in them; His spirit animates them and Holy Communion binds them sacramentally in that unity. Hence, it is Christ whom we must see and love in all. Whatever the faults of the members, they are unable to eclipse the Head.

The Holy Ghost inclined Therese to the practice of charity from her early childhood. From her early youth she sympathized with the sufferings of the poor and loved to console them. After her entrance into Carmel she practiced it even more ardently, understanding from the start that "if we want to live a life of love of God, we must not fail in our love towards our neighbor." [1]

Nevertheless, however well-intentioned we may be and though we consider that we must practice charity, we sometimes find this a difficult commandment. We cannot help seeing our neighbor as he truly is. All men are imperfect and we are frequently annoyed by the faults and conduct of others.

Therese had quickly realized that the practice of charity demands a great deal of self-denial and that it requires that we act in a spirit of faith. She could not help noticing the natural shortcomings of her Sisters. She saw their imperfections, their frailties and their faults. But *she endeavored to look only at the virtues of her Sisters.* "Charity," she said, "consists in disregarding the faults of our neighbor, not being astonished at the sight of their weakness, but in being edified by the smallest acts of virtue we see them practice."

She desired to have only charitable thoughts and sought excuses for what might appear to be reprehensible in her Sisters. She left to Jesus the task of passing judgment on them. She knew by experience that we often make erroneous judgments, that what seems to be a fault may be even an act of virtue because of the person's particular intention. On the other hand, she held "that there is nothing sweeter than to think well of our neighbor." [2]

She would have liked to see the closest union reigning at all times in her community. That is why she avoided or repressed everything that might disturb that peace.

She had a horror of quarrels. There was one religious who usually expressed views that were contrary to her own. Therese let her say those things and turned the conversation in another direction. "It is better," she declared, "to let others keep their own opinions and preserve the peace."

She disapproved of criticisms. "You are wrong" she taught, "to criticize this or that, to desire that everybody should adopt your view of things. Since we want to be little children, little children do not know what is best. Everything seems right to them." [3]

When some trouble arose in the community, *she did her best to restore peace.* The presence in a monastery of four and then five members of the same family was bound to cause certain difficulties. Therese sometimes had to suffer on this account. "We must seek forgiveness, she told her sisters, for living under the same roof."

Considering that it is a property of charity to expand the heart, *Therese tried to animate all souls with joy*. "Jesus," she proclaimed, "loves a cheerful heart. He loves persons who are always smiling." [4]

That is why she urged the novices to struggle against unevenness of disposition. She wanted them to present a calm and serene demeanor for, in her opinion, nothing makes community life more depressing than sad faces and beclouded brows. She preached this by her own example. Her face was lit up with a perpetual smile. She was the soul of gaiety during recreations. Faithful to the recommendations of her holy Mother, St. Teresa, she wanted this exercise to serve more for the recreation of others than for her own relaxation. She had a good sense of humor and did not disdain witticisms and even giving "little digs" provided they did not hurt anybody. More than once, when she was absent, the sisters remarked: "Well, we shall not laugh so much today!"

True charity makes us forget ourselves and seek the welfare of others. Therese wished to render service to those about her. She put herself at the disposal of all. She was always ready to help any one who asked her and would interrupt her own work to do so. Sometimes service is asked for in an unpleasant or unreasonable way. "Then a soul that is not firmly established in the practice of charity finds a thousand reasons for refusing, or at least she is not disposed to grant what is expected of her, and she makes sure that the petitioner be made to understand her lack of delicacy." [5] That is an imperfect attitude and very unlike the charity of Christ. "We must never refuse anyone," said Therese, "even when it costs us much pain. Think that it is Jesus who is asking this service of you; how eager and friendly you will then be in granting the favor requested!"

However, *there is something that is even better than to*

give to him who asks; we can offer ourselves. "I must antici-
pate the desires of others," she wrote; "show that we are
much obliged, very honored to be able to render service. The
good Lord wants me to forget myself in order to give pleasure to others." [6]

Her sister Genevieve (Celine) testified that she never
neglected an opportunity to render service: "My dear little
Sister," she reported, "never did anything to please herself.
Whatever little free time she had at her disposal, was spent in
the service of others. While she was sacristan, I noticed that
on free days when her own work was finished, she would
remain near the sacristy so that she might be called on to
help others to finish theirs. She put herself in the way of the
sister who distributed "charges" so that the latter might ask
her to undertake some task—as she invariably did. Knowing
that in reality this cost her a great deal, I often showed her
how it could be avoided. But it was all in vain. She wanted
to be at the beck and call of everybody." [7]

When working with others, she tried to please them in
every way. However strange the tastes or the opinions of her
companions might be, she adjusted herself to them to such
an extent that she seemed to share their views.[8]

As might be expected, when she was novice mistress, she
devoted herself still more completely to the young Sisters of
whom she had charge. She allowed them almost to "devour"
her. According to one statement, "they disturbed her in season and out of season, to the point of pestering her with endless questions that were unnecessary and often indiscreet."
But Therese always maintained the calm and gentle manner
with which she treated everybody.[9]

In training the novices, however, Therese pointed out
that no one should impose on the charity of one's neighbor,
nor ask for assistance from others unless it was necessary.[10]
She also warned them against rendering service to others for
unworthy or selfish motives: "I must not be obliging in order
to appear so, or with the hope of forcing another Sister to

render me service in her turn." She invoked, in this respect, the words of our Lord who teaches us to lend to others without expecting a return from them.

Sometimes, of course, our neighbor who asks us a service, promises spontaneously to repay us at the first opportunity: "They come and tell you with a convincing air," she writes with a turn of humor, " 'Sister, I need your help for a few hours, but don't worry, I have our Mother's permission and I will make up for the time you give me.' Since we know very well that the time thus lent to another will never be repaid, we feel inclined to say, 'I *give it* to you!' But where, then, would our charity be?" Moreover, whether they made a return for her services or not, she was never defrauded: "I lose nothing; what I do is done for God . . . to give pleasure to Our good Lord . . . so I am always paid for the trouble I take in serving others." [12]

This habit of always putting oneself at the disposal of one's neighbor may become very burdensome. People learn to run for favors to those who, they know, will grant them. "It does not matter," says Therese; "I must not avoid the Sisters who readily ask for my services. Does not the divine Master tell us, 'To him who asks of you, give, and from him who would borrow of you, do not turn away?' " (Matt., 5:42) [13]

There are times, of course, when one cannot grant the favor that is requested. In that case, we must remember that "there is a way of refusing that is so gracious . . . that the refusal gives as much pleasure as the gift."

In virtue of the vow of poverty, everything is held in common in religious life. No one has the right to possess anything as his own. Nevertheless, because of one's occupation or for other reasons, certain objects are put at the disposal of an individual religious. Now it happens sometimes that a Sister takes something that has been put at the disposal of another and fails to inform the person concerned. Or, again, she enters the office of another and upsets things there.

Patience is severely tried on such occasions and it is difficult to preserve one's spirit of detachment. Therese recommends that in such circumstances we act with humility. We should ask for the return of the article in question as if we were poor beggars. If, even then, we are met with refusal, we should be prepared to accept that and waive our personal claims. Nothing is to be preferred to peace and the joy which will flood the soul of one who knows how to be truly poor in spirit.

This charitable behavior must exist toward all without distinction. It stands to reason that we find it easier to practice charity towards some persons than towards others. There are persons to whom we feel attracted on account of the natural character or the spiritual qualities that we find in them, whether it be something felt naturally or based on the other person's moral or spiritual qualities. There are others towards whom we feel a certain antipathy; we are not inclined to seek their company, nor do they seem drawn towards us. Neither of these tendencies is evil in itself. Jesus and the Saints have had a particular love for certain souls and have manifested their affection for them. In religious life, however, the manifestation of special affection or antipathy can interfere with the exercise of charity. It can interfere with the harmony of a community and might even lead to serious trouble. Hence, we must watch the one and be on our guard against the other.

Therese deliberately sought the company of the sisters who, on account of their imperfections, were shunned by others, or those who pleased her least. One of these was very difficult to live with on account of her crotchety character and disagreeable manner. Therese forced herself to treat her "as she would the person that she loved most." At times when she was tempted to give a sharp answer, she treated the Sister's rudeness with a friendly smile. This puzzled the nun so much that she asked the Saint one day why she was so attracted to her. Therese replied that she smiled each time they met because she was "glad to see her." In recounting this incident later, she added with a twinkle in her eye: "Of course I didn't tell her that I was acting from a supernatural motive." [14] We learn from the Saint herself that her charity towards that Sister gained for her so great a grace that, from that time, she had no further difficulty in practicing that virtue.

When others complained to her about the unpleasant character of that nun and the annoyance they suffered on her account, she replied: "Be very kind to that Sister. It is both an act of charity and an exercise of patience. We must not allow our own souls to be upset and yield to interior bitterness. We must sweeten our minds by charitable thoughts. After that, the practice of patience will become almost natural." [15]

When engaged in work with other nuns, our Saint chose as her companions sisters who seemed to be depressed or sad. Not being allowed to break the silence, she smiled affectionately at them. She knew that a smile is often enough to gladden a human soul. Should one of the nuns be ill, she would hasten to her side; but she was prepared to be rebuffed, knowing in advance she might not be welcome and that "a word said with the best intentions is sometimes taken amiss."

When she found it impossible to console or help a sister, she prayed that God do it. [16] To those who were tempted to anger against a sister who had offended them, she counselled prayer for the benefit of the offender and advised them to ask God to reward her for the suffering she had procured for them. How could we prove our love to Jesus, she asked, if we did not act with gentleness and charity towards those who make us suffer? [17]

When she herself had suffered from others, she kept silence and did her best not to worry about it. [18] Her charity was so delicate that she tried to spare others the humiliation they might have felt when they realized the mistake they had made.[19] She was so generous that she offered to nurse an invalid sister whom no one else could please. The description of this experience written in her own delightful style shows how God blessed her patience and her charity.[20] In this case, she was successful in a task at which all the rest had failed. She admitted, however, that the practice of charity had not always been easy for her: Sometimes she had "to grasp her patience with both hands, lest it should escape" her or she "had to run away like a deserter, so as not to go down in defeat." [21] But grace crowned her efforts and she always triumphed in the end.

The acts of charity we have recorded are certainly noteworthy, yet her practice of that virtue during her last illness was even more remarkable. For charity is so much more perfect when it is more delicate and when more effort is required for its practice.

Therese suffered horribly during her last illness. And yet, however great her physical exhaustion or her moral affliction, she did her best when receiving a visit to be cheerful and agreeable in her manner.[22]

The visits she received at that time were not always pleasant. One ill-advised Sister came every evening to look and smile at Therese, remaining at the foot of her bed for a considerable time. However good the Sister's intentions might have been, her frequent and protracted visits were very trying to the patient though she made no complaint, and even managed to smile at her visitor. One day, however, she was asked whether those indiscreet visits did not fatigue her. "Yes," she replied, "it is very painful to be looked at with a smile while one suffers, but I say to myself that our Lord on the Cross was much gazed at in that way in the midst of His sufferings." [23]

After she had received Extreme Unction and Holy Viaticum, the sisters pressed around her without leaving her time for her act of thanksgiving. She greeted them immediately, without showing the least displeasure. She later confided to Mother Agnes: "I was greatly disturbed during my thanksgiving. But I remembered that when our Lord withdrew into solitude, the people followed Him and He did not send them away. I wanted to imitate Him by receiving the sisters graciously." [24]

Finally, here is a case that borders on the heroic. It was during the last night Therese passed on earth. She was reduced to a state of exhaustion. Her own sisters were watching with her. One of them had fallen asleep. The other, in turn, dozed off while Therese was sipping slowly the drink she had been given. The Saint, through compassion for her sisters, kept the glass in her hands until one of them awoke.

THERESE'S PERFECT CHARITY

However perfectly Therese had practiced charity throughout her life, in June 1897 she wrote that up to the time of her last illness she had not fully understood the extent of that precept. She had, no doubt, read the text of St. John where our Lord bade His apostles to love one another as He had loved them. But, she writes, she had not penetrated the depth of its meaning. Since she was aspiring for a love that was truly perfect, Jesus revealed to her "that it was His will that she should practice this new commandment."

God, in the Old Law, had ordered His people to love their neighbor as themselves. Considering the great selfishness inherent in human nature, He was asking a great deal when He prescribed that rule of conduct, before He had given them the example of His own life on earth.

But when Jesus came among us, He was no longer satisfied with even that measure of love. He demanded that we love our fellowmen as He had loved them, as He will love them to the end of time. Now, says St. Therese, "I put myself to the task of finding out how Jesus had loved His disciples.

I realized that it was not for their natural qualities, for they were ignorant and full of worldly thoughts. And, yet, He calls them friends, His brothers. He desires to see them near Him in the kingdom of His Father and, in order to open that kingdom, He chose to die on a Cross, saying that there is no greater love than that of laying down one's life for those whom one loves."

Enlightened by these reflections, Therese understood that, if until then she had loved Jesus in her sisters, trying even to sow joy and peace in their hearts,[25] henceforth, in order to fulfill the new commandment, she would have to cultivate a personal love for each one, forming in her own heart the same feelings that Jesus had for them.

Always conscious of her own littleness, she asked herself how this could be achieved. She felt that she was incapable of realizing such an ideal of love, so she begged that Jesus Himself would implant His own love in her heart. Since He gave us the commandment of loving as He loves, that meant that He was prepared to give us the grace to do so.

Hence, from that time she endeavored to remain more closely united to Him, for she was convinced that the more intimate that union would be, the more also she would realize the precept of charity. Jesus would then love in her, and she would love through Him and like Him.[26]

Considering on the other hand that Jesus is present in the soul of her sisters, she endeavored to love Him also in them.[27]

To practice charity in the manner in which Therese practiced it, is not the work of unaided man. Divine grace is necessary. She herself wrote that without grace it is impossible to practice supernatural charity or even to understand all that it requires.[28] To those who found such a practice difficult she replied: "It is only the first step that is difficult." God will help us when we have good will. Just the desire alone of practicing charity gives peace to the soul.[29]

Let us end with one case which will serve as a suitable

conclusion of this study. It was towards the end of her life and Therese was very ill. When the weather permitted it, she was brought to the garden and there worked on the final pages of her autobiography. The sisters who passed near her, while showing friendliness, constantly disturbed her. At every interruption Therese put down her pen, closed her copybook and replied to the sisters with a smile. Mother Agnes asked her how she found it possible, under such conditions, to connect even two consecutive thoughts. Therese replied: "I am writing about fraternal charity. This is a case of practicing it. . . ." And she added these words which are perhaps the most beautiful ever written on the subject: "My dear Mother, fraternal charity is everything on this earth. We love God in the measure in which we practice charity." [30]

This sentence is both an echo of the Gospel teaching and a revelation of a fundamental attitude of Therese. May we always keep it in mind and translate it into our own conduct.

THERESE'S ZEAL FOR SOULS

Charity is not confined to those with whom we live or with whom we come in contact. Just as God's love extends to all men and Christ has given His life for all, so must our love be universal. When love is strong, it engenders zeal,[31] zeal for the glory of God, zeal for the salvation of souls.

Being a worthy daughter of the Prophet Elias, Therese was always inflamed with a most ardent zeal. It is not without reason that the Sovereign Pontiff made her the patroness of the missions. "The love of God had taken hold of her from her infancy;" zeal for souls was kindled in her heart from her tender years.

On the feast of Christmas, 1886, she received a grace which "changed her heart . . . charity entered her heart with the desire of always forgetting herself." She experienced a fervor unknown until then, a great desire to labor for the conversion of sinners. Jesus made her a fisher of souls.[32]

Some time later—it was a Sunday of July, 1887—while closing her missal at the end of Mass, a picture of the divine Crucified slid from its pages, showing her a hand pierced and bleeding. That sight made her experience an ineffable wave of feeling that was quite new to her. "Her heart was filled with sorrow at the sight of that precious blood falling to the ground without any one hastening to collect it." [33] It was not simply a feeling of compassion towards the divine Sufferer of Calvary, nor yet a thought of the ingratitude of men who ignore so great a love, that was predominant in her mind. It was rather that she was struck with sorrow to see how that precious blood was wasted because there was not one to collect it and pour it out over the souls of men.[34]

Henceforth, she understood the part that God assigned to her in the work of redemption, the kind of consolation He expected from her.

It would be her role to remain constantly in spirit at the foot of the Cross and to cooperate in the work of redemption by collecting the precious blood and pouring it out for the benefit of souls. From that time onwards, she thought she heard constantly the cry of the dying Jesus expressing His thirst. The suppliant cry enkindled in her an ardor she had not known until then. She burned with the desire of saving sinners.

The conversion of Pranzini, which was the fruit of her prayers, helped to intensify that desire.[35] She considered herself to be the intermediary "in a veritable exchange of love." She poured out on souls the blood of Jesus and offered Him the souls purified by the blood that He had shed.

Seeing that Therese was animated with such sentiments, we might imagine that she would have wished to enter a missionary Congregation. She, however, preferred the cloistered life "so that she might give herself more completely to the good Lord." She considered that in the cloister she could consecrate herself more fully to a life of self-denial and mortification and that her sacrifice would be all the more fruitful for souls,[36] as she would be deprived of the consolation of working actively amongst them. She, therefore, entered Carmel to give herself totally to God, to love Jesus more perfectly and to belong entirely to Him.

We must also remember that the Carmel of St. Teresa of Avila has a well-defined apostolic purpose, specified by the saintly reformer. It was that purpose which Therese proclaimed at the canonical examination which preceded her profession, when she was asked why she had come to Carmel. "I came," she replied, "to save souls and especially to pray for priests." [37]

After her entrance she applied herself to the pursuit of that end with all the ardor of her generous soul. "When we want to reach a certain goal," she wrote, "we must use the proper means. Jesus made me understand that it was through the cross that He would give me souls; so the more my suffering grew, the more I loved it, and that was my main objective for five years. Nothing, however, revealed to others the sufferings I endured and they were all the more painful because they were known only to myself." [38]

Therese knew that God has made us His helpers in the work of salvation and that, in virtue of the Communion of Saints, the prayer of an insignificant soul, a sigh of our heart, can save the souls of our brethren.[39]

That is why she made the resolution of offering everything for that purpose and to keep nothing for herself. "I don't know how to save up" she declared; "all that I have I immediately spend for the purchase of souls.[40] All that belongs to me belongs to everyone (of my brother missionaries). I feel that God is too good to give us only measured portions. He is so rich that He gives without measure what I ask of Him!" [41]

And at the end of her life, she said: "I don't know whether

I shall go to purgatory, and I don't worry about that in the least, but if I go there, I shall not regret that I did nothing to avoid it. I shall not regret at any time that I have labored exclusively for the salvation of others. How happy I was to know that our Mother St. Teresa thought likewise." [42] Therese even desired that the prayers said to obtain some relief for her in her cruel sufferings, should be offered for the salvation of souls.[43]

Knowing that there were souls who did not have the Faith, she wanted to "be seated at the table of sinners." To bring them back to God, to prevent or to make reparation for one single fault against the Faith, she declared her readiness to eat the bread of suffering until it should please God to bring her into the kingdom of His glory. She was willing to renounce all joy on earth in order that God might bring heaven to unbelievers.

Therese sought to enkindle the same zeal in others, especially in the heart of Celine: "Lately a thought has come to my mind which I must reveal to my dear Celine." And she went on to remind her of the words of Jesus urging the Apostles to ask the Lord of the harvest to send laborers into His harvest. "What a mystery!" she exclaimed. "Why does Jesus say this? Is He not all-powerful? It is because He has such an unfathomable love for us that He wants us to have a share with Him in saving souls. He does not want to do anything without us. The Creator of the universe awaits the prayer of an insignificant human being to save others who, like herself, were redeemed at the cost of all His blood. . . ." And she proudly recalls the share of Carmelites in that work: "Our special vocation is not to work in the harvest fields ourselves. It is something still more sublime. Listen to the words of Jesus: 'Lift up your eyes and see: see how in heaven there are empty places. It is your task to fill them. Become like another Moses praying on the mountain; ask for laborers and I will send them. I await but a prayer, a sigh of your heart.'

Is not the apostolate of prayer, as it were, more sublime than the work of actually preaching?" [44]

To one of her brother missionaries she said: "A Carmelite who is not an apostle abandons the purpose of her vocation and ceases to be a daughter of the seraphic St. Teresa, who desired to give a thousand lives to save one single soul." [45] "Let us then work together for the salvation of souls. We have only this short life to save them and thus to give to the Lord the proof of our love." [46]

This zeal for souls was marked by a special note that is not so clearly defined in other saints. All saints are devoured by zeal for souls but at the end of their lives their greatest aspiration seems to be to partake of God's beatitude and repose in Him.

Therese, of course, also experienced this desire; it comes from God Himself. But her apostolic ardor was so great that it seemed to her that her happiness would not be perfect if, notwithstanding her repose in God, she were not allowed to return to earth to continue her apostolate: "I cannot reflect much on the happiness that awaits me in heaven. One thing only causes my heart to throb: namely, the thought of the love I shall receive and the love I shall be able to give. I think of all the good that I would like to do after my death. . . . If my wishes were granted, my heaven will be spent on earth until the end of the world. Yes, I desire to spend my heaven in doing good on earth. I shall not be able to take any rest as long as there are still souls to be saved. But when the Angel shall have said, 'Time is no more' then I shall take my rest. Then I can be happy, for the number of the elect will be complete and all shall have entered into joy and eternal rest." [47]

That is why she asked that, after she had gone to heaven, others would often fill her hands with small sacrifices and prayers, so that she might have the pleasure of pouring them on souls like a shower of graces.[48] Her zeal was so great that she affirmed one day that, if in heaven she were no longer able to work for the glory of God, she would prefer to be exiled from that heavenly fatherland. This, of course, is but a forceful manner of speech, for she knew, as she wrote elsewhere, that in heaven she would be more useful to souls than she had ever been while on earth.[50]

Therese was interested in the souls of sinners. For them she desired to suffer. But, above all, she was interested in priests and missionaries. It was for them that she had entered Carmel, as she proclaimed at the canonical examination before her profession. This she afterwards repeatedly affirmed: "O my Mother," she wrote to Mother Agnes, "how beautiful is our vocation! It is the function of Carmel to preserve the salt of the earth. We offer our prayers and our sacrifices for the apostles of the Lord. We ourselves must be their apostles, while they, by their words and example, evangelize the souls of our brethren. What a noble mission is ours!"

She told Celine: "Our mission, as Carmelites, is to form evangelical workers who will save millions of souls of whom we shall be the mothers. Why, then, should we envy priests?" She felt the need of praying for them all the more, because she knew that their love and virtue do not always correspond with their sacred character. "Celine," she continued, "during the short moments that still remain to us on earth, let us not waste our time. . . . Let us save souls; let us be apostles, and especially let us save the souls of priests. Their souls should be more transparent than crystal. . . . Alas! how many are bad priests, priests who are not saints . . . who give to others their hearts that belong so absolutely to Jesus. . . . Let us pray and suffer for them. . . . May our life be consecrated to them!"

She told her also: "O Celine, I feel that Jesus asks of us both to quench His thirst, by giving Him souls, especially the souls of priests. He makes me feel this every day and wants me to tell you. Our mission is to forget ourselves, to annihilate ourselves. We are so insignificant and, yet, Jesus wants the salvation of souls to depend on our sacrifices, on our love. He begs souls from us. He wants us to produce many priests who know how to love Him."

Therese realized that by praying for priests, she was laboring for a much wider field, for "by preserving the salt of the earth" that is, by cooperating for the sanctification of priests, she contributed to the efficacy of their ministry. For the holier the priest, the greater is his radiating power.[51]

Finally, let us note that when, in conformity with the fundamental tendency of her life, she thus applied herself to the salvation of souls even unto self-immolation, it was, above all, in order that God might be loved: "There is but one thing for us to do in the night of this life and that is to love, to love Jesus with all the energy of our heart and to save souls so that He may be loved by them. O let us cause Jesus to be loved by men!" [52]

To love Jesus and make others love Him, such was the objective of her whole life, the continual aspiration of her soul, her preoccupation of every moment. May this be true also of us! Charity is genuine only when it embraces souls as well as God.

Jesus came down among us to glorify His Father and for Him He sacrificed Himself. But He came also to save us and for us He shed His blood to its very last drop. It follows that he who thinks only of his own sanctification cannot claim that He acts in conformity with Christ's designs and imitates the life of Jesus. It is not enough to live in God's presence while remaining unconcerned about the lot of so many souls that are heading towards perdition. Realizing how little God is loved and to what extent Christ's sufferings and death are rendered useless, or at least fruitless, for many souls, how can we refuse to apply ourselves with all our heart to the task of consoling the heart of our Savior by bringing the infinite merits of Jesus Christ to our fellowmen?

If so many virtuous people fail to make progress in spiritual life, is it not often on account of their lack of charity? They show no interest in the spiritual good of others. They have no zeal for souls. A more perfect practice of charity, a greater devotedness to the salvation of souls would help them become more detached from self-love and forget their personal interests. By that means they would advance in the love of God and strengthen their union with Him.

CHAPTER VII

Spirit of Renunciation and Sacrifice

WHOEVER desires to love God as He deserves to be loved must reject everything that might impede or weaken that love. For we love God truly only when we love Him alone and love Him with all our heart; furthermore, any love we have for creatures must be centered in Him and be for Him. To this law there is no exception.

Now, in consequence of original sin, we find in ourselves a tendency to seek ourselves in all things. It is this inordinate self-love that pulls us hither and thither and prevents the full unfolding of our love of God and our growth in Christ. That is why Jesus demands of those who wish to be His disciples that they deny themselves.

Therese had chosen love as the first and absolute objective of her spiritual life. She had resolved to love God alone with complete generosity. It was imperative, then, that she should practice a radical renunciation. In fact, she never yielded to the demands of selfish nature. Neither did she tolerate concessions to that nature in her teaching and direction of her novices.

WHAT IS THIS RENUNCIATION?

When renunciation is mentioned, many people immediately picture to themselves a most unpleasant series of mortifications. They are frightened by such a prospect and the sight of the many deprivations they will have to impose on themselves. Now, this is not what is meant by renunciation. No doubt, its practice implies a succession of privations, but renunciation is, above all, an interior disposition, a spiritual attitude.

Renunciation consists principally in mortifying that self-love which makes us seek our own pleasure and satisfaction in everything we do. It means that we practice self-forgetfulness.

Again, renunciation is not an end in itself, but as self-seeking is incompatible with love, we must practice renunciation and self-forgetfulness before love can reign in our hearts.

Renunciation appears painful because we, too, often look upon it solely as on a sort of amputation, a cutting off of the things we like and to which we are attached. We should view it rather as a process of liberation; it frees us from slavery to self and disengages us from everything that obstructs the development of love. We renounce ourselves because we love God and want to love Him progressively more; we want Him to act freely in us so that we may conform to Christ and attain close union with Him.

Therese explained this one day to a novice who had exclaimed: "Alas, when I think of all that I still have to acquire!" Therese answered: "Say rather 'to lose' . . . it is Jesus who takes charge of filling your soul according to the measure in which you get rid of your imperfections." [1]

When we consider renunciation under that aspect, it becomes easy and we find that Christ's burden is truly light. It is love that lightens burdens. No doubt, we shall have to give up certain satisfactions and cut off certain attachments; but the process of purification is a gradual one and it seldom demands a hard sacrifice. The nearer we approach progress, and the more clearly we recognize the obstacles that are impeding our progress, the more anxious we feel to free ourselves from everything that arrests our flight towards Him and our transformation into other Christs.

THERESE'S RENUNCIATION DURING HER CHILDHOOD

Like all children, Therese had natural shortcomings. Actions springing from her nature occasionally escaped from her control, but this happened rarely and she immediately corrected her conduct. "It took me but an instant to acknowledge my faults," [2] she said afterwards, and once I was told a thing was not right, I no longer had any desire of committing that fault a second time." [3]

Moreover, after the death of her mother, her sisters devoted themselves to the training of her character. Pauline, in particular, "allowed none of my imperfections to escape her." Jesus, on His part, "watched over His young bride and took care that everything, even her faults, should be turned to her advantage. The fact of their being corrected at that early age helped her to grow in perfection." [4]

From her earliest years Therese had applied herself to the practice of sacrifice. She had learned this first of all from her sisters but later she was led to it by a special grace from God. At the age of three she had already her 'beads of mortification' on which she counted her acts of renunciation. When some article was taken away from her, she let it go without complaining. If she was accused, she preferred to keep silence instead of offering excuses. She also applied herself to the task of curbing her self-will. She refrained from answering back as children are so prone to do and rendered little services to others without seeking an acknowledgement of them. In the beginning, she did not always meet with immediate or easy success. Therese, like the rest of us, had to struggle against herself, but grace made triumph. Her victory is traceable especially to the reception of her First Holy Communion and later to the special favor she received on the feast of Christmas, 1886. "On that day," she declared, "I felt my heart being filled with love and with the desire of forgetting myself in order to give pleasure to others. From that time on I have been happy." [5]

Her conversations with Celine in 1887 confirmed her in these dispositions: "Virtue from that time on became sweet and natural to her . . . renunciation became easy so that it seemed spontaneous." [6] Moreover, as her love for God increased, the vanity of earthly things became more evident to her eyes: "On earth, we ought not to attach ourselves to anything, even to things that are most innocent. . . . It is only that which is eternal that is capable of satisfying our heart." [7]

THERESE'S RENUNCIATION IN CARMEL

It may seem strange to say that religious life gave Therese occasions for practicing virtue under circumstances more painful than anything she had previously experienced. She herself was not surprised by this. Before she entered the convent she knew that religious life would be hard, with its constant obedience and submission and the daily trials that must be borne unnoticed by others. She understood "how easy it would be to withdraw into one's shell, to become self-centered and forgetful of the sublime end of one's vocation." [8]

It is not surprising that religious life, life in a religious community, should have its difficulties. It was meant to train its subjects to imitate in their lives and to reproduce in their souls the model set by our suffering Redeemer. Whatever be the rigors or ascetical practices that are special to any particular Order, the very fact of living in community entails certain trials, mortifications, and sufferings that are not found elsewhere. This is especially true in the cloister where one's whole life is spent with the same set of persons and in a frame of circumstances that is narrow and rigid. The causes of friction are numerous. They spring from differences of temperament, of background, of education and training to be found in every community. There are the imperfections, the defects and the faults of each individual soul. One may have to deal with people who are lacking in sound judgment and occasionally with a crotchety character who can get on with no one at all. The very trials of our neighbors may make their company hard to bear. They may be depressed or worried. They may suffer from ill-health or fatigue. Yet, always the law of charity bids us love our neighbor as ourselves and show unwearying kindness and consideration to all our fellowmen.

Therese was particularly predisposed to suffer acutely from causes such as those we have mentioned. Her sensitive loving nature had been fostered by home life in a family where affection reigned supreme. She was still young when she entered the Carmel and she was determined to realize the Carmelite ideal in its full perfection. She understood that in order to become a saint she would have "to suffer much, to aim constantly at perfect holiness and to forget herself; that there are several degrees of perfection; that each soul is free to respond to our Lord's invitation to a greater or lesser extent, that is, to choose the degree of self-sacrifice from among the sacrifices He asks for." But Therese did not want to be a "half-baked saint"; "(O God) I am not afraid to suffer for Your sake. I fear one thing only, that is clinging to my own will. My choice is to do what You wish me to do. Take away from me all self-will!" [9]

Therese also declared that "we ought to avoid lessening the martyrdom of religious life by allowing ourselves or obtaining permission from others for a thousand things that would make life pleasant and comfortable: [10] We should endure as much as we can before we make any complaint." [11] Therese did not mean by this that we should exhaust our physical strength but that we should show our generosity by bearing courageously the inconveniences and fatigues that are inherent in religious life and persevere in our efforts even if that were to cause us real suffering.

Therese then had foreseen all the self-denial that religious life entails and, having once accepted it wholeheartedly, no sacrifice seemed too great to her in the pursuit of her ideal. She placed her happiness "in living a hidden life, ignoring all created things, detaching herself from creatures, conquering her own self-will." She rejoiced in being forgotten and being considered as a person of no account: "Let us allow Jesus to rob us of all that is most dear to us," she wrote, "let us not refuse Him anything." In her own home she had often got up in the morning with sadness of heart at the prospect of a day that would be filled with annoyances; but in the cloister "she arose with all the more gladness because she foresaw the many occasions she would have for practicing self-denial and renouncing her own self-will."[13]

The day of her profession marked an important date in her life of abnegation and sacrifices. Feeling that she was truly a "queen," she took advantage of that title to express to her King all that she desired for souls and for herself. On a note which she carried on her heart she had written: "O Jesus . . . let me seek and find but You alone! May creatures be nothing to me and may I be nothing to them. . . . Let no one be interested in me. May I be trodden under foot, forgotten like an insignificant grain of sand!"[14]

Knowing that a mere gesture inspired by love is dear to the heart of God, Therese attached great importance to minor acts of renunciation. The "little sacrifices" that she offered to Him so frequently were small acts of loving self-denial or mortification which thwarted the natural demands of self and gave her endless hidden opportunities of expressing her deep love of God and of practicing virtue.

Therese by nature loved beauty and neatness. In the beginning of her novitiate she was delighted to be assigned clean and neat clothes. Later, learning to esteem poverty, she began to seek the oldest and most darned clothes. Her "alpargates"[15] had been so patched that when she died a lay sister took them from the hands of Therese's oldest sister and threw them in the fire; her pitcher was chipped; she had to use a pin to turn up the wick of her lamp.

She mortified herself especially at table. Her delicate stomach did not digest easily the austere meals of Carmel. Some foods she disliked or were hard to digest (beans, milk). As the sisters did not know this and as she was urged to eat well—she has written that she never ate so much as in Carmel —her indigestion, naturally, increased. She never complained, however, and they never did learn what foods she disliked. A sister who sat near her at table tried to discover what her preferences were but never succeeded. Next to Therese at table was a sister who was ill. This nun suffered from an insatiable thirst, and poor Therese had to suffer from this very disagreeable companion. For many months this sister monopolized the small bottle of cider which was intended for both of them. Therese accepted the privation without making any complaint, even abstaining from mentioning it lest she might hurt the sister's feelings.

The sisters in the kitchen, knowing the indifference that Therese showed with regard to food, often sent her warmed dishes that would have been unacceptable to other members of the community. For Therese, ill-treatment of this kind was the occasion of spiritual progress but, ultimately, it was bound to have an undermining effect on her health.

The sister who took such devoted care of Therese during her last illness was unable to find out what food her patient found appetizing. The nurse, thus, saw herself obliged to make her own choice and this gave Therese many occasions for mortification. It was only after she had been ordered to make known what foods caused her pain that the nuns began to realize the extent to which she had mortified herself when she had lived on community fare.[16]

As novice mistress, the Saint had trained the young sisters to the same detachment in the matter of food. Recommending, for instance, that they should not seek mere gratification of the sense of taste, she suggested that they finish most of their meals with something that was not too agreeable, such as a morsel of dry bread: "These little things do no harm to our health. They remain unnoticed and keep the soul in a state of supernatural fervor."[17]

Therese suffered terribly from the cold. At the end of her life she confessed that "I have suffered so much from the cold that I almost died from it." [18] But she had never made that known to anyone. "If I had known that," declared her directress, "what would I not have done to remedy her condition!" [19] Therese did not wish her novices to suffer as she had done, but she wanted them to harden themselves against variations of heat and cold. She told them not to double up nor to rub their hands like people who feel very cold and to try not to shiver.[20]

During the first three or four years of her religious life, she was not allowed to practice any mortification except that of her self-love. But, declared Therese, this did her more good than corporal penances.[21]

Nevertheless, she did take the discipline. From 1892 or 1893 she was allowed to wear the hairshirt, the iron bracelet, and a cross with points. She practiced these penances until 1896. But she never had recourse to the extraordinary mortifications which were practiced by several members of her community.[22] She was severe[23] towards herself when taking the discipline: "I do not believe," she said, ""in doing things in a half-hearted way. I take the discipline so that it will cause me pain and hurt me as much as possible." She added that the more keenly she felt the blows, the more she smiled in order that the good Lord might see even on her face that she was happy to suffer for Him.[24]

She was not satisfied with practicing the acts of renunciation and penance that are implied in religious life. *She seized every opportunity for mortification that came her way.*

One day a sister, while re-fastening her scapular with a pin, fastened Therese's skin as well as the cloth! Our Saint said nothing and continued her work in spite of the pain this caused her. She revealed this only several hours later for fear that she was failing in obedience by practicing a penance that had not been authorized.

She said also that "for a long time, during meditation, I was close to a sister who never stopped rattling her beads or fidgeting in a most irritating way. . . . I cannot find words to express the fatigue that this caused me. I was tempted to turn towards the offender and make her stop the noise. But I felt in my heart that I should suffer this annoyance with patience, for the love of the good Lord and also to avoid giving pain to this sister. So I remained still, but sometimes I was covered with perspiration and my suffering was my only prayer. I tried to bear it with peace and joy, at least in the depth of my soul. I endeavored to love that insignificant and disagreeable noise and I offered that concert to Jesus." [25] This might seem childish but those who have had such experiences know how much effort is required to practice that kind of continual renunciation.

She chose for herself the most painful and disagreeable tasks. One washday her neighbor inadvertently sprayed Therese's face several times with dirty water. "My first tendency," she recounted later, "was to withdraw while wiping off my face so as to say, 'Sister, do me the favor of keeping quiet.' But I immediately reflected that it would be very foolish to refuse the treasure this sister so generously offered me. So I carefully avoided showing what conflict was going on in my soul. On the contrary, I did my best to receive as generous a sprinkling of dirty water as was possible, so much so that at the end I had come to like it and promised myself I would return to that blessed place where favors were so prodigally distributed." [26]

She went so far in her abnegation that she deprived her-

self of things that were helpful to her in her spiritual progress.
A sister had asked her for a loan of a book which Therese was
reading at that time and which she found profitable to her
soul. Our Saint gave it up immediately and never asked that
sister to return it to her.

*Her spirit of abnegation and sacrifice was especially mani-
fest during her painful illness.* We can affirm without fear of
exaggeration that in this she was truly heroic. She never complained. She never asked for anything except what she considered herself in duty bound to say to her Prioress or her
nurse. She never asked for a dispensation from the observances nor the Office. On the contrary, she regretted being
relieved from those tasks when her superiors had found out
that she was unable to fulfill them. We shall see farther on
in more detail how she bore her illness.

In a cloistered community, where silence and solitude are
habitual, news from the outside world rarely enters and religious are easily inclined to inquire about what had been said
or done during their absence. Therese did not experience that
kind of curiosity. She did not question others when they failed
to report what had been said during recreation or to inform
her about anything that was new. She only asked questions
about things that it was her duty to know.

When we suffer we like to tell others about it and receive
consolation from them. Therese kept her sufferings and sorrows to herself. It was her opinion that discussing such things
upsets us rather than gives relief, while by renouncing ourselves we draw down upon us light and assistance from God.

Her life seemed to flow peacefully and pleasantly but, in
reality, she was at all times practicing a profound and total
abnegation. The following example may serve to show to
what extremes she was led by her spirit of sacrifice. One day
shortly before her death, when her three sisters were with
her, two of them suggested that she should direct her last
glance to the eldest of them, Mother Agnes, whom she had

always called her "little mother." "No," she replied, "that would be yielding too much to human nature. If the good Lord permits it, I shall give my last glance to my Prioress" (who at that time happened to be Mother Marie de Gonzaga.) A few days later she told Mother Agnes once more: "I shall be happy to die in the arms of our Mother (de Gonzaga,) because she represents the good Lord. If I were to die in your arms, there might be a too-natural affection in it. I prefer to have everything on the supernatural plane." [27]

Therese made no concessions to nature. She renounced even the most legitimate inclinations of her heart. She was convinced that without renunciation, nothing could have a stable foundation: "It is necessary for me to meet abnegation and sacrifice in everything . . . for it seems to me that we cannot accomplish any good while we indulge in self-seeking." [28]

She felt certain, above all, that it is impossible to love truly and give ourselves entirely to God without complete self-forgetfulness. "Recall," she said, "that profoundly true word of the Imitation: 'As soon as we begin to seek ourselves, at that very moment we cease loving.' " [29] And to another she said: "True love is found only in complete self-forgetfulness, and it is only after we have detached ourselves from every creature that we find Jesus." [30]

To one of her spiritual brothers she said: "At this moment when I am ready to appear before God, I understand better than ever that only one thing is necessary: to work solely for Him and not to do anything for oneself or for creatures." [31]

There are frequent opportunities for renunciation in any kind of life. We do not have to seek for them; they are at every step on our road. Let us not waste any of them. These are the "little sacrifices" of which Therese speaks. These—better than more important actions—enable us to prove to Jesus that we love Him, and by means of them we become sharers in His work of saving souls.

One sentence recalled by her sister shows us to what

extent she had applied herself to such sacrifices: "At my death, when I shall see the good Lord and His willingness to fill me with His tender love, for all eternity; when I shall no longer be able to prove my love by means of sacrifices, if I have not done all that I could have done to please Him during my mortal life, that thought will be unbearable to me." [32]

Therese had no reasons for such fears for we know that she always did everything possible to please God. She loved Him with all her heart and gave herself completely to Him to the very last moment.

PEACE—THE REWARD OF SPIRITUAL COMBAT

The consistent practice of self-denial, while giving Therese the means of proving her love for Jesus, also established her in perfect peace of soul. When writing her first manuscript in 1896, she recalled the great peace she enjoyed when she entered Carmel: "That peace has been my inheritance for eight and a half years. It has never left me even in the midst of my greatest trials." [33] This is significant when we recall what sacrifices she imposed on herself during those years.

It was not without a struggle that Therese attained to that peace. She has repeatedly confessed that it cost her a great effort to counteract the tendencies of her natural tempearment.[34] A short time before her death she declared: "I had a nature that was hard to conquer; people were not aware of that but I felt it keenly. I can assure you that I have had many struggles and that no day has passed without suffering, not a single one." [35]

On one occasion she had to make so violent an effort to restrain herself from rebutting charges made against her that her forehead was bathed in perspiration. On another, she had to seek refuge in flight but violent palpitations forced her to sit down until she regained control of her feelings.[36]

She refers also to a time when she was so overwhelmed by temptation that the grace of God alone saved her from a revolt against obedience.[37]

With the help of God, however, she always conquered the tendencies of nature and at the end of her life she was able to say that she was no more attached to self-esteem or self-love than she was to any other earthly creature and that she found it no longer necessary to fight against them. Borrowing an expression from St. John of the Cross "her home was completely at peace." [38]

Her equanimity and serenity were noted by her own sisters. To one of them who asked her how she managed to be always calm and cheerful, she replied: "I was not always that way; but from the time that I gave up self-seeking, I have been leading the happiest life one can imagine.[39] If people only knew what one gains by renouncing oneself in all things!" [40]

If we, too, wish to enjoy peace of soul, we must practice self-denial and self-forgetfulness. That will demand a struggle, no doubt, but as Therese says, "let those who are frightened by the undertaking make an effort. God never refuses the first grace which gives us the courage to overcome ourselves. If the soul corresponds with that grace, she finds herself immediately in the light. The heart is strengthened and she goes from victory to victory.[41] The more you advance ... the less combats you will have to sustain, or rather you will have more facility in overcoming the difficulties. Your soul will rise above creatures."[42]

KEEP SMILING

The practice of self-denial would not be perfect if it failed to translate itself in proper comportment and manner. There are people who practice it in a harsh and repellent way that is quite alien to the gentleness of Christ.

Therese did not act like that. She practiced mortification with such unaffected simplicity that it often passed unnoticed. Her abnegation did not make her difficult or disagreeable in her dealings with others. She had learned to do and accept the most painful things with joy, with a smile, even with a song: "I always see the bright side of things. There are people who always take everything from the most painful point of view. I do just the opposite. If I am faced with pure suffering; when heaven is so black that there is no bright spot to be seen anywhere, I then make that itself a source of joy." [43]

The smile which constantly lit up her face seemed to many her natural expression. In reality, it was the sign of a will that was generous to the extreme, and caused her to offer everything to God with a joyful heart. "Jesus," she said, "loves cheerful hearts; He loves a soul that is always smiling." [44] She was cheerful always and everywhere, in recreation and in her correspondence, amidst sufferings and interior sorrows. "I will always sing," she wrote, "even when I must gather my roses amidst thorns, and the longer and sharper those thorns, the more melodious my songs shall be." [45] In the infirmary, whatever her state of health, she gave visitors such a friendly welcome that it was a joy for them to pay her a visit.

LOVE—THE SOURCE OF HER GENEROSITY AND SERENITY

Where did Therese find the strength, the generosity that made her smile in all circumstances and offer with a joyful heart the sacrifices she was asked to make at every step? She drew it from her love, a love always burning in her heart and which was her answer to Christ's own love.

Following Therese's example let us generously practice renunciation. He who practices it frees himself from himself and from the dominion of creatures. He thus reserves all his powers for the services of God. But he who is unable to free himself from self and from creatures, remains a slave to both. However small his unruly attachment may appear, he does not give his heart to Jesus alone.

Let us, then, apply ourselves to complete and constant self-abnegation and use every opportunity God gives us, to offer Him the proof of our true and effective love. He cannot rest satisfied with nice protestations of love which are not translated into deeds. Like Therese, we can draw the strength we need from the love of One who loved us infinitely, from the love of a God-man who was willing to be crucified out of love for us.

To love means to forget ourselves for the One whom we love.

CHAPTER VIII

Abandonment

THROUGHOUT her life Therese applied herself with constant generosity and unwavering fidelity to the accomplishment of what was agreeable to God. It was her constant concern to conform to God's will and to have no other will than His will.

It was out of love for that divine will that she did her very best to live religious life in all its perfection. She knew, too, that it was God's will that we should love one another, and, hence, she always did her best to love her neighbor as Jesus has loved us. She had a great desire for suffering because she considered it as the supreme proof of love, the most adequate way of becoming identified with the divine Savior, and the best means of realizing God's will to save the souls of men. (Fr. Combes).[1]

Nevertheless, towards the end of 1895, she came to the conclusion that there is a degree of love that is even higher than the desire of suffering. While putting the finishing touches to her first manuscript, she realized that all her desires were satisfied, "not only her desires of perfection but also those which she considered vain, although she had not experienced it. "This," she said, "was a gift to her of divine mercy."

But the time had come for all her desires to be reduced to one alone. "I have now," she exclaimed, "no longer any desire except that of loving Jesus unto folly. Yes, it is love alone that attracts me. I no longer desire suffering nor death, and, yet, I love both. I have desired them for a long time.

I have had suffering and I have come close to dying. . . . Now, abandonment is my only guide. I can no longer ask ardently for anything except that God's will may be perfectly accomplished in my soul." And, inspired by St. John of the Cross, she concluded: "My Mother, how sweet is the way of love! No doubt, we are liable to fall, to fail in constancy, but love knows how to draw profit from everything. It quickly consumes anything that may be displeasing to Jesus, leaving only a humble and profound peace at the bottom of our heart." [2]

By these words Therese made it clear that henceforth abandonment would be her guide, that she no longer had any desires. Does abandonment, then, exclude all desires? Not necessarily. When a thing is manifestly in accordance with the divine will, to desire it is not contrary to abandonment to God. Desire, in this case, is one with God's will. This explains why Therese, after declaring that she no longer desired suffering and death, said, a few days before her departure for heaven, that she wished to suffer even more. It was the expression of her conformity with the divine good pleasure.[3]

From that moment, however, abandonment remained her rule of conduct. "I follow the way traced for me by Jesus," she wrote. . . . "He wants me to practice abandonment, like a little child which does not worry about what others might do with him. . . .[4] I try to be no longer occupied with myself in anything and I abandon to Him whatever He wants to accomplish in my soul." [5]

It is certain that such a disposition is a superior one. Whatever the motive or the love that may inspire us in our activities, there is no greater proof of love of and confidence in God than to abandon ourselves fully to Him. There is no better means of honoring Him than to acknowledge the supreme role of His Providence in the government of the universe and of our own lives.

Abandonment, on the other hand, gives us a better means of realizing our destiny and of attaining the holiness to which we are called. God has special designs regarding each and every soul and He alone knows what they are. When we try to guide ourselves, we risk putting obstacles in the way of divine action as a consequence of our meddling and deviating from the path marked out for us by God; whereas when we abandon ourselves to God, we walk on the safe road. We enter the way that leads most quickly to the goal that He has set for us.

Therese was convinced that nothing happens without the will of God. "I understand better now than I did at any time before," she wrote, "that the most insignificant events of our life are under God's direction." [6] "It is Christ's hand that guides everything. We must see Him alone in everything." [7] "I love all that the good Lord gives me" [8] is an expression she liked to repeat. That also is why she refused to express any personal preferences. She preferred what God chose for her.

Speaking of the conduct of Jesus in her regard, she declared mischievously: "I am pleased with what He does. When He seems to mislead me, I pay Him all sorts of compliments. He then no longer knows what to do with me." [9]

She considered that this complete, unconditional acceptance of the divine will is the true means of always preserving our souls in peace: "My heart is full of the will of God; so if anything else were poured over it, it could not even get in. I still remain in a state of peace that nothing can disturb."

Indeed, he who fulfills God's will, dwells in peace [10] and "outside the divine will, we can do nothing for Jesus or for the salvation of souls." [11]

Finally, she affirmed that in order to know better the will of God, she preferred to keep her eyes constantly fixed on Jesus, so as to discover what was most pleasing to Him.

To abandon ourselves does not mean that we become slothful and inactive. Abandonment always implies effort on our part to cooperate with grace. It supposes correspondence with grace. Therese never failed to give that cooperation. All we have recorded offers perfect evidence of this fact.

Our Saint did not reach perfect abandonment all at once: "It took me a long time before I became established in that degree of abandonment," she confessed to Mother Agnes, "but now I have reached it. The good Lord has taken me in His arms and has placed me there." [12]

It was at the end of 1895—as we have mentioned before —that Therese, enlightened by the Holy Ghost, saw clearly the superiority of this way and recognized in it the true means of reaching the perfection of love. "Jesus is pleased," she said to Sister Marie of the Sacred Heart, "to show me the one and only road that leads to the Furnace of Love. This is the abandonment of a little child that goes to sleep without fear in the arms of his father." [13]

Nothing could have been more helpful to her in that period of her life when she had to endure peacefully the most terrible trials. In fact, she preserved an unalterable peace throughout that long ordeal. To those who were wondering at the sight of so much calmness at the height of her sufferings and dereliction, she said: "My heart is full of the will of Jesus. When anything is poured over that, it does not penetrate deeply. It is, at most, a superficial scum which floats like oil on limpid water. Oh, if my soul were not thus filled beforehand (with the will of Jesus)! If it were subject to the rapid alternating waves of joy and sorrow that we experience on earth, I would be overwhelmed by a flood of bitter grief. But those transient feelings touch only the surface of my soul and I still remain in a profound peace which nothing can disturb."

When the Carmel of Hanoi appealed for sisters to the Carmel of Lisieux, Therese would have accepted to go there, if she had not been prevented by her illness. She would have felt the exile keenly, but she was, nonetheless, determined to go. "For a long time," she said, "I have no longer belonged to myself. I have delivered myself completely to Jesus. He may do with me what He pleases. He has prompted me to desire a complete exile." [14]

She looked upon that abandonment as on a detachment, a liberation that would facilitate her flight to heaven. "My Mother," she said to Mother Marie de Gonzaga, "it seems to me now that there is nothing left to prevent my flight, for I no longer have any great desires except to die of love. . . . Oh! how sweet it is to abandon oneself in the arms of the good Lord, without fears or desires!"[15]

Even the thought of eternal beatitude did not make her relinquish that attitude of abandonment. And, yet, how ardently she had longed for heaven in former days! "If you knew," she confessed, "how calm I remain at the thought of soon going to heaven! And, yet, I am very happy, but I cannot say that I feel transports of gladness or joy." [16]

She wrote to her sister Leonie that she did not want to enter heaven one minute earlier, if that were done by her own will, for she felt that "the only happiness here below consists in always finding joy in whatever Jesus gives us." [17] Mother Agnes, having expressed the thought that, notwithstanding all these sentiments, Therese would prefer to die rather than to live, she exclaimed: "O my dear Mother, I repeat: 'No! I do not prefer one thing to another. Whatever the good Lord wishes and chooses for me is what pleases me most. . . . It is what He does that I love!' " [18] She expressed the same idea to Mother de Gonzaga: "I am quite satisfied to remain ill all my life if it is agreeable to the good Lord, and I would even agree to live for a very long time." [19]

Nevertheless, when one day someone remarked that she might recover her health, Therese avowed that if that were to happen, she would consider it as a sacrifice although, of course, she would wholeheartedly accept it. "If it were God's will," she replied, "I would be most happy to offer Him that sacrifice; but I assure you that this would not be a small thing, to go so far and then to return from such a distance."[20]

One might object that some of her desires, such as not wanting to die during the night, and that of hoping to leave soon, apparently weakened her attitude of perfect abandonment. Actually, those wishes were but the expression of her charity towards her sisters. She did not want them to suffer on account of her protracted illness and she feared they would be disturbed if she died at night. As far as she herself was concerned, her abandonment remained complete.[21]

Moreover, she addressed these desires to the Blessed Virgin and not to God. This was her custom when she was not certain that her petition would be pleasing to God. "To ask something of the Blessed Virgin," she said, "is not the same thing as asking the good Lord. She knows well what to do with my small wishes, whether to transmit them to her Son or not. . . . Finally, it belongs to her to examine those wishes so that the good Lord may not, as it were, be forced to hear me but that on the contrary He may feel free to do everything according to His will." [22]

Because she was so firmly established in abandonment, Therese enjoyed perfect happiness. "I have no disappointments," she confessed, "for I am pleased with everything that the good Lord does." [23]

To Live the Present Moment

In order that one might practice abandonment in a more perfect way, she earnestly recommended that one should, as it were, enclose oneself in the present moment. One day the novices told her, "how it grieves us to see you suffer so much, and to think that perhaps you will suffer even more." "Oh," she replied, "do not grieve on my account. I have reached the point where I can no longer suffer because all suffering has become sweet to me. Moreover, you are quite wrong in imagining what painful things might happen to me in the future, for that is like interfering with God's work of creation. We run in the way of love, must never worry about anything. If I did not accept my suffering from one minute to another, it would be impossible for me to remain patient. But I see only the present moment, forget the past and take good care not to visualize the future. When we become discouraged and sometimes despair, it is because we think of the past and the future.[24] "To think of the painful things that might happen in the future means that we are lacking in confidence."[25]

Moreover, how often do the things of the future that we fear most really happen? God gives grace only for the present moment. Hence, it is not to be wondered at if we lose our peace when we leave the present. It was in that spirit that Therese sang:

"For tomorrow, I cannot pray,
Cover me with Thy shadow, just for today."[26]

Is it not because we do not follow these principles of wisdom that we are often perturbed? We formulate many desires. We address to God all sorts of petitions without even considering whether they are in harmony with His will. Sometimes we want to plan out our lives and arrange things according to our own views. At others we are worried about the past or apprehensive of the future. After the example of Therese, let us live in the present, and think only of today. Let us do what we have to do each day that is given to us by God, leaving all else in His hands. "Sufficient for the day is the evil thereof";[27] tomorrow will have worry of its own. That is what Jesus taught and that should be our guide.

God has designs full of mercy towards us. He has disposed all things for our good. If we are truly abandoned to Him, faithfully accomplishing His will, whatever the road on which He leads us, and the accidents we meet with, we shall march in peace and reach the repose He has prepared for us.

CHAPTER IX

Simplicity

W E do not need to prove that simplicity must, of necessity, belong to a Way of Spiritual Childhood. The child
is simple by nature. It is simple in its thoughts, simple in the
way it expresses its feelings. It says simply what it thinks
and how it feels towards its parents. It is simple in its actions.
Now this is also true of a child of God.

In fact, simplicity is an outstanding characteristic of the
"Way of Spiritual Childhood." But it is important to understand this properly. It does not consist, as some might believe,
in being commonplace and performing only actions that are
ordinary. Theresian simplicity is, above all, an attitude of
mind. He who is inspired by the Theresian spirit of simplicity
considers all things and all events as they are in their relation to God. He knows that all things come from God and
that everything ought to be referred to Him. Hence, he
accepts equally the joys, the labors and the sufferings that
come his way, and he orders all things towards God. He dis-
likes what is complicated, devious, extraordinary, but is
pleased with what is ordinary and in that way his life is
wholly simplified. His spiritual life is simple; he goes straight
to God as a child to his Father, animated by filial confidence.

There is no artificiality in his prayer, nothing extravagant
in his penitential practices. He accepts with equanimity the
trials and joys sent or permitted by God. When an important
charge is entrusted to him he does his best to acquit himself
of his duty, with the naturalness with which he undertakes
everything else.

Therese was perfectly simple. "I love only simplicity," she said, "and have a dislike for what is contrary to it." [1] This was confirmed by her sisters: "In Therese everything was simple and natural." This was the more necessary because her Way was destined for "little ones." Others had looked upon perfection as on something complicated, a summit that could only be reached by means of a multiplicity of exercises, rigorous penances and after passing through high degrees of prayer. Therese's concept was quite different from that: "Perfection," she writes, "seems easy to me. I realize that it is sufficient that we acknowledge our nothingness and abandon ourselves like a child into the arms of our good Lord." [2] She frequently repeated that teaching, though using a variety of expressions. To be a saint it is sufficient to be little, to love to apply ourselves to giving pleasure to Jesus and to have confidence.

But the text which most clearly explains her thought is the one in which she affirms that "holiness does not consist in this or that practice; but it is a certain disposition of the heart which makes us humble and small as we rest in God's arms, which makes us realize our weakness but, at the same time, gives us confidence to the point of audacity in the goodness of God as our Father." [3]

SIMPLICITY IN HER PRAYER

Therese was simple in her prayer and she had a dislike for borrowed and stiff formulae. Her prayer principally consisted in telling Jesus that she loved Him and desired to do His will in all things. "I don't have the energy," she said, "to hunt for beautiful prayers that are found in books. Not knowing which ones I ought to choose, I act like children who cannot read. I say simply to the good Lord what I want to tell Him, without constructing nice sentences, and He always understands me. For me, prayer is a lifting up of my heart.

It is a simple glance heavenwards. It is a cry of gratitude and of love, in the midst of trials as well as amidst joys. It is something great, something supernatural, which dilates the soul and unites me with Jesus." [4]

She did not waste time in explaining to God in detail her own intentions or those that had been recommended to her. She feared, she said, that she would never come to the end of her litany of intentions and again that she might forget some of them. Such litanies she considered useless complications, declaring "simple souls don't need complicated means." [5]

In the fulfillment of her obligations she followed the suggestions given her by Jesus. She had learned that by saying simply: "Draw me," she could cause all the souls whom she loved to follow after her. "To ask to be drawn," she wrote, "means that we desire to be united intimately to the object which captivates our heart. I ask Jesus to draw me into the flames of His love, to unite me so intimately to Himself that He truly lives and acts in me." She felt certain that in this cry she obtained the same grace for those whom she loved. [6]

Sometimes, however, wishing to be charitable to a sister who had recommended an intention to her, "she very quickly addressed herself to God, but after that gave it no more thought." [7]

She did not specify to whom she destined the merits of her works: "I cannot force myself to say, 'My God, this is for the Church . . . give this to Peter, give that to Paul.' The good Lord knows well what to do with my merits. I have given Him everything in order to please Him." "When I pray for my brother missionaries, I do not offer my sufferings but say simply, 'My God, give them what I myself would like to receive.'" [8]

She did not worry about her distractions in prayer. We cannot help having distractions in our relations with God. Our wandering imagination, the images so easily recalled by our memory, our mental curiosity and our senses that are always collecting impressions are sources of multiple distractions. Many good persons grieve over that fact but they are wrong, for if they reject them as soon as they are noticed, such distractions are not faults. Therese "didn't bother her head about them." She accepted everything that came along, out of love of God, even outlandish thoughts.[9] To a novice who worried about her distractions, she said: "I, too, have many distractions, but as soon as I notice them, I pray for the persons who occupy my imagination and in that way they draw profit from my distractions."[10]

One of her companions complained because she was not able to direct her will often to God. Therese reassured her: "That 'direction' is not necessary for those who are entirely dedicated to our Lord. No doubt, it is a good thing to recollect our mind, but we should do that gently, for constraint does not glorify the good Lord. He is well acquainted with the nice thoughts and the elegant expressions of love which we would like to address to Him, but He is satisfied with our desires. Is He not our Father and are we not His little children?"[11]

Simplicity in Therese's method of mental prayer. Although she was repeatedly favored with high mystical graces, she never became attached to them nor did she aspire to such things.[12] She even considered it contrary to humility to entertain a desire for such graces: "To all ecstasies she preferred the monotony of an obscure sacrifice."[13] Hence, she did not like it when others expressed their belief that she was favored with extraordinary graces, or when they hoped she would receive some.[14] Having been asked whether she had an intuition regarding her approaching death, she replied: "O Mother! Do you say 'intuition'? If you only knew my poverty! I see only what you yourself know. . . . I guess only what I actually happen to see and feel."[15]

On the eve of the feast of Our Lady of Mount Carmel, a

novice remarked that if Therese were to die on that day, after receiving Holy Communion, it would mean so much less suffering for her. "Oh!" replied Therese, "that would not be like my Little Way at all. It would mean that I am abandoning that Way in my own death! To die of love after my Communion! Little souls would then be unable to imitate me in this. In my Little Way all things are common and ordinary. It is necessary that all that I do, little souls should be able to do also." [16]

One day some one mentioned the interior light which certain souls receive concerning heaven. "As for myself," she answered, "I have only lights that make me see my nothingness, but this does me more good than the lights concerning matters of faith." [17] She wanted to walk solely in the darkness of faith and this, also, she taught to "little souls."

Being a faithful disciple of her Father, St. John of the Cross, she had learned to appreciate the superiority and the certainty of this way: "It is so sweet, to be able to serve the good Lord during the night of trial. We have only this present life on earth when we can live a life of faith." These words reveal how well Therese had grasped the excellence of faith.

However obscure faith may be, it is, nevertheless, a true light that guides us on our journey here below and by it we find God; for, as St. John of the Cross expresses it, "faith contains God and gives Him to us. God is hidden in the obscurity of faith." That is why Therese "preferred not to see God and the Saints, but to remain in the night of faith in contrast with those who are anxious to see and understand everything." "Remember well," she continued, "that it is in conformity with the spirit of the Little Way, not to desire to see anything." [18]

These words do more than affirm that we ought to be willing to live by faith in the present life. They demand that we love to live in the obscurity of faith; for when we live by faith we establish our spiritual life on the word of God, on the revelation given us by Christ. We render homage to God as infallible Truth. Faith, according to God's plan, is sufficient to draw us to God. "It is," writes St. John of the Cross, "the proximate and proportionate means of union of our soul with God." For all that it teaches us about God is so true that the difference between faith (here on earth) and vision (in heaven) is only a matter of our mode of apprehension: on the one hand there is faith (God is believed), on the other vision (God is seen); but in either case, it is the same object, God, who is known by us. Thus, in very truth, though veiled, faith is a light that makes us know God.[19]

Simplicity in her actions and in the practice of renunciation and penance. Therese's Way, according to her own testimony, normally demands only actions that are ordinary and commonplace, things that are, therefore, not a source of envy.[20] She considered herself "a very little soul, one who can only offer insignificant things to God." [21] "God," she said, "has no need for brilliant deeds, for beautiful thoughts. . . . It is neither intelligence nor talent He is looking for on earth. He loves simplicity. We would indeed deserve pity if we were required to do great things." [22] "I don't despise profound thoughts which nourish the soul and unite us to God, but I have understood for a long time that we do not need to build on such foundations, nor does perfection consist in receiving many lights. The most sublime thoughts are valueless without works." "God made me realize that in order to attain true glory we do not have to accomplish brilliant works, but we must hide ourselves and practice virtue in such a way that our left hand does not know what our right hand does." [23]

That is why all her conduct consisted in pleasing Jesus, in doing perfectly the actions which form the texture of our ordinary lives. She made acts of virtue and renunciation as circumstances suggested them, and offered Him the little nothings which alone remain to a soul that lives in spiritual dryness: "I have no other way to prove my love," she wrote, "than to strew flowers, that is, to use every opportunity for making little sacrifices, be they a look or a word; to use all the most insignificant things and do them out of love. . . . Hence, I pluck every flower I find on my way, for Jesus. And then as I strew my flowers before Him I desire to sing, although I have had to pluck them among thorns. And the sharper and longer the thorns, the sweeter is my song."

Similarly, she reaffirms her joy in slight renunciations: "Would religious life be meritorious without these sacrifices? No! On the contrary, these small crosses constitute all our joy. They are commonplace but they prepare our hearts to accept the great crosses when such is the will of our good Master." [24] "Let us not refuse Jesus even the most insignificant sacrifice! Everything belonging to religious life is truly great." [25]

We are often inclined to neglect or underestimate the little sacrifices and the small ordinary acts of daily virtue. Our esteem goes to important works and we are inclined to admire the big and the obviously difficult. By this somewhat artificial standard of values, we lose much and show but little love. Nothing is insignificant or negligible in the service of God; for definitely the value of an action does not come from the importance of its object. It comes from the intention with which we perform it and the love with which it is animated. "Little things done out of love," said Therese, "are those that charm the Heart of Christ. . . ." On the contrary, the most brilliant deeds, when done without love, are but nothingness." [26]

It is true, of course, that the importance and the difficulty of a work, the degree of renunciation it requires of us can be the occasion for greater merit. Nevertheless, the true value of such actions springs from the quality of the love that animates them.

On the other hand, our daily routine offers us opportunities for nothing more than ordinary renunciations and the exercise of ordinary virtues. We rarely have an occasion for doing extraordinary things and we find ourselves incapable of performing the penances we read about in the lives of many saints, nor does God expect them of all. The lives of most people permit only the exercise of the duties of their state of life. A good life consists principally in the acts of virtue and the sacrifices that belong to its daily routine. We might be led to consider this insignificant, but we should not judge things by their appearances.

When we examine the conduct of such an "ordinary" good life more carefully, we realize that it is no small thing to remain faithful during a whole lifetime to the petty performances that constitute the round of daily duty; to accept day in and day out, with unfailing generosity, the sacrifices that are so constantly demanded and, yet, never to lose the opportunities for good that are offered hourly. Neither must we forget that such an existence is often passed amidst dryness of soul, with serenity hampered by moral trials from which God seems to be absent, while the soul appears to be abandoned to itself and can offer Jesus but this "little nothing." "If I felt that I had nothing to offer to Jesus," said Therese, "I would offer Him that nothing." [27]

These "nothings" constantly offered, these insignificant acts and sacrifices faithfully made, are a true martyrdom according to Therese.[28] (It may be proper to note here that Therese's own life was not entirely made up of little sacrifices and ordinary actions. She underwent extraordinary sufferings, both in body and in soul, and her last years on earth were like a continuous ascent of Calvary. It remains true, nevertheless, that the texture of her life in the world and even in the cloister was woven of ordinary actions that are in the reach of all. In the great trials of her life, however, God's hand was plainly visible, for she had a special mission

to fulfill, and her apostolic heart, in turn, longed ardently
for suffering.)

Therese grew in simplicity. Therese made a point of
recording in her autobiography the fact that she did not at
first understand the great value of simplicity. That was quite
natural; for as the saints do not attain sanctity all at once,
so neither do they immediately find the rule best suited to
lead them to the attainment of that goal. Such knowledge is
the fruit of experience and depends on light from above.
Experience comes to us progressively and, as St. Therese
said, "Jesus does not like to show us everything all at once. . . .
He ordinarily gives light little by little." [29]

Light and experience of life are especially necessary for
one who desires to act with simplicity. Unquestionably, he
must avoid a rigidity which would fetter and oppress his
soul, by exacting too much from himself and by putting too
much emphasis on penance. Likewise, with equal earnest-
ness he must refuse to cater to nature at the expense of the
spirit, under the specious pretext of acting with simplicity.
Simplicity holds a middle course. It is the fruit of reason and
of the spirit of the Gospel. It is a gift of God.

It is possible that Therese learned this from her holy
Mother Teresa of Avila; for we are told that she was fond of
quoting these words of the holy Reformer: "God does not
look for a multitude of minutiae, as some might think. We
must not fetter our souls in any way . . . for such a method,
instead of leading us to holiness, would be the occasion for
a multitude of imperfections." [30]

Enlightened by the Holy Ghost, Therese changed her
views in the matter of penance and mortification. The reading of the lives of the Saints had first inclined her to imitate
their example. Moreover, a certain number of her religious
companions were devoted to the practice of extraordinary
penances. But it so happened that Therese fell ill because
she had worn too long a small cross which had sharp iron

points. Enlightened by heaven, she realized that the austerities of the saints were not meant for her nor for those who were to walk in the Way of Childhood.[31] She understood that the mortification of the mind and the heart are incomparably more crucifying. So she went to war against herself in the spiritual sphere by means of renunciation and hidden sacrifices." She applied herself to the practice of self-forgetfulness and avoided seeking herself in anything." [32]

In a letter to Father Belliere she wrote: "I know that there are saints who spent their lives practicing extraordinary mortifications . . . but, after all, there are many mansions in the house of our heavenly Father. Jesus has told us so and that is why I follow the way He has traced out for me. . . .[33] In those extraordinary penances there easily creeps in that which is inspired by nature rather than by virtue, whereas, in the hidden struggle of interior renunciation, nature cannot get such a hold on us and we can more easily attain humility and peace." [34]

We know that our Saint here teaches sound doctrine. Are there not numbers of persons who imagine that they are mortified because they practice bodily penances, while they fail to renounce themselves in the ordinary things of daily life or in the life of a religious community? Such persons are often lacking in humility of mind and are unwilling to obey. They do not practice self-forgetfulness nor do they practice charity towards their neighbor. They seemingly try to lead a spiritual life. Some may even live in religion for many years and, yet, never succeed in giving the deathblow to their self-love; and they may never be able to make an efficacious resolution of forgetting themselves once and for all.

Therese tells us that at the beginning of her religious life, wishing to mortify herself at meals, she mingled bitter herbs with the foods she had a particular liking for, or she tried to think of things that would make her have a disgust for them while she was eating them. But "Later", she said, "I found that it was more in conformity with the virtue of simplicity to offer them to the good Lord and thank Him for the things which I found to my taste." She adds, however—and here we see once more her predominant intention—"but when something was wanting, I was much more satisfied, because I was then truly giving up something." [35]

Therese also rejected mortifications that might interfere with her attention to God. One day when someone spoke to her about a priest who suffered greatly from an irritation of the skin and, yet, refused to alleviate the pain, she remarked: "I would not have been able to practice that sort of restraint. I prefer to practice mortification in a manner that leaves my mind more free (for God)." [36]

Her sisters testified that as she was nearing the end of her life on earth, she practiced even greater simplicity in this matter of penance.[37] We have recalled with what violence she used to administer the discipline to herself; and also her answer to Sister Genevieve when the latter spoke of the natural tendency to stiffen one's body so as to soften the pain of the blows. Therese first replied that, as far as she herself was concerned, she held herself in the position that would make her suffer the most. But she added that she did not counsel anyone to follow her own example: "Do such things with great simplicity," she declared.[38] She made a similar remark in regard to the cold from which she suffered so intensely. Finally, Mother Agnes, who knew Therese's thoughts so very well, declared that her sister's heroic action should not be considered a rule which all should try to follow: "The best rule is that we should follow what love inspires us to do from moment to moment, with the sole desire of pleasing the good Lord in everything He asks of us." [39]

Nevertheless, while accepting Therese's rule of prudence which takes account of our weakness and makes us practice a simplicity that favors "little souls," we must avoid a softness that would go counter to essential prescriptions of the Theresian doctrine. Descretion and simplicity must never lead us to spare our nature in a manner that would falsify the Little Way. As Mother Agnes explains it, the supernatural spirit, the love of Jesus, must always remain the rule of all our conduct.

At the beginning of our supernatural life, and even later, we may not feel drawn to mortification nor have the courage to practice penance as it should be practiced, and this in spite of our good dispositions. With a heart turned towards God and docile to His inspirations, let us, in all simplicity, give what we are able to give Him. If we are supple and faithful, and if God expects more of us, He will give us the light and strength that are necessary to accomplish more in the line of penance.

Her simplicity in illness. It often happens in religious communities that the sick, considering that they are a physical burden to those who are taking care of them, and a financial one to their community, yield to anxiety and fear that their illness might be prolonged. Therese also experienced such thoughts and feelings. But when God had established her in abandonment, she understood that it was more simple to accept what God sent her: "I am willing to be ill all my life, if that pleases the good Lord," she wrote. "I even consent to live a very long life (in this condition)." [40] And in the matter of medication, she confessed: "I grieved much because I had to take medicine that was expensive, but at present, that no longer bothers me. Quite the contrary, for I have read that those who are doing good to us benefit by their charity." Hence, she "asked in all simplicity for everything she needed, but for nothing more." [41]

Her simplicity in the acceptance of joys. In the Theresian way one has only God in view. All our actions are intended to give Him pleasure. We must lose sight of ourselves and refuse to become attached to anything whatsoever. It would seem to follow, then, that we would not be free to enjoy even legitimate pleasures. But this is not so. This would be contrary to Therese's teaching, particularly in the practice of simplicity.

Therese knew too well the Heart of our heavenly Father and the Heart of Christ, who Himself did not reject earthly pleasures, to imagine that God wants to draw us away from the few small joys we meet in this valley of tears. "The good Lord," she said on one occasion, "Who loves us so much, already suffers enough because He sees himself obliged to leave us on earth to go through our time of trial, and He must be glad when He sees us smile." [42] "It seems that if we can say that our sacrifices are like locks of hair that captivate the heart of Christ, we must likewise say that our joys affect Him in a like manner. In order that this may be so, it suffices that we refrain from indulging in a selfish sort of happiness, and offer to our Spouse the small joys He strews on the path of our life to delight our souls and raise them even to Himself." [43] Hence, the only condition Therese demands of us when we accept joys is that we take no selfish complacency in them, but make of them means to raise our hearts to God.

Therese herself accepted with simplicity whatever joys God sent her, whether they were occasioned by spiritual favors, by her family or by the contemplation of nature. She accepted her pleasures "out of love" just as she accepted her sufferings. She would have considered it a fault against simplicity, if she had refused to enjoy the charms of nature or of music or of art, or of whatever moved her to thoughts of love and gratitude towards God.[44]

Towards the end of her life, speaking about the joys of the heart, she explained that, while she had mistakenly deprived herself of them at the beginning of her religious life, she no longer felt it necessary to refuse them "because her soul was strengthened by Him Who was truly her only love." From her rich personal experience she makes this significant reflection: "I am glad to recognize that when we love God our heart expands, and we can give incomparably more tender love to those who are dear to us than when our love is selfish and barren. . . . Love is fed by and develops from sacrifice. The more we deprive ourselves of natural satisfaction, the stronger and the more disinterested our love (for others) becomes." [45]

Simplicity in regard to God's gifts. Therese was simple in the matter of God's gifts. The humiliations to which He had subjected her had so deepened her humility that, as she said, "If all creatures stooped down to her, admired her and covered her with praise, all this could not add one bit of false joy to the true joy she felt when recalling that in God's eyes she was but a poor little nothing, nothing more! She felt that she was too little to be vain, quite incapable of turning out nice sentences making others believe that she was very humble. She preferred to admit in all simplicity that the Almighty had done great things in this child of His divine Mother and that the greatest of these was that He had shown her her littleness, her incapacity."

To acknowledge God's gifts is not pride, but it is pride to attribute the merits to ourselves.

On the other hand, Therese was fully conscious of the obligations that accompany the gift of graces. She wrote to Father Belliere: "Do not imagine that humility prevents me from acknowledging the gifts of God. I know He has done great things in me and I joyfully recall it in song every day. But I also remember that more love is required of those who have received more. Hence, I do my best to make my life one act of love." "Instead of making me vain, the recollection of God's gifts to me leads me to Him."

Therese affirmed that she was able to enjoy without trouble or fear the expressions of love and confidence which she received, because she referred all these gifts of God to God. "Moreover," she added, "if it pleases Him to make me appear

better than I am, that is not my concern. He is free to do what
He likes." [46]

Simplicity in the manner of correcting her faults. Finally,
she practiced simplicity in the way in which she acknowledged her defects and endeavored to correct them. "How
easy it is," she said to Celine, "to please Jesus. We have
merely to love Him without paying attention to ourselves,
without examining too intently our defects. With one glance
towards Jesus comes the realization of our own wretchedness,
and everything is in order once more." [47]

As her functions became more numerous, so, also, were
there more occasions for imperfections, but she did not worry
about them because her will was centered upon God. She
even felt that she was coming closer to God in spite of
her faults.[48]

Therese, let it be well understood, does not say that we
must not be on our guard against our faults, for otherwise,
how could we correct them? But she does maintain that we
must not—to use a more recent expression—psychoanalyze our
conduct, weigh our imperfections with anxious care, nor lose
our time bewailing our wretchedness. Having recognized our
faults, she advises, let us humbly regret them and, prompted
by love, make reparation for them. Love is our best means
for correcting our faults as it is also our best safeguard against
future failing.

*Simplicity in important works and extraordinary situa-
tions.* Thus far, we have spoken of ordinary actions. They
form the fabric of our lives. But occasionally we have to deal
with things of importance and must assume a greater responsibility. Everybody may sometimes be faced with extraordinary situations. Therese herself performed both ordinary and
extraordinary actions and she had the opportunity to make
great sacrifices. Her Little Way is, thus, practical for all situations and for all kinds of work. She affirmed that if she should
live to be eighty and should be burdened with great responsi-

bilities, she would, nevertheless, remain as little as she was at the eve of her death.[49] Pius XII declared that "the Little Way is as suitable for those who bear the heaviest responsibilities for souls, as for 'little ones,'" while Pius XI proclaimed "that there is no one who is not able and is not obliged to follow it."

Simplicity, then, extends to all circumstances of life, whether it requires great deeds or ordinary actions.

Therese had practiced the way of simplicity so perfectly that most of the sisters were unaware of the perfection she had attained. This fact is revealed by the remark made by one of them a few days before the death of our Saint: "Sister Therese of the Child Jesus will die soon and I wonder what our Mother will be able to say about her after her death. She will find it difficult, for this little sister, however friendly she was, has certainly not done anything that is worth re-telling." [50]

This judgment astonishes us, but it proves to what extent Therese's virtues had remained hidden and the sublimity of her life had remained unnoticed.[51] Nevertheless, all the members of her community honored Therese with an esteem and a veneration which they gave to no others.[52]

Therese had received enlightenment from above and had understood the excellence of the Way of Simplicity. This way, she knew, is not merely free from illusion, but it leads to a holiness that is in the reach of all.[53] We know to what degree of sanctity it led her. We have every reason, therefore, to practice simplicity in our relations with God.[54]

CHAPTER X

Act of Oblation to Merciful Love

THIS act of oblation is of capital importance in the spiritual doctrine of St. Therese of the Child Jesus. She had known from childhood that Jesus desires to be loved for Himself and above all things, and she had done her best to give Him such a love. But on the Feast of the Holy Trinity, June 9, 1895, while assisting at Mass, she received the grace of understanding more than ever before, how very much our Lord desires to be loved. But she realized at the same time that "the hearts on which Jesus wishes to bestow His love, turn to creatures begging them for a miserable affection of one fleeting moment, instead of seeking the bliss of the ardent 'Furnace' of infinite Love."

She next let her thoughts run to those who offer themselves as victims to divine justice. There had been such souls in the Carmel of Lisieux, and she could not help knowing it. Moreover, a book which was well liked by the nuns of her convent, taught—though mistakenly—that such an offering was one of the purposes of the Carmelite Order. Therese considered that such an offering was "noble and generous," but she did not feel inclined to make such an offering. It did not agree with her mentality. Those who offer themselves to divine justice are struck by the outrage which sin attempts to inflict on God and the chastisement which the guilty draw upon themselves. This thought prompts them to make reparation, to satisfy divine justice and save sinners.

Therese, on the contrary, was principally attracted by divine mercy whose wonderful ways God had revealed to her. For, as she has told us, she had for a long time asked herself why all souls do not receive an equal amount of grace, why God has preferences in regard to certain souls, bestows extraordinary graces on great sinners, and fondles others from the cradle to the grave, permitting no obstacle to prevent their flight to Him. She had asked why there are great saints and lesser saints and why some souls have no other guide than the natural law.

Jesus showed her that it was His wish to have this variety of great saints and "little ones"; this very variety adds to the beauty of the world of souls and He finds delight in such an order; He has a particular care for each individual soul and adjusts everything to the good of each.

He made it particularly clear to her that His merciful love shines in the soul that is most simple and in no way resists His grace, as well as in souls that are most sublime; and that this merciful love is, in fact, proportionate to the degree of a soul's self-abasement. After all, is it not a property of love that it should desire to stoop down to wretchedness? Therese herself was keenly aware of the number of preventive and gratuitous graces with which merciful Love had favored her.[2]

All this should help us to understand why on that ninth of June she offered herself as a victim to merciful Love rather than to divine justice. On that day she realized more fully how much Jesus desires to be loved and how many souls refuse Him that love. That is why she composed the following prayer:

"O my God, will you confine your merciful Love to your heart? Is it only your justice that will receive holocausts? Does not your merciful love also deserve to receive them? If your justice demands that it be exercised, does not your merciful love clamor more loudly for its application to souls so that it might enkindle them? It seems to me that if You should find souls that offer themselves as victims of holocaust to your merciful love, You would quickly consume them; You would be glad to release the floods of infinite tenderness that are contained in You." And, translating her words into deeds, she exclaimed: "O Jesus, let me be that blessed victim! Consume Your little victim in the fire of divine love."

Therese realized, moreover, that by offering herself to the merciful Love rather than to divine justice, she would be able to be more beneficial to souls. For, loving God with His own divine love, she would have so much more power over His Heart in her prayers in their behalf.

When the sisters had left the choir after Mass and thanksgiving, Therese approached Celine, who had been novice mistress for a few months, and asked her to accompany her to visit Mother Agnes the Prioress. With Celine at her side, she knelt before Mother Agnes and asked the permission for both of them to offer themselves as victims to merciful Love. The Prioress did not hide her surprise but, seeing in this only a devout action inspired by the Feast, she granted their request. Therese after that composed a form of oblation which is still preserved; and two days later, on the eleventh of June, prostrate with Celine before the statue of the miraculous Virgin who had restored her health, she renewed her consecration.

Let us analyze its main lines.

The offering properly so-called comprises only the three last paragraphs. What comes before serves as an introduction. The Saint addresses herself to the Blessed Trinity and expresses the fundamental desires of her heart, summarizing at the same time the fundamental principles of her Little Way. She first recalls what had always been the chief objective of her life: to love God, to cause Him to be loved by others, to glorify the Church and save souls.

She expresses once more her desire to be a saint, to attain the degree of glory which God has destined for her. In order that she might accomplish this she is resolved to fulfill perfectly God's holy will. But she realizes that she is incapable of reaching that perfection by her own unaided efforts; hence, she asks God to be Himself her sanctity. She offers Him the infinite merits of Jesus which, after all, are her possession. She begs Him to look at her only through the eyes (the Holy Face) of Jesus and with the sentiments of His Heart burning with love.

Next, to insure a favorable reception of her petition, she implores the Blessed Virgin to present her offering personally to the Most Holy Trinity.

Therese hopes, in fact she feels certain, that all her heart's desires will be fulfilled, for it is God Himself who has inspired them. That does not mean that she is sure that she will not commit faults from time to time, for she knows that she is weak; but she begs God to purify her immediately (after a fall) by a glance of love. She tells Him how grateful she is for all the graces she has already received and for the gift of suffering. She hopes that the latter will procure for her in heaven a greater likeness to the divine Savior. Regarding heavenly beatitude and the possession of God, she firmly hopes to enjoy them some day and, yet, she does not expect them as a reward for her own meritorious deeds. She offers her merits for the benefit of other souls. She wants to owe her happiness solely to God's love.

After this preamble comes the oblation itself.

Therese first proclaims why she is making it: "In order to live in one great act of perfect love," or, what amounts to the same thing, to live as a saint, for sanctity is but the exercise of perfect charity.

She offers herself as a victim to merciful Love, so that God may flood her soul with His infinite tenderness and she may love Him as He loves us, that is, with His own love which is the Spirit of Love.[3] This love will constantly consume her, purify her, cause her to suffer a veritable martyrdom of love. And when she has attained the degree of perfection to which she has been called, love will tear the veil and her soul will take its flight to the eternal embrace of merciful Love.

Therese concludes saying that she wants to renew this offering an infinite number of times, with every heart beat. It is not then a passing act of devotion, but her entire life must be one act of perfect love. She wants to build up an habitual disposition, a continuous donation to God, an entire abandonment to His operation of love in her soul, a perfect correspondence with His divine wishes.

This, then, is the admirable formula in which Therese sums up her Spiritual Way; and the effects she was aiming at in making this offering soon became manifest. Her love, however fervent it had been until then, increased wonderfully; and God was evidently responding to her gift of herself.

Five days later, while making the Stations of the Cross, she suddenly felt wounded by so ardent a dart of fire that she thought she would die. An invisible hand seemed to plunge her into a furnace of fire, and so great was her love that she thought she would be unable to bear its ardor one second longer without expiring.[4] And then came "rivers, oceans of graces," which for ten months—until April 5, 1896 —flooded her soul. Merciful Love had penetrated and enveloped her, purifying and renewing her at every moment, leaving in her no trace of sin.[5]

After Easter of 1896, God willed that she should be once more afflicted by spiritual trials, but love continued to burn in her soul. This we know from repeated confessions she made to those around her. To Mother Agnes she said that she did not see very well what more she would have in heaven than what was given her on earth: "True enough, I shall see the good Lord, but as for being with Him, well, I already have that completely."[6] And a few days later she wrote: "Dear Mother: Jesus does well to hide and to speak to me only from time to time and even then 'through bars,' for I feel most keenly that I could not bear more than that.

My heart would break, being unable to stand so much happiness." [7]

To her own sister Marie of the Sacred Heart she said that if, in the end, she failed to reach the highest regions of love to which her soul aspired, she would, nevertheless, have tasted more sweetness during her earthly martyrdom than she would experience amidst the joys of heaven, unless Jesus erased the memory of her earthly hopes.[8] And to Mother Marie de Gonzaga she repeated, at the end of June or the beginning of July, 1897, that her love was an abyss, and that Jesus could not possibly fill a soul with more love than He had given her.[9]

Finally, she confided to Sister Marie of the Trinity: "My desires are boundless; the things the good Lord has in store for me after my death, and the glory and love I foresee, so greatly surpass all that can be conceived that I sometimes have to stop my thinking, for it makes me dizzy." [10] It was this love that sustained Therese during her most terrible physical and mental sufferings; and, ultimately, she would die a death of love, carried away in an act of love.

This act of oblation to merciful Love which Therese was the first to make, was not meant to be something personal and reserved for herself. In a letter to Sister Marie of the Sacred Heart, now found in Chapter XI of the *Story of a Soul*, she asks God to choose for Himself "a legion of little victims that are worthy of His love." This means that not only fervent souls but all who have nothing and are keenly aware of their poverty and wretchedness can offer themselves to divine Love. In fact, that offering has the definite purpose of remedying imperfection; it makes up for their indigence by replacing their personal love with God's own love. "It is my weakness," said Therese, "that gives me the audacity of offering myself as a victim of His love." [11]

It is clear that if we want to draw from that offering to merciful Love all the fruit which it is destined to produce, we must not be content with pronouncing the words, even if that were done with fervor. We must live our offering. Therese herself warns us about that, as can be seen in what she said to one who had an excessive fear of God's judgments: "It seems to me that there will be no judgment for the victims of love but that the good Lord will hasten to recompense with eternal joys His own love which He will behold shining in their hearts." And to a sister who had asked her, "in order to enjoy that privilege, is it enough to recite your act of obla-tion?" She answered: "Oh! No! Words are not enough! In order to be truly a victim of love, we must give ourselves entirely. We shall be consumed by love to the extent that we surrender ourselves to love." [12]

He who has offered himself to merciful Love must do his best to live in a continuous act of love. He must endeavor to please God by fulfilling to perfection His smallest wishes and offering Him all the sacrifices he meets with. When that act is translated into generous and faithful practice, it facilitates the acquisition of perfection and enables us to attain that perfection more surely and more speedily.

Nevertheless, this takes time. Faults and falls are inevi-table as long as we are journeying on earth. Therese herself said that love continued to purify and renew her. It is also worth remembering that our faults are not always an indica-tion that we have come to a standstill, for we can fall while continuing to walk. If, after we have fallen, we make repara-tion for it by humility, "love, which can draw profit from everything, soon consumes everything that might displease Jesus. He will even make our faults serve our progress, and all that will be left will be a humble and profound peace abiding in the depths of our hearts." [13]

Does not offering ourselves to merciful Love commit us to suffering? It does not, for we do not offer ourselves to suf-fering but to Love. Everything in that offering is inspired by love and tends to love.[14] Therese, by offering herself, had no other objective than to draw to herself the love of God, so that she might love God with His own love. Her sisters, Mother Agnes, faithful interpreter of her thought, and Sister Genevieve, her associate in that offering, understood it also in this sense. Moreover, they have affirmed that Therese believed that God had accepted her as a victim, a holocaust, not because of her martyrdom of the heart, but because she had felt in her soul an excessive outpouring of the floods of God's infinite tenderness.

Again, the act of oblation makes no allusion to suffering. The terms "victim of holocaust" and "martyrdom" which, at first sight, seem to suggest it, merely express the effect of love in a soul that is afire and consumed by that love. St. John of the Cross, speaking of souls that are consecrated to love, expresses himself in similar terms in his *Spiritual Canticle* and his *Living Flame of Love*.[15]

Sister Genevieve relates a significant fact bearing on this subject. When the liturgical Office of our Saint was published, the ninth Lesson for Matins, in its shorter form, read: "Inflamed by the desire of suffering, Therese, two years before her death, offered herself as a victim to merciful Love." Mother Agnes, after reading this, exclaimed: "If it is possible even in our lifetime, to distort in this way Therese's thought, what may we not expect to happen after our own death!" Hence, she did not feel at ease until she had obtained the correction of that error from the Sacred Congregation of Rites. She was successful in having this correction made four years later. The passage mentioned above was replaced by the words: "inflamed by divine charity." [16]

On the other hand, however, it is true that Therese herself suffered much. Her last days on earth were a veritable martyrdom. But we must remember that she had "asked for" suffering; she had desired to die the death of Jesus on the Cross; she had offered herself for souls so that those who had the faith might preserve it and that others who had lost it might recover it.

In conclusion we must say, therefore, that the act of oblation does not necessarily entail suffering, although suffering may constitute its crown and completion. Suffering is a gift of God to those whom He loves, the means He uses to sanctify them. It is also the object desired by all who want to prove their love to God; it is the thirst of all who have contemplated the divine Crucified and desire to associate themselves with His redeeming work. Hence, it is normal for a soul that has offered itself to Love, to undergo suffering. Therese herself has said that "when we engage ourselves in the way of love and offer ourselves as victims, we are not entering a road that is all repose, but, on the contrary, we are invited to surrender ourselves without reserve to God's good pleasure . . . even to the extent of sharing with Jesus His cup of bitterness."

However, when God, in His wisdom and love, gives suffering to the soul which has offered itself to Him, He proportions that suffering to the strength of the sufferer. This is the sense of the answer given by our Saint to Sister Marie of the Sacred Heart, who refused to offer herself to merciful Love, for fear that her sufferings might be unbearable: "If you offered yourself to Divine Justice," said Therese, "you might entertain fear, but merciful Love will have compassion on your weakness . . . from this love we should expect nothing but mercy." [17]

The act of oblation to merciful Love is a basic element of the spiritual doctrine of St. Therese of the Child Jesus. It is the means par excellence of realizing the "Little Way of Childhood."

Aware of our poverty, our weakness and imperfection, we realize "that of ourselves we are unable to love God as He should be loved. Knowing, too, that God holds floods of infinite tenderness which He is unable to pour into hearts that turn away from Him, we offer ourselves to Him so that He may fill us with this love which others despise. Our intention, while making this oblation, is that we may make our lives, henceforth, one great act of perfect love; that we may love God with His own love; that we may strive for a holiness that will cause Love to be loved by others.

Our imperfection is not an obstacle to such an offering. It is, in fact, because we are poor and miserable that we offer ourselves so that merciful Love may make up for our indigence. This Love will purify us, and burn up our imperfections. Jesus will clothe us with His justice, will consume us, provided we be faithful. For it is not enough to have made that act of oblation in order to enjoy its effects. We must, on the contrary, show ourselves more and more faithful and generous to God proportionately as we are possessed by His greater love.

Hence, while constantly remembering our littleness and weakness, we shall apply ourselves to the task of doing as perfectly as possible the most insignificant actions. We shall not neglect any opportunity for making sacrifices. We shall rise confidently, when we have fallen, and remain fully abandoned to all God's wishes and intentions. "We are consumed by Love only when we deliver ourselves to Love" and respond to Love.

ACT OF OBLATION TO MERCIFUL LOVE
(A Short Form)

(This act, is not from the pen of St. Therese of the Child Jesus, but it certainly expresses her thought.)

O my God, Blessed Trinity: Father, Word and Holy Ghost, I adore You, praise and bless You. I thank You for all the graces You have granted me and in particular I thank You, Father, for the gift of your Son. I thank You, Son of God, because You became one of us, sacrificed yourself for me, and have given me the Eucharist to transform me into You. I thank You, Spirit of Love, because You have established yourself in me, together with the Father and the Son, causing me to participate in the divine nature and making me a child of the heavenly Father.

I ask Your pardon for my many faults and negligences, and I offer You in reparation, the satisfactions, merits and love of Jesus, our divine Savior. I want to love You from now on as You deserve. Nevertheless, poor and powerless as I am, how can I fulfill such a desire? But You are merciful Love precisely because we are miserable. Hence, I pray You to make up for my poverty by Your own love.

Hence, in order that I may love You in one great act of perfect love, I offer myself as a victim of holocaust to Your merciful Love. And I beg You to fill my soul to overflowing with the floods of infinite tenderness that are contained in You. May that love purify me, consume unceasingly my imperfections and my faults, inflame and transform me!

My one and only aspiration is to love You and make others love You. My most ardent desire is to become holy and to attain to that degree of glory which You have prepared for me. But I do not rely upon my own works. All that I have I abandon to You. I desire to rely solely on the merits of Jesus. I expect everything with confidence from Your mercy.

And that I may realize such a life of love, I resolve to apply myself to the task of fulfilling Your will to perfection, even in the smallest details. I resolve not to refuse any act of virtue or sacrifice. I resolve to forget myself in all things and, thus, to live united with Jesus and to act through Him and like Him for love of the Father and for souls.

May that love consume and perfect me ever more and accomplish in me the degree of likeness to Jesus for which

You have predestined me. And, finally, may I die in an act of perfect love for You.

O Virgin Mary, Mother of Jesus and my Mother, and you, Sister Therese, deign to present to God this offering, and help me to fulfill it. Amen.

CHAPTER XI

Vocation Within the Mystical Body

THERESE was truly consumed by divine Love. Her desires knew no limits; her ardor constantly increased and she suffered a "veritable martyrdom" of love.

Not satisfied with being a Carmelite, a bride of Jesus, a mother of souls, she would have liked to have all vocations, to accomplish the most heroic deeds and shed her blood to the last drop so that Jesus might be loved by men.

Because of the spiritual pains which her zeal caused her to suffer, she opened the epistles of St. Paul, hoping to find in them counsel and comfort during her martyrdom. She came upon Chapter XII of the First Epistle to the Corinthians and read there that the Body of the Church necessarily comprises several members, each having its own special functions. But this was not enough. Continuing to read, she learned from Chapter XIII that all gifts, even the most perfect, that are distributed to the various members, are valueless unless they are animated by love and that charity is the great way that leads securely to God.

This time she understood. She realized that the Church is a Mystical Body composed of diverse members, diverse organs. It must have a heart, a heart burning with love, as with us; it is the heart of the Mystical Body which has the function of giving life and energy for action to the other members.

From that moment she saw clearly her own vocation. Since love is everything and contains all vocations, she had only one thing to do: to love. This would enable her to give to Jesus all that He desired. Hence, she exclaimed in an ecstasy of joy: "O Jesus, I have finally discovered my vocation. My vocation is LOVE. . . . In the heart of my mother, the Church, it shall be my function to love. In this way I shall be able to be all things, to have all vocations." [1]

It was after September 8, 1896, probably on the fourteenth of that month, that Therese discovered this "vocation"; for it is truly a vocation and not merely a way of pleasing God. Throughout her life she had given God nothing but love.[2] All her conduct was inspired by love. She had even offered herself as a victim to merciful Love so that she might love God with His own love. Hence, it was not merely a matter now of loving Him more. What Therese was looking for was the kind of role she ought to play in the Church. She wanted to find the means of so loving God and causing Him to be loved that it was equivalent to the task of all other apostolic laborers and all vocations.

Now she had the answer: it was simply love. By loving God with the Love to which she had offered herself, the love which, from that moment had possessed her heart, she would render to God love for love and fulfill all vocations. "Is not the smallest movement of pure love more useful to the Church," wrote St. John of the Cross, "than the sum total of all other works?" While her brother missionaries were laboring and struggling in mission fields, she would remain near God's throne, loving in their stead.

Love is proved by works; hence, she tried not to neglect the least little sacrifice or any glance or word . . . but to make good use of every opportunity for doing good. She would suffer and, yet, rejoice always, because she was always full of love. She was confident that such "little nothings" offered by a loving heart would please Jesus. Nevertheless, in order to increase their value and efficacy, she asked the Saints to present them to Him, that He might clothe them with His merits and then pour them out over the Church Militant and the Church Suffering.[3]

Having found the means to satiate her immense desire, Therese enjoyed profound peace. The word "peace," she tells us, expresses better her dispositions than the term "delirious joy" which she had used first, although she was still inflamed by the same extraordinary fervor, as she relates in the ardent pages she wrote on that occasion.

She goes so far as to say that "if in the end she does not attain the highest regions of love to which her soul aspires, she will, nevertheless, have tasted more sweetness in her martyrdom than she would have tasted amidst eternal joys, "unless," she adds, "Jesus takes away from me the memory of my earthly hopes." It was on that occasion that she wrote the ardent apostrophe which must be numbered among the most beautiful pages of Christian literature:

"O Divine Word! You are the Eagle I love, the Eagle who draws me to Himself. Plunging down to this land of exile, You chose to suffer, that You might attract souls to the eternal Furnace of the Blessed Trinity. And, although You have re-ascended to Light inaccessible, your permanent abode, You deign to remain in this valley of tears, hidden under the appearances of a white Host. . . . Eternal Eagle, You desire to nourish me with your divine substance, who am poor and little and would return to nothingness, were it not that your divine glance sustains my life at every instant. . . . O Jesus! allow me to declare to You, in my boundless gratitude, that your love is folly! And how could I fail to take my flight to You while I contemplate such a folly, or place a limit on my confidence in You?

"I know that the saints have also indulged in folly in their love for You. They have done great things! My own folly consists in hoping that your love will accept me as a victim. . . . My folly consists in begging the 'eagles,' my spiritual brothers, to obtain for me the favor of flying to the sun of Love, on the wings of the divine Eagle Himself. My Well-Beloved, for as long as You may desire, your little bird will remain without energy and wings, keeping His eyes constantly fixed on You. He wants to be fascinated by your gaze and become the prey of your love. I trust, O my adorable Eagle, that some day, You will come and take your little bird and, mounting with him to the Furnace of Love, You will plunge him for all eternity in the flaming abyss of that Love to which he has offered himself as a victim. . . ." [4]

All true love of Christ is apostolic: it generates zeal. Hence, at the moment when her love reached an exceptional degree of fervor, Therese's thoughts turned towards souls. She prayed Jesus to reveal to other souls the secret of His love, to choose for Himself a legion of souls who would walk her own Little Way and become victims of divine Love. Their imperfection would not be an obstacle. Even if they were weaker and more insignificant than herself, they would be even better suited for the action of merciful Love, provided they abandoned themselves to Him with complete docility and full confidence.

At this stage of her life, Therese understood better than ever before that love is everything, that "it makes up for everything, even for a long life" [5] in this land of trial, that when a soul is truly delivered to love, all its actions, even the most insignificant, are marked with that divine seal.

This does not mean that hitherto she had not understood this; for at the very beginning of her religious life, she had written to Celine: "There is only one thing for us to do during the night of this life: to love, to love Jesus with all the strength of our heart, and to save souls for Him that He may be loved. Oh! the joy of causing Jesus to be loved!" [6]

About the same time, she had taken for her rule of conduct [7] the words of St. John of the Cross: "It is very important for us in this life to consecrate ourselves to acts of love, in order that, being more quickly consumed, we may not have to wait long here or hereafter, before we are granted the vision of God." (THE LIVING FLAME, Str. I, 96).

The experiences of religious life served but to confirm her intuitions and the truth of the words of her spiritual Father. She had understood the value of love, because she had tasted it and lived it. Hence, when on the eve of her death, Sister Genevieve asked her for a word of farewell, she contented herself with the reply: "I have said all. All is fulfilled. It is only love that matters." [8]

Let us remember those words! They are the last will and testament of a Saint who was commissioned by God to teach us a new way of spiritual life. "It is love alone that matters" because it is the root principle and the end of all, in heaven and on earth. Everything comes from love; it is the soul of all things, and to all works it gives the perfection which consummates them. It makes us find God, unites us to Him, transforms us into Him. It is the source of the only happiness, the only true happiness. "Because I have never given anything to God but love," said Therese, "He will render love to me." [9]

Let this principle be the inspiration of all our actions! May everything in our lives proceed from and be done out of love!

It will be one of the principal titles to glory of St. Therese of the Child Jesus that she has taught us the precious truth that to be holy we have merely to love God with the heart of a child.

CHAPTER XII

Therese's Sufferings

SUFFERING held an important place in the life of St. Therese of the Child Jesus. She did more than accept it; she passionately loved it. This love of suffering, like her other virtues, was the effect and, as it were, the natural prolongation of her love of God. In order that divine Love might take possession of her soul and develop within her, she had pushed her practice of renunciation to the limit. Desiring to respond to the love of Christ, she had consecrated herself without reservation to the love of her neighbor. But a love that has its source in the divine Furnace of Love, does not stop there. It desires to give itself in complete immolation. It cries out for suffering so the self might be entirely consumed by it.

This had happened in the life of Jesus. This was also the aspiration of Therese. She wanted to suffer and sacrifice herself so that she might love more and cause Love to be loved by souls.

We know that suffering was not a part of God's original plan for man. He had protected us by a preternatural gift against the suffering that might result from our nature and from earthly conditions. Suffering, then, is a consequence of sin. In God's wisdom, however, it has been transformed into a means of sanctification, a proof of love, an instrument for the salvation of souls. It is, thus, one of the most admirable provisions of divine mercy.

God, in His love, decreed to save us from the eternal loss which we had brought on ourselves, and to restore, according to an even more magnificent plan, the order we had destroyed. Now, it was through the voluntary Passion of His Son that God chose to accomplish this merciful design. Suffering and the cross thereby acquired an inestimable dignity. They were to have their specific role in the supernatural order, in every effort of the soul towards its conformity with Christ. Nothing great would be accomplished without them. Until then they had inspired nothing but fear and horror. Henceforth, they were to become objects of desire for all loving souls, one of the best means of manifesting one's love for God.

God has bestowed the gift of suffering on His Son. He would likewise bestow that grace on those whom He loved in a special way. "Far from complaining to Jesus because He sends us crosses," wrote Therese, "I cannot fathom the infinite love that prompted Him to deal with us in this way." [1] "Suffering is, of all the things God can give us, the best gift. He gives it only to His chosen friends."

However, because suffering and the cross have become objects of love, it does not follow that they no longer cause pain, that crosses have ceased to be crosses. They continue to be a load on our nature and may even make us cry out in anguish. A suffering that is not felt is suffering no longer, and it is hard to see how, under such conditions, it could still fulfill its special Christian role.

Therese had learned the meaning of suffering. She was only fifteen when she wrote to her sister Celine: "What is this sweet Friend doing? Does He not notice our anguish and the weight that oppresses us? Where is He and why does He not come to console us? If He is 'begging for this sadness we suffer, it must be because He needs it. . . It grieves Him because He sees the need of filling us with sadness. Our suffering never makes Him happy. He sends it to us and, as it were, turns away His head while so doing, but suffering is a thing that is necessary for us."[2]

1. First, *suffering is necessary as a means to detach us, to purify us and dispose us for union with Jesus.*

God has loved us to the extent of desiring that we should become conformed to the image of His Son and be united with Him. But because we are miserable, stained with sin and immersed in earthly things, we cannot attain this end without a perfect purification of our soul and the acquisition of the virtues that make union with Christ possible. Now, only physical or mental suffering penetrates sufficiently to the core of our being to purify it and to enrich it so as to enable us to become similar to Christ.

"Suffering," said Therese, "is necessary to detach us from the earth and make us look up higher than this world . . ." to detach us "from all that is created . . ." "from all that is not Jesus, and to purify us," [3] to make us acquire the virtues and particularly charity. "I have often remarked," she said, "that suffering makes us good; it makes us indulgent towards others, because suffering brings us nearer to the good Lord." [4]

Suffering is especially necessary to make our heart turn to Jesus alone, for "we must suffer much if we want Him to possess us completely." [5] "It is suffering which makes us resemble Him. A spouse of Jesus must resemble Jesus. And He is covered with blood and crowned with thorns." [6]

2. *Suffering is also a matter of love. It is God's proof that He loves us.*

"Jesus tries those whom He loves," said Therese. "Suffering is the greatest proof He can give us of His tenderness towards us. He gives it only to His chosen friends. He even increases it according to the greater measure of our love for Him." [7]

Suffering is also the response of our love to His love. "God is admirable," wrote our Saint, "but He is, above all, lovable.

Let us, then, love Him! Let us love Him to the extent of being ready to suffer for Him whatever He may wish us to suffer, even the sufferings of the soul. . . .[8] Is there any greater joy than to suffer out of love of God?"[9]

But we owe a special debt to Christ, for He emptied Himself and sacrificed Himself for us, and because, in spite of so much love, He receives so little love in return: "Jesus," says Therese, "became poor that we might practice charity towards Him. He longs for our love and begs for it. . . . He looks for souls who will console Him but finds none. . . . He, as it were, puts Himself at our mercy. . . ."[10] "Let us, there-fore, make our life a continual sacrifice, a martyrdom of love to console Jesus. He asks only a glance, a sigh, but a glance and a sigh that are for Him alone!"[11] "What a joy to be able to suffer for Him whom we love!"[12]

3. *The third reason for suffering is that without it we cannot reach heaven.*

Again, the reward in heaven will be proportioned to the measure and quality of our suffering here below.

From the day when Therese had read in a work of Father Arminjon the glowing description of the reception which God has in store for those who have labored and suffered for Him, suffering had become dear to her. "If it be necessary to suffer and weep in order to reach heaven," she said, "well, I want to suffer whatever may please Jesus!"[13] "If Jesus, in spite of His love for us, makes us suffer; if He does not spare us, it is because He looks beyond time, because He already beholds us in the state of glory. He rejoices in our eternal beatitude. He so greatly desires to give us a rich recompense! He knows that suffering is the only means to prepare us so that we may know Him as He knows Himself, and, thus, make us gods."[14] She wrote, likewise, to Mother Agnes: "I desire only one thing as long as I shall be in Carmel and that is to suffer always for

Jesus. Life passes so quickly. How much better to have a beautiful crown at the expense of a little pain than to have an ordinary one without pain. Think of it, for one pain borne with joy, I shall love God more perfectly for all eternity!" [15]

Hence, her firm resolution: "Let us embrace suffering, otherwise Jesus will not be able to say 'now it is my turn to give you something.' "[16]

4. Finally, *suffering is necessary for the salvation of souls.*

"Without shedding of blood, "writes St. Paul," there is no remission of sins." [17] For our salvation Jesus 'annihilated' Himself and suffered the most excruciating pain. He allowed Himself to be crushed by sorrow and died covered with blood flowing from numerous wounds.

But the work of redemption is not finished. It will last as long as there are souls to be saved. This work Christ continues through the members of His Mystical Body. "I fill up in my flesh for his body," says St. Paul, "what is lacking of the suffering of Christ." [18] Christ has suffered. Christ's members must now take their share of suffering. By that means they will cause Christ's merits and satisfactions to be applied to souls.

Therese had a profound comprehension of the role of suffering in the work of saving souls. "It is only suffering," she wrote, "that can beget souls for Jesus." [19] She recognized in that cooperation which our divine Savior expects of us, a special love for us: "Jesus," she said, "has for us a love so incomprehensible, so delicate, that He does not want to do anything without associating us with Him. He wants us to participate with Him in the work of saving souls. The Creator of the universe waits for prayers, for the immolation made by a poor insignificant soul, to save other souls which, like that soul, were bought at the price of all His blood. . . ."[20] Oh! how happy I would be, if, at the moment of my death, I were able to offer one soul to Jesus! There would be one soul which had been saved from hell and which would praise God for all eternity!" [21] Hence, she had scarcely entered Carmel when she gave away all she had without counting the cost: her actions, prayers, sufferings; and she never made any reservations; she "even exhausted her very substance in that gift."

Children have a natural horror for suffering and their capacity of bearing it is limited. But Therese was not an ordinary child. The Holy Ghost had taken possession of her from her early childhood and progressively enlightened and strengthened her.

She had begun by simply accepting suffering, but after a short time she fell passionately in love with it and longed for it. She tells us that "at first she had not realized that it is necessary to suffer much if we want to attain holiness." But the trials which very soon came to afflict her, made her understand that "it is only the complete immolation of self that can be called love, and it is by means of suffering that we sanctify ourselves." [22]

Therese's Suffering Before her Entrance into Carmel

Therese met with suffering at an early age. "The cross has followed me from the cradle," she said, "but Jesus has taught me to love it passionately." [23] However, as we shall show, it was only at a later date that she actually loved it with true passion.

God made her understand why He was sending her suffering so early. "Since I was to become soon the betrothed of Jesus," she wrote in 1895, "it was necessary that I should suffer from my childhood." [24] These pains had, therefore, also for their purpose to prepare her for her spiritual espousals. They were a training for divine union and served as an introduction to passive purifications.

Death of Therese's Mother.

The first poignant trial which Therese had to undergo was the death of her mother (August 28, 1877). Though she was then only four years old, this loss inflicted so deep a wound in her heart that it made her suffer for many years. So grievous was her sorrow that she thought she would die of it. "I had the feeling from my tender youth," she said later, "that the 'little flower' would be plucked and carried away in its spring-time." [25] It was only through divine intervention that she was left on earth,[26] but her thoughts and aspirations were riveted on heaven.

Therese, nevertheless, found consolation in her home and family, but she was happy only in their company. While with them, she could enjoy an atmosphere that was in harmony with her own profound aspirations and her heart was at peace. But as soon as she left the family circle, she felt like an exile and her great sorrow found expression in bitter tears.

Departure of Pauline for the Convent.

For four years Pauline played the part of a mother for Therese. But on October 2, 1882, she left home to enter Carmel. This was a new and most severe trial for the poor child. The whole edifice of her life seemed to fall to pieces. Her principal support was now taken away from her. "In one instant," she wrote, "my life appeared to me in its true reality: I understood that it was but a round of suffering and a series of separations. I shed very bitter tears, for I did not know the joy of offering a sacrifice. I was weak, so weak that I regard it as a great grace that I was able to bear a trial that seemed far beyond my strength. . . . I now realize clearly that my sorrow should not have taken on those proportions, but my soul was far from mature and I would have to pass through many crucibles before I could reach the desired goal." The fact is, however, that even in the midst of that early suffering her mind developed to an astonishing degree.[27]

Her Mysterious Illness.

Before long she became grievously ill. She first suffered severe headaches and then suddenly grew worse at the recollection of memories concerning her mother. She said things she had not thought of saying and did things she did not want to do. She was, at times, subject to crises, during which she fell to the ground in a kind of vertigo. Sometimes she remained unconscious for several hours. And, yet, she never lost the proper use of her reason during her waking hours.[28]

One day, the statue of the Virgin, before which she was praying to obtain her cure, seemed to come alive. Mary appeared full of ravishing beauty; her face glowed with ineffable tenderness. She smiled at Therese and relieved her of a trial that had lasted from March 25 to May 13, 1883. However, this cure did not mark the end of Therese's sufferings. It became, rather, the occasion of prolonged trials of another character.

On the occasion of a visit to Carmel, Therese became aware of the fact that her sisters had an erroneous idea of the apparition of the Virgin to her. She began to blame herself for it and imagined she had told a lie. A sentiment of profound humiliation took hold of her and she was horrified every time she thought of it. This worry lasted four years (from 1883 to 1887). It left her during a pilgrimage to the Church of Our Lady of Victories: "The Blessed Virgin gave her to understand that it was truly she who had smiled at her and had cured her."

Later, she began to fear that she had simulated her illness, that "she had fallen ill on purpose." This notion was the "source of a veritable martyrdom" which ceased only after

her entrance into Carmel, when Father Pichon "took away
all her doubts as with the wave of the hand." [29]

The Desire of Suffering.

The year 1884 ushered in a new period in the life of
Therese. It was the year of her first meeting with Jesus in the
Holy Eucharist. She made her first Holy Communion on May
8th. Some time later, on the feast of the Ascension (May
22nd), her sister Marie, who prepared her for her communions, told her that in all probability the good Lord would
spare her from sufferings and that He would always carry
her in His arms. Instead of accepting her sister's prophecy,
Therese, after receiving Communion, felt a lively desire for
suffering: "I felt the dawning in my heart of a great desire
for suffering. At the same time, Jesus seemed to assure me that
He had reserved a great many crosses for me. I was filled
with great consolation and consider that as one of the greatest
graces of my life. Suffering became an object of attraction for
me. It had charms which ravished me, although I did not
yet understand this well." [30]

Here, then, was considerable progress. Until then, Therese
had adjusted herself the best she could to the divine will; but,
being still too weak to bear her sufferings properly, she suffered with sadness and tears. But notice, once Jesus had
entered her heart, instantly there was a radical change in
her dispositions. Suffering became attractive. She fell in love
with it, though not fully understanding the reasons for its
attractiveness. "Until then," she said, "I had suffered without
loving suffering. From that day I felt a true love for it." [31]

At the same time, let it be noted, her soul was flooded with
such great consolations that she did not experience the like
of them during the remainder of her life. God apparently
desired to strengthen her in preparation for her 'passion,' for

she felt sure that the future held many crosses in reserve for her.

To those graces was added another, which came as their crown and complement. "I felt another desire," she wrote, "that of loving God alone" which for her meant that she would "no longer find joy anywhere except in God alone." But to find joy in Him alone, it is necessary to give up enjoying creatures. Hence, from that moment, in her acts of thanksgiving after Holy Communion, she began to repeat the words of the Imitation: "O Jesus, Who art sweetness unspeakable, turn into bitterness to me all fleshly delights!" (Whitford-Klein Translation).[32] She notes that it was as if those words were whispered to her: "I uttered them like a child who repeats without proper understanding what a friend suggests to her." [33] God, without letting her know where He was leading her, made her ask for detachment, for absolute poverty, so that He might be able to accomplish His loving designs in her soul.

Therese was, thus, converted to a love for suffering, but that does not mean that she found her delight in it. "Until the age of fourteen I practiced virtue without feeling its sweetness. I desired suffering without thinking of making it my joy. This is a grace that was granted to me only at a later date." [34] She had not yet reached the degree of perfection which would make her face immediately, and with proper generosity, the trials which were once more to afflict her. These were to be as varied as they were numerous. God had heard her prayer and seemed to have taken her petitions literally.

Therese's Scruples.

She suffered especially from severe scruples. "I cannot describe," she wrote, "what I have had to suffer for one and a half years (from her retreat for her Second Communion,

May, 1884, to mid-August, 1885). All my thoughts, and even
my most ordinary actions, became for me a source of trouble. I found relief only in reporting my worries to Marie (her
sister). And this cost me too much, for I thought I had the
obligation of telling her the extravagant ideas I had about
her. As soon as I had put down my burden before her, I tasted
a momentary peace, but it left me immediately with the rapidity of lightning and my martyrdom quickly started all over
again." [35] It finally caused her to become ill and she had
to leave the boarding school when she was no more than
thirteen.[36]

Marie's Entrance Into Carmel.

Amidst all her afflictions, Marie, her godmother,"the sole
support of my soul," her "only oracle," without whom she
"could not live," decided to enter Carmel also. (October
15, 1886).

This was too heavy a cross. Therese burst into a deluge
of tears. Because she had been so often disappointed, she
resolved "to take no more delight in any earthly things." To
whom could she go now to confess her scruples? Who would
be able to give her the help she needed so badly?

Suddenly inspired, she turned in her distress to her four
little brothers and sisters who had already gone to their
heavenly reward. To them she addressed a prayer that was
so simple and heartfelt that she thought they would find it
hard not to do something about it. She told them that she was
the youngest of the family, that she was loved and fondled by
all, and that surely if they had remained on earth, they would
have acted kindly to her in her distress. Now, the fact that
they had entered heaven was no reason for forgetting her.
Hence, she begged them to show that in heaven one can still
love his own, and to prove it by drawing from the divine
treasures the peace of which she was presently so much in

need. Her little brothers and sisters responded perfectly to her appeal. She had scarcely finished her prayer when "peace came and inundated her soul with its delightful waters." [37]

Therese's Great Sensitiveness.

Therese's victory was not yet complete. She had still to conquer her excessive sensitiveness: "I greatly desired to practice virtue, but I was truly unbearable on account of my excessive sensitiveness. When I had unwillfully caused a little pain to another . . . I wept like a Magdalen and, afterwards, when I began to console myself thinking that perhaps I had not caused pain after all, I cried because I had cried for nothing. All reasoning about it proved useless. I was unable to correct myself of this ugly fault." [38]

The reason for this lack of success was that until then the grace of suffering well was but a "spark hidden under the ashes." Hence, in spite of her desire for suffering, in spite of her prayers and her own efforts, she did not succeed in gathering the fruits for which she had hoped. The flowers faded and fell to the ground before their time and she said to herself with sadness and astonishment: "Shall I never have anything but desires?" [39] But the moment was approaching when God, touched by so much suffering and perseverance in her efforts, would reward her, granting her the grace of bearing, henceforth, with courage, the trials she was to meet.

The Grace of Christmas—Her Conversion

It happened on the night of Christmas in the year 1886. From her childhood Therese had been accustomed to find her shoes full of sweets when she returned from midnight Mass. But on this particular night, when she was returning upstairs to her room, she heard her father say in a tone of dissatisfaction: "That sort of surprise is too childish for a big girl like Therese. I hope this will be the last year for this sort of thing."

This was a hard blow for one so sensitive as Therese, and it was natural to expect that she would react with a flood of tears. Celine understood this well and she asked Therese to wait a little before she went up to get the candy. But Therese "was no longer the same. The dear little Child one hour old had transformed the darkness of her soul into a torrent of light. On this night when He became weak and began to suffer for love of her . . . He prompted her to put away her swaddling bands and the imperfections of childhood . . . and made her strong and courageous." [40]

Repressing her tears, and the excited throbbing of her heart, she came down to the dining room and joyfully drew forth from her shoes the surprises they contained. Celine, seeing Therese's calmness, "thought she was dreaming at such a sight." In fact, God had granted Therese "the miracle she had so long prayed for." The fountain of her tears dried up and from then on they flowed but rarely and with difficulty: "Little Therese had recovered the strength of soul she had lost at the age of four-and-a-half years, never to lose it again." Not only did she regain her former vigor, but she found it reinforced by a supernatural energy that would enable her to face her future trials unflinchingly.

From 1891 on, Therese "began to navigate with full sails the waters of confidence and love" [41] and no disquieting fears that came to disturb her soul were able to weaken her resolution. She would, henceforth, "advance from victory to victory, running a race fit for a giant." [42]

This turning point in the life of Therese enables us to better understand her conduct in times of suffering during that earlier period from 1877 to 1886.

A careful study of her autobiography and of the statements left us by those who had lived with her, show us that Therese was truly not the "crybaby" and difficult child that some have seen in her; nor was her extreme sensitiveness due to any organic or psychic cause. In judging her, let us remember that Therese's severe trial began when she was four-and-a-half years old, a mere child, and that it left her when she was only thirteen, a very young girl indeed.

It is also necessary to remember that she was endowed with an extreme delicacy of feeling and with an exceedingly tender heart. The slightest things caused her to suffer greatly. It is natural, then, that during those ten years she was repeatedly shaken by events that were so painful that they produced violent repercussions in her. There was first the death of her ardently-loved mother—a loss over which she grieved so greatly that she would gladly have taken the flight to heaven with her. Next, came the departure for Carmel of Pauline and Marie, who had been her support during her trials. The last of these upsetting ordeals was a terrible illness, and then a year of scruples. Furthermore, we should not forget the disappointments God sent her in answer to her petition and for the purpose of perfecting her in the practice of virtue.

She would have liked to be able to bear those trials with unflinching courage. She wished to respond immediately to God's grace and give Him the proof of a generous love. But her virtue had not yet reached the development that is required for the exercise of so great a perfection. Hence, her tears and her sorrow at the sight of her imperfection.

Therese has been rather severe in her judgment of her own sensitiveness.[43] Her appreciation of her own conduct is of the same order as the reproaches which saints are accustomed to make to themselves while weeping over their faults. Hence, we should not accept her testimony too literally.

During the process of enquiry conducted by the ordinary, Celine made a report which sheds much light on this period of Therese's life. She said: "From the age of four-and-a-half years, that is, after the death of her mother, until Christmas, 1886, when she became fourteen, Therese went through a period of darkness. A veil seemed to hide the qualities God had given her. Her teachers recognized her intelligence but, in the world, she was considered awkward and lacking in ability. The thing that occasioned and seemed to justify that opinion was, especially, her excessive timidity which made her hesitate and paralyzed her at every step. My uncle, Mr. Guerin said that Therese's schooling had been shortened and that her education was incomplete. It is true that she gave cause for such unfavorable interpretations, for she said scarcely anything herself but always left the talking to others. Contrary to appearances, her life was filled with trials from her infancy. She underwent a true martyrdom of the heart and suffered much in body also. She had almost constant headaches; however, her extreme sensitiveness and the delicacy of her sentiments constituted the most prolific source of her sufferings. All this she bore without complaint, but it made her sad. It is important to note that, even during that period of her life, she was fundamentally a strong character, in spite of the apparent weakness caused by her sensitiveness. This remarkable strength was evident to me from the fact that her sorrows never turned her away in the least from the discharge of her duties. For my part, even during that period, I never noticed any fault of character, a too lively word, a weakness in the matter of virtue. She mortified herself every moment and in the most insignificant things. It seems to me that she never neglected a single occasion for offering sacrifices to God." [44]

That "grace of Christmas" which Therese calls "her conversion" deserves that title only in a relative sense. It clearly did not mark the passage from a state of wickedness to one of virtue, but it was an ascent from a less perfect to a more perfect state. We should, rather, call it a transformation.

Certain authors have considered that transformation as the fruit of ten years of effort and struggle in which, of course, she was aided by grace; but they see in it also a victory for

Therese. This is not the Saint's own view of the matter, for she attributed the victory entirely to Jesus. "In one instant," she writes, "Jesus accomplished what I had been unable to do for several years, having been content, on my part, with my good will, which had never been wanting." She confirms her judgment by the example of the miraculous draught of fishes: "Just like the Apostles, I was able to say, 'Lord, I have fished all night and taken nothing.' Being more merciful towards me than He was towards His disciples, Jesus Himself took hold of the net, cast it out and drew it in filled with fishes. He made me a fisher of souls . . . I felt a great desire to labor for the conversion of sinners. . . . In a word, I felt charity enter my heart, the need to forget myself that I might please others, and from that time I have been happy." [45]

In her opinion, therefore, all her efforts had no other effect than to prove her good will. Although she acted with all the energy she possessed, she was forced to recognize the impotence of human virtue in respect to the goal of perfection that has to be attained. Her transformation was purely a grace given her by Jesus. Hence, she said: "When I recall the past, my soul overflows with gratitude, seeing the favors heaven has bestowed on me. This has caused so great a change to take place in me that I am no longer recognizable." [46]

But a new period of tribulation was about to begin. From the age of two, Therese had been thinking about entering the religious life and "from that time on her resolution had never changed." [47] At the age of nine, she felt certain that she was called to Carmel: "She felt this so strongly that she had not the least doubt about it." [48] Following the "Christmas grace," her desire to enter Carmel became more ardent: Christ's call became more pressing.[49] She would have liked to join her sisters, who were already in the convent, the following year and on the very day and hour when she had received the "grace of conversion."

It was in the afternoon of the feast of Pentecost, May 29, 1887, that she approached her father and asked his permission. Repressing his grief, he granted it to her. But she had also to obtain the consent of her uncle and guardian, of whom she was very much afraid. It was not until October that she summoned the courage to speak to him about it, and then only to meet with a point-blank refusal, which, of course, caused her great sorrow. However, encouraged by her sister Pauline, she soon returned to the charge, although her fears were aggravated by a painful crisis her soul was passing through: "It seemed to her she was in the midst of a frightful desert for three days. . . . A night, a deep night, as of death, came over her. Finally, on the fourth day, October 22, she spoke to her uncle again. This time he acceded to her wishes. Love re-entered her soul and inflamed it to such a degree that she sometimes felt an ardor such as she had never before experienced; this was truly a transport of love." [50]

But the case was not settled by any means. The Superior of Carmel, having been informed of her plans, categorically opposed her entrance because of her age, and the Bishop adopted the Superior's view. Only one other possibility remained—to have recourse to the Sovereign Pontiff. This was tried but here, also, with failure. All she could do now was to abandon herself to God.

Added to this was the fact that Jesus "seemed to be absent; nothing revealed His presence to me." [51] And, yet, in spite of the "bitterness that filled her soul to overflowing, in the depths of her heart Therese had an intimate feeling of great peace" because she sought nothing but the will of the good Lord.[52]

When at long last it was decided that she would be permitted to enter at the end of Lent, Therese prepared herself by greater seriousness and mortification. She endeavored to break her own will and rendered little services to others while avoiding any credit for them. In this way, she tells us, she grew in abandonment, humility and the other virtues.[53]

THERESE'S SUFFERINGS IN CARMEL

Therese made her entrance into Carmel on April 9, 1888. It is there that we must now follow her to see how continued suffering enabled her to satisfy her love of the cross.

"From the moment of my entrance into Carmel," she wrote, "suffering stretched out its arms to me and I embraced it with love. During the solemn examination which preceded my profession, I declared what I was seeking by entering Carmel: 'I am come to save souls, in particular to pray for priests.' He who wants to attain a certain goal must make use of the proper means for it. Jesus made me understand that it was through the Cross that He desired to give me souls and, thus, I felt more and more attracted to suffering in proportion to its increase." [54]

She became so thoroughly convinced of this truth that she affirmed that "suffering with love is the only thing truly desirable . . . and the only thing that I want in this life." She considered that for a Carmelite, a day without suffering was a day lost.[55] Not satisfied with embracing only the sufferings that came to afflict her, she invited more and went to meet them.

Martyrdom had been the dream of her youth. On the day of her profession she placed on her heart a note on which she had written: "Jesus, may I die a martyr for You; give me martyrdom of the heart or of the body, or, rather, give them both to me." [56] This desire for the crucifying martyrdom of the heart in one so young, shows how ardent was her thirst also martyrdom of the soul. We shall now consider those for suffering. We shall see that God gave her even more than she had asked for; not only martyrdom of body and heart, but three martyrdoms in detail.

A. *Martyrdom of the Body:*

Therese began by suffering in her body. Although she had physical sufferings during her life in the convent, for the life of a Carmelite is inconceivable without such sufferings, her corporal martyrdom began especially with her illness. In a letter to Celine, she shows that she did not suspect at that time how crucifying bodily sufferings can be: "Why worry about exterior crosses! The true cross is the martyrdom of the heart, the intimate suffering of the soul." [57] She would later be forced to change her views about that.

In June, 1894, appeared the first signs of an illness that was to prove serious. She developed persistent sore throat and was treated with cauterization by silver nitrate. This caused her great pain but no one suspected the gravity of her illness. From that time on (April, 1895) "the feeling that God had given her from her childhood that she would die young" became more definite,[58] for she told one of her companions: "I shall die soon. I do not say that it will be within a few months, but within two or three years. I feel, because of all that is taking place in my soul, that my exile will soon come to an end." And in the course of her illness, she more than once repeated (at the end of 1896 and in 1897) that her death was near.

During the winter of 1895-1896 there were no disquieting signs in regard to her health. When Lent came, Therese, considering herself "stronger than ever," desired to practice its penances with all the rigor that is customary in Carmelite monasteries. But she had over-estimated her strength.

It was in the night between Holy Thursday and Good Friday of the year 1896 that appeared the first symptoms of the illness that was to lead to her death. She had remained in adoration before the Blessed Sacrament until midnight. After returning to her room, she had scarcely stretched out on her pallet, when a stream of blood rushed to her lips. She thought she was going to die, and this filled her soul with joy. In the morning, when she discovered that her handkerchief was full of blood, she felt certain that she had received the first call from Jesus, and she eagerly revealed to her Mother Prioress what had happened. She passed the whole day in a spirit of jubilation at the thought of the blessedness that awaited her. Because she had said that she did not feel tired, she was given permission to fast the whole day and took nothing but dry bread and water. She even washed the panes of the large windows of the cloister. One novice, having noticed her pallor and tired look, offered to take her place, but Therese refused, saying that she could very well bear a slight fatigue on the day when Jesus had suffered so much for her. In the evening, she took the discipline during the time required for three *Miserere's*. But when she returned to her cell and made ready to settle down to sleep, she had a second hemmorrhage. The physicians were consulted but they declared that there was nothing serious in her condition at that moment.[59]

After that first crisis, her condition seemed to improve for a while but this did not last long. The illness once more took the upperhand, causing a state of exhaustion in the poor sufferer; but in spite of it she continued to assist at the Canonical Hours, even taking part in night Offices. Sometimes her courage almost failed her because of the heroic effort it required for her to hold out. At the end of Matins, as she painfully made her way to her cell, passing through icy corridors or under open cloisters, she was transfixed with cold. Then, shivering from the cold and fever, it took her half-an-hour to undress. She stretched out on her pallet under her two badly worn blankets which were far too thin to give her the warmth she needed. There was a certain week during that winter when she shivered almost continuously. She even admitted one day that she suffered "unto death" from the cold.[60]

Nevertheless, she prepared herself with confidence for

even more severe sufferings: "I am not at all afraid of the last struggles nor of the sufferings of illness, however serious they may be. The good Lord has helped me and led me by the hand from my most tender years. I count on Him. I feel certain that He will continue to assist me until the end. I may have to suffer extreme pains, but I shall never have too many; of that I feel sure." [61] To this feeling of assurance she gave expression on several occasions.

Noticing that her condition was getting worse, she had little doubt that her illness would be the cause of her death. But, faithful to the rule of conduct she had chosen, she paid attention only to the present moment, for she knew it is only for this that grace is given to us. She was also confident that as the seriousness of her malady increased, God would give her proportionately greater graces.[62] Again, realizing that God willed this suffering, she took delight in pleasing Him by courageously accepting it.[63]

Her illness now took a more alarming turn. Tuberculosis had invaded the intestines. The physician who had failed to diagnose her illness correctly, now tried to help her by cauterizations and other violent remedies, which proved fruitless.

It had been Therese's wish to remain in her cell as long as possible because she thought she would be too well taken care of in the infirmary. Besides, she had borne so much suffering in that room that she would have liked to die there also. But on July 8 she was asked to leave her cell and this was a great sacrifice for her.[64]

Her body was rapidly wasting away. "I notice," she said, "that I am becoming a skeleton." Far from grieving over it, she took pleasure in witnessing this disintegration.[65] She had aches and pains in many parts of her body. A cold sweat exhausted her. Coughing spasms sometimes lasted for hours and left her breathless. Gangrene ate away her intestines and she lost blood two or three times a day. Drinking only intensified her burning thirst. She had a terrible feeling of suffocation which could not be alleviated by the administration of ether. Finally, her bones protruded through her flesh to such an extent that, when she was made to sit upright to get some relief, it seemed to her that she was seated on iron spikes.

Very soon the only thing left her was the free use of her hands, and her face alone remained intact. But she found encouragement in the thought that the more grievous her sufferings, the greater would be her eternal happiness.[66] Because her hemorrhages were becoming more frequent as the month of July drew to a close, it was judged proper to give her Extreme Unction. This sacrament she received on July 30.

Before receiving the Holy Oils, she asked pardon from the community for the faults she had committed or the dis-edification she had given, and this she did in terms of such great humility that the sisters were unable to restrain their tears. After the ceremony she exclaimed, radiant with joy: "The door of my somber prison is half open. I am full of joy, especially because our Father Superior has assured me that my soul resembles that of a little child after the reception of Baptism." [67]

But she was to live two more months afflicted by ever increasing sufferings. This, however, did not deject her. On the contrary, with staunch courage, she wanted to bear everything without alleviation. One day when she had exclaimed, "Oh! how my shoulder hurts me!" she was asked: "Shall we put some cotton on it?" "No," she replied, "do not take away this little cross from me." [68] Nevertheless, she accepted and even asked for such remedies and care as had been prescribed, remarking, "it is for the sake of obedience." It cost her a great deal to accept such comforts.[69]

Therese's one great concern was not to lose the merits of suffering or, it might be better to say, she was most eager not to diminish in the least the quality of her love. "I suffer much," she remarked, "but am I suffering in the proper spirit?" [70]

So intense were her sufferings that she confessed: "I feel that I would become discouraged if I did not have faith, or, rather, if I did not love the good Lord." [71] And, as her charitable thoughts went out to her neighbor, she added: "My little sisters, pray for the sick who are at the hour of death! Oh! how much we should pray for the dying! If you knew what takes place, how easily we become impatient. We ought to be charitable and indulgent towards all without exception. . . ."[72] I understand very well why those who don't have the faith commit suicide when they are undergoing severe sufferings. See to it when you are taking care of sick people who are the prey of violent pains that you don't leave poisonous medicines in their reach. I assure you, when one is suffering, it takes but an instant to lose one's head." [73]

In the last days of her life, her suffering became truly excruciating; hence, the doctor who took care of her advised: "Do not wish to keep her, seeing what condition she is in. Her suffering is truly horrible."

Her weakness was so great that she was no longer able to hold a conversation. "Not . . . even . . . talk . . . any more . . . with you," she said sadly to Mother Agnes. One day she almost fainted at the mere sound of the *Miserere*, as it was recited in a low voice before she was given Holy Communion. It was then that she sighed: "I shall perhaps lose my senses. This night, not being able to bear it any longer, I asked the Blessed Virgin to take my head in her hands and to support it. . . ."[74] People do not know what it means to suffer like this. . . . I never thought that I could suffer so much. . . . Oh! how good God must be since I am given the strength to bear all that I suffer." [75]

Having been asked whether she had lost her courage, she replied: "No, and yet everything is for the worse," but immediately taking this back, she added: "No, everything is not for the worse; everything is for the better."[76]

During the last month of her life, a month of martyrdom,

the poor sufferer confessed: "How much courage I need just to make a sign of the Cross! My God, my God, have pity on me; that is all I can say any more!" [77] And, yet, she affirmed that she was not tired of suffering, "that she did not want to suffer less. . . . When I can go no further, well, I cannot go further!" [78] And to a sister who had remarked: "You are suffering dreadfully," she replied: "No, it is not dreadful. A little victim of love cannot look upon something her Bridegroom sends her as being dreadful. He gives me from moment to moment what I am able to bear; no more." [79]

She also wanted the infirmarian to keep up her courage. Sometimes when she was out of breath, she sighed: "I suffer." But she had asked her nurse: "Every time I say, 'I suffer,' please reply 'so much the better'; for that is what I would like to say, but I don't always have the strength to say it." [80]

Up to two days before her death, she desired to be left alone during the night but, in spite of her request, the infirmarian visited her several times. On one of these visits, she found Therese with hands joined and eyes raised heavenwards. "What are you doing?" she asked; "you should try to sleep." "I cannot sleep, Sister, I am suffering too much; so I am praying."

"And what do you say to Jesus?"
"I say nothing to Him; I just love Him." [81]

On the morning of September 28, her agony seemed to be close at hand. A most painful rattle in her throat made her breathing difficult. At midday, she asked the Mother Prioress: "Mother, is this the death agony? What must I do to die? I shall never be able to die." In the afternoon she suffered a severe crisis which made her say: "I can't endure any more. Oh! pray for me. If you knew!" It was thought that she would not live through the day, and Sister Genevieve hastened to ask her for a parting word. It was then that Therese spoke the words which give the keynote of her whole life, of her spiritual doctrine: "I have said everything; it is LOVE ALONE THAT COUNTS." [82]

After Matins, as she was undergoing a true martyrdom, she joined her hands and murmured: "Yes, my God! Yes, my God, I accept anything." The Mother Prioress asked her: "You are suffering unbearably, aren't you?" She replied: "Not unbearably, Mother, but much, much . . . just what I can endure."

The following day, the day of her death, she was breathing very heavily. Joining her hands and gazing at the statue of the Blessed Virgin, she exclaimed: "Oh! I have prayed fervently to her. But this is pure agony without any admixture of consolation!"

The whole day she endured indescribable pains: "If this is agony," she said, "what, then, is death? But the good Lord will not abandon me. . . . Yes, my God, everything You wish, but have pity on me." Towards three o'clock she held out her arms as on the cross. The Mother Prioress having placed a picture of Our Lady of Mount Carmel on her knees, Therese looked at it and said: "Mother, present me very quickly to the Blessed Virgin. Prepare me for a good death." The Prioress told her that her preparation for death was already complete, to which Therese, after a moment of reflection, replied: "Yes, I have understood what it is to be humble of heart." And then, as if God, at that supreme moment, wished her to summarize in a few words the profound thoughts which had inspired her life, she added: "I am not sorry because I have surrendered myself to Love. Oh, no! I am not sorry for having delivered myself to Love; quite the contrary!"

Finally, expressing more explicitly the role of her sufferings, she remarked: "I would never have believed that it was possible to suffer so much! Never, never! I can explain this only because of my ardent desire to save souls." [83]

All her aspirations, all she had striven for throughout life, was summarized in those last words: humility or truth, the foundation of her doctrine; love which is its soul; zeal for souls, which constituted her apostolic mission; lastly, as a sign of her love, as well as a means of saving souls, suffering, ardently desired and generously borne.

These are thoughts that should inspire every Christian life. Our spiritual life, our relations with God should be based on truth. We please God only to the extent that we are true and, therefore, humble. Our life has no value unless it is animated by love. St. Paul expressed this fundamental principle in the words: "Practicing the truth in charity, in order to grow in Christ, in all things." (Eph., 4:15) On the other hand, we cannot truly love God without loving our neighbor and desiring his salvation; nor can we truly love Him without bearing our cross and suffering after His example.

Towards five o'clock in the evening her death agony began. A horrible cough racked her chest, her face was congested, her hands turned purple. She trembled in all her members, and sweat ran from every pore of her body, wetting the bedclothes and the mattress. This condition lasted for two hours. At six o'clock, at the sound of the Angelus, she opened suppliant eyes and gazed at the statue of the Blessed Virgin. A little after seven, to her question whether this was the end, the Mother Prioress answered that God might still prolong her agony for a few hours. "Well . . . so be it . . . so be it . . ." she repeated. "Oh! I would not want to suffer less (than what has been appointed by God)" And then, looking lovingly at the Crucifix, she exclaimed: "Oh! I love Him . . . my God! I love You!" Scarcely had she uttered these words than her head fell gently back on the pillow. She had sealed her martyrdom by an ACT OF LOVE.

One question that we might wish to ask in regard to Therese's sufferings is whether proper care was given to her during her illness. This is a delicate matter and several elements must be kept in mind if we wish to answer it fairly and objectively.[84]

We must note, first of all, that at that time tuberculosis was not as well known as it is today, nor were the physicians well acquainted with the suitable means to take care of it.

It was in July 1897 that a doctor whose competence cannot be doubted was consulted regarding her condition. After examining her he said that he did not think that Therese had contracted tuberculosis. Her appearance certainly did not betray her true condition. Her face remained unchanged and her loss of weight was not apparent because of the ample habit. Again, no one, until April 1897, not even her own sister, Mother Agnes, was aware of the gravity of her illness. The remedies ordered by the doctor were always administered to the patient and on several occasions she was given what were supposed to be "body builders" such as meat, wine, grapes.

On the other hand, Therese, faithful to the rule of conduct she had chosen for herself, never asked for anything. She was satisfied with anything that was offered to her. Nevertheless, she made known to her Prioress what she considered herself in duty bound to reveal, but this she did in such moderate terms that it was easy to get the wrong impression about her true condition.[85]

She had at one time suggested to her novices the rule of conduct to be followed in such circumstances: "When you are ill, say it simply to Mother Prioress, and then abandon yourself to the good Lord without any anxiety, whether they take care of you or neglect you. You have done your duty in notifying those in authority and that is enough. The rest does not concern you any longer; it is God's concern. If He permits you to be wanting in anything, this is a grace. It means that He trusts that you are sufficiently strong to suffer something for Him. . . .[86] If God judges it necessary, He will enlighten the Superiors."

Those words shed light on Therese's own case. Her Prioress did not suspect the gravity of her illness; and since Therese wished to attend to her exercises and her functions until the end, she was permitted to assist at the Office of Matins. She was even seen going to the laundry at a time when she had a burning fever. Another time her chest and back were racked by open wounds and, yet, she went to help others hang up the wash. On one occasion, she even lay down on her hard pallet after the doctor had applied no less than 500 spots of cauterization.

One day, however, when she was suffering more than usual, she admitted to one of her novices, who was assistant infirmarian, that she often lost courage because of the violent efforts she made to sing and stand erect during the night Office. The infirmarian wanted to go and inform the Prioress of Therese's condition, but the latter, who had already told the Prioress, but probably without making it clear to her how thoroughly exhausted she was, replied: "Our Mother knows that I am tired. It is my duty to tell her all that I feel, and since she chooses to allow me to follow the exercises with the community, she is inspired by the good Lord, Who wishes to grant my desire to keep going to the very end." And she added with a laugh that she usually shook off her fatigue with the words: "If I die they will surely notice it." [87]

This novice and infirmarian, instead of heeding Therese's request not to carry the matter to the Prioress again, did go and consult her about it. The latter, following to the letter the principle of the old school regarding the care of one's health replied with words that were directed as much to the novice as to Therese: "We have never met young people who are so fussy about their ills as you are. In the old days one would never have missed Matins. If Sister Therese of the Child Jesus can't hold out any longer, let her come and tell me." [88] The sister infirmarian later remarked: "There was no danger that the servant of God would thus go and complain."

Therese, therefore, continued to assist at the night Office and to perform all the duties assigned to her, except the most fatiguing. "I am still able to walk," she said; "I must be at my task." [89]

But towards the end of March or the beginning of April, 1897, she revealed to the assistant infirmarian what an effort she had to make to climb the stairs and to get undressed. This infirmarian, in spite of Therese's prohibition, informed Mother de Gonzaga and Mother Agnes. "From that time on," said the infirmarian, "she was well taken care of" and was dispensed from the observances. "Oh!" exclaimed Therese, when she learned this decision, "I had begged God so earnestly to let me follow the community exercises until my death. He has not desired to hear me. It seems to me, nevertheless, that I could assist at all of them. I would not die one minute sooner. I sometimes even imagine, that if I had not said anything, they would not consider me ill." [90]

Since, at that time, she was not yet in the infirmary, she came down every day to receive Holy Communion in the Chapel. One day, when Mother Agnes went to her cell after thanksgiving, she found Therese exhausted, seated on her poor bench, with her back resting against the wall. Mother Agnes reproached her for having tired herself out like that but Therese replied: "I don't think it is too much to suffer, for the sake of gaining one Communion." [91]

What, then, ought we to conclude from these facts?

It is my opinion that we must admit that Therese did not receive the care that anyone as sick as she was for so long a time should have had. While it is true that some rest and medical care were given her, these were in no way proportionate to the gravity of her illness. On the other hand, it also seems true that those responsible did not realize that she was afflicted with tuberculosis. Moreover, by not revealing how much she suffered, and by her persistent desire to acquit herself of her tasks and to be present at the common exercises,

Therese helped to hide her true condition. Finally, we must remember that the mental attitude of people of that time towards suffering, especially that of those living in religious houses, was much more austere than it is today; consequently, personal health was apt to be neglected.

With all this in mind we can find, perhaps, partial excuse for those who belonged to her community. In any case, her associates were not guilty of deliberate ill-treatment nor of grave negligence towards Therese. Nevertheless, knowing Therese's generosity and the drastic sort of treatment imposed on her by the physician, they should have watched her more carefully, spared her, and taken better care of her.[92]

Therese did acknowledge that she had not always received sufficient care. When Mother Agnes, at the end of Therese's life, reproached her for not having informed her earlier of the gravity of her condition, the patient replied: "Oh! my Mother, thank God for it. If you had known my condition, seeing how little care I received, you would have grieved too much." [93] At the risk of distorting its meaning, we had best accept this sentence literally.

It is true that on another occasion (when they failed to serve her an egg prescribed by her diet) she said to Mother Agnes: "Do not worry on my account; I am still too well cared for." But this answer, which applied to a particular case does not weaken the judgment she expressed in the text previously quoted.

God, however, had permitted all this in His wisdom and love, for Therese had been destined for suffering.

B.   *Martyrdom of the Heart:*

Before she had experienced the severe pains of her corporal martyrdom, Therese had asked for the martyrdom of the heart, because she considered those other external crosses insignificant. Her request was generously granted.

Community life is sometimes pictured as family life, where the religious taste the sweetness of fraternal unity and love. This conception is only partially true for, as Therese writes, it is only through sacrifice that such unity can be achieved.[94] Although the members are striving for perfection, they do not always have the same idea of what perfection is, nor do they all strive toward it with the same fervor. Moreover, they cannot realize their ideal overnight. Hence, because of the diversity of minds and characters, conflicts easily arise. A religious who truly seeks God, uses these very difficulties as means of ascent to Him.

Therese, no doubt, was referring to this sort of vexation when she wrote to Celine: "We shall find here more than anywhere else the cross and martyrdom. . . . We shall suffer together, as the early Christians suffered, keeping close together in order to encourage one another during our periods of trial." [95]

First of all, Therese had to suffer from her Prioress.

Mother Marie de Gonzaga had genuine qualities but she had also some serious defects. She was dictatorial, very impressionable, by nature distrustful and inclined to melancholy. She was often wanting in balance and consistency. All this made her government painful to her subjects.[96]

Therese's relations with her Prioress, during her novitiate, were very painful. As she herself confessed, "the good Lord permitted her (the Prioress) to be very severe towards me without being conscious of it. . . . I had to kiss the ground whenever I met her. . . . So it was also on the rare occasions when she gave me direction (of conscience). What grieved me most was the fact that I did not know how to correct my faults, for example, my slowness, my little devotion during the Office." [97] Besides that, she felt unable to open her heart to her Mother Prioress.[98]

This severity of her Prioress was especially evident during the first two years. We should be sinning against historical truth if we maintained that Mother de Gonzaga always acted with a good intention. But we also would do her an injustice if we refused her the benefit of an excuse.

The Prioress had recognized from the very beginning the superior qualities of this young postulant. "I would never have thought it possible," she said, "that a child of fifteen could possess such maturity of judgment. There isn't one word that I feel obliged to say to her. Everything is perfect." [99] The day after Therese's profession, she wrote: "This angel is seventeen-and-a-half years old, but she has the understanding of a person of thirty, the consummate perfection of an advanced novice and the self-possession of an old religious." [100]

We have already recorded that she had Therese help her in the work of the novitiate. She even judged her capable of being Prioress, despite her youth.[101] But precisely because she discerned these qualities and exceptional virtues in her novice, she wished to subject her to severe discpline. "This is not the kind of soul," she affirmed, "that one should treat like a child, and fear to humiliate at every turn." [102] However, the Prioress could have shown greater discretion, and used more suitable means for her purposes of discipline. If a serious formation demands that no fault should be overlooked in a novice, that does not dispense the mistress of novices from the duty of being a mother to them. At a later date, Therese would give a concrete example of the proper treatment of novices.

Later, especially from 1893 on, there was an improvement in Therese's relationship with the Prioress. She herself has acknowledged that her Mother Prioress gave signs of her love and confidence.[103] And this was so true that the members of her community generally believed that the Prioress was spoiling her. Mother Agnes has confirmed this fact.[104] However, the skies, even then, were not always cloudless.

After Mother Marie de Gonzaga had entrusted the direction of the novices to Therese, while remaining titular Novice Mistress, there were new occasions for friction. She was jealous by temperament, and when she thought that too much affection was being shown to the Sub-Mistress, or that the latter was transgressing her authority, she yielded to ill humor and humbled her assistant. Therese always accepted this without complaint. But this did not prevent her from making the proper observation to the Prioress—and this she did both with firmness and respect—when, on certain occasions, she considered that the latter was going beyond her rights.

The Prioress confessed later that she treated Therese during the first years with great severity but that the Saint had found in her discipline occasions for joyful sacrifice.

On the other hand, Mother Agnes declared that Therese had accepted those humiliations not only with generosity but even with joy. One day, her "little mother" had told Therese how much she pitied her when she noticed how frequently she was subjected to humiliations. Therese replied: "You should not have had so much pity on me. I was lifted up to such heights that I felt an increase of strength after suffering each humiliation." [105] These admirable words show the depth of Therese's virtue of patient obedience.

Therese and her Mistress of Novices, Mother Marie des Anges.

Mother Marie des Anges was a saintly person, very kind, even condescending. She fulfilled in herself the characteristics of the first Carmelites. But she was also absent-minded, was sometimes wanting in perspicacity and inclined to worry. She would give directives to her novices and later forget all about them; or she would fail to inform the Mother Prioress about these directives and, as a consequence of all this, Therese had to suffer. While Mother Marie des Anges was supervising Therese's work in the linen room, she frequently gave the latter lengthy spiritual conferences which were not in harmony with the Saint's inclinations. On this account, for the first two years, Therese felt unable to confide in this Mother. Later, however, the most intimate relations were established between their souls.[106]

Trials of Therese from her community.

The Carmel of Lisieux was a fervent religious community and, yet, it comprised some religious who, although doubtlessly good, were hard to get along with. We meet that sort of person in the best of families.

At Lisieux, the situation was rendered more difficult because of a very special circumstance. Knowing the great qualities of the Martin sisters, Mother Marie de Gonzaga had consented to accept four of them. Marie Guerin, their cousin, joined them on April 15, 1895. Five religious of one family in a monastery which had not more than eighteen choir nuns, constituted a group whose influence could have been considerable. In conformity with the custom of a number of French Carmels, the right to vote in conventual chapters had been restricted to two of the Martin sisters. In this way, Therese never received the place in the chapter that belonged to her by right, and she had in it neither voice nor function. Being charged with the formation of the novices, under the authority of the titular Mother Mistress (Mother de Gonzaga), she remained among them as their "dean" until her death.[107]

In spite of these restrictions, the existence of the Martin group remained capable of stirring up feelings. This explains many of the disagreeable experiences of which Therese was the victim. Mother de Gonzaga thus noted her difficulties: "Sister Therese is perfect. She has only one fault: she has three sisters in our convent." [108]

Those trials of the heart began to afflict Therese from the moment of her entrance into Carmel. "My first steps," she said later, "met more thorns than roses." [109] She learned from personal experience how very painful are the little pinpricks which companions see fit to administer.

During her retreat before receiving the habit, she wrote to Mother Agnes: "Ask Jesus that I may be very generous during my retreat. He riddles me with pinpricks. The little ball cannot stand it any longer. It has so many small holes that it suffers more from them than from one large one. From the part of Jesus it receives nothing, but at least there is silence. Silence does a lot of good to one's soul . . . but creatures, oh! those creatures! The little ball trembles. . . . When it is her sweet Friend Himself who pricks her, suffering is sweetness, for His hand is so gentle . . . but creatures. . . . And, yet, I am happy to be able to suffer what Jesus desires me to suffer. If He does not Himself directly prick His little ball, it is true nevertheless that He guides the hands that prick it." [110]

On another occasion she remarked: "I can only be crushed and tried by the righteous, for my sisters are pleasing to God. . . . It is less bitter (however) to be broken by the sinner than by the righteous; but, O my God, I ask You, out of compassion for sinners and that they may be converted, let me be broken by the holy souls among whom I live. . . .[111] I desire this anguish, these pinpricks." [112]

Therese attributed these indelicacies to the natural imperfections of her companions, to their lack of judgment and upbringing, to their touchiness.[113] This was true in the case of a lay sister who was very generous and edifying in her conduct but also quick by nature and easily aroused. More than once she chided Therese, who was then a young postulant, with sharp words because of her slowness and awkwardness in manual labor. At Mother Genevieve's death, while Therese was arranging flowers around the coffin, this same lay sister remarked with indignation: "It is plain to see that those large bouquets were given by your own family. Those given by poor people will remain hidden." Therese immediately rearranged the flowers. The lay sister was so touched by it that she went and confessed her fault to the Mother Prioress.[114]

Other nuns also, and in particular one sister, "was the cause of struggles." The latter was neurasthenic and Therese, having asked to be her companion, took care of her for a period of three years. Some of the less fervent were even annoyed by the virtue of our Saint, by her meticulous observance of every point of convent regulations.

Among the remarks that grieved her most deeply were those that were addressed to her during her father's illness.[115] The novices themselves, although they loved their Sub-Mistress dearly, did not always spare her and told her what they disliked in her.[116]

These trials of the heart, which Therese called pinpricks, were ordinarily no more serious than that, but our Saint had a heart that was both very sensitive and very charitable. Hence, she felt those "pinpricks" very keenly. All the members of the community, who made her suffer in this way, later acknowledged and regretted their mistake, trying at that time to outdo one another in praising Therese's renunciation and humility, her patience and her charity. Mother Agnes also said that the nuns who lived with Therese "had for her an esteem and a veneration which they did not have for any other. . . . If the sublimity of her life was not understood by most of them, it is because she was so simple and so humble." [117]

Relations with her own sisters.

Therese's heartaches came to a great extent from the restrictions she imposed on herself in her relations with her own sisters. "You know," she wrote to Mother Marie de Gonzaga, "that Jesus has offered me more than one bitter chalice (in regard to her beloved sisters) . . . I did not come to Carmel to live with my sisters. I realized that my refusal to grant anything to nature while dwelling with my sisters would be a source of continuous suffering for me." [118]

Therese imposed a law upon herself never to give in to a natural impulse. She had also resolved never to ask for permissions that might tend to lessen the burden of religious life. Hence, her reserve. She could at times have asked permission to have a heart-to-heart talk with her "little mother," but she did not consider it proper to do so. Even when Mother Agnes happened to talk to her, she preserved such a silence about the affairs of her own soul that this poor Mother grieved over it. One day, recalling the restrictions she had imposed on herself during the five years that preceded the Priorship of Mother Agnes, Therese said to her: "Oh! my little mother, how much I suffered at that time! I thought you no longer knew me—that is, that you no longer knew my soul —I would not open my heart to you!" Besides being conscious of what God demanded of her, Therese, no doubt, also considered it proper to act as she did as a matter of discretion, since so many of her sisters were living in the same Carmel.

On the day on which Celine, whose entrance into Carmel she had so much desired, stepped into the cloister, Therese embraced her, but, fearing that she might yield too much to her natural inclinations, she immediately ran off. The Mother Prioress had to call her back and tell her to take her sister to the cell that had been designated for her.[119]

At the beginning of her religious life, she had been given as an assistant to Mother Agnes for service in the dining hall.

Naturally, their meetings here would offer opportunity for exchanging a few spiritual words. But neither she nor her sister ever spoke about anything except the care of the table.

She never saw her sisters nor did she speak to them outside the times of recreation. Even then, she continued to mortify herself by sitting near the first religious who came along, or by seeking the company of those for whom she felt the least attraction.[120] She practiced the same self-effacement in the parlor, letting others do the talking while she said scarcely a word; and, at the end of the half-hour, she was the first to leave. She deviated from her rule of silence only in favor of her sisters Leonie and Celine, when it happened they were in need of consolation from her.[121] One day one of her own sisters asked her whether she would have paid a visit to the infirmary during recreation, should one of her sisters have been ill. "I would have gone straight to recreation," she answered, "without inquiring how you were, but I would have done this simply so no one could detect my sacrifice. If I had been asked to visit the infirmary, I would have purified my intention, visiting you to give you pleasure but not to satisfy myself. In that way, I would have hoped to draw graces upon you which you could not have received from my own self-seeking. And I myself would have drawn great strength from renunciation." [122]

Therese's rigor in her relations with her own sisters seemed at times so great that one day Mother Genevieve spoke to her about it and reproached her for not having a right understanding of charity.[123]

When the question came up of sending her sisters, her "little mother," and her "beloved" Celine to the Carmel of Saigon, Therese's heart was deeply affected; but, though she knew that they would suffer there, and had her private doubts about this departure being the will of God, she did not say one word to prevent it. For herself, she had expressed a desire to be sent to the Carmel of Hanoi in case her malady

were cured, and this not so much that she might render
service as that she might do God's will by sacrificing herself
for Him according to His wishes: "If some day I had to leave
my dear Carmel, it would not be without suffering a wound.
Jesus has not given me an insensitive heart, and it is precisely because it can suffer that I desire it to give to Jesus all
that it can give. . . . Here I am loved by you, my Mother,
and by all my sisters, with an affection that is very sweet to
me. That is why I am dreaming of a monastery where I would
be unknown, where I would have to suffer poverty, lack of
affection, and, finally, the exile of the heart. Oh! It is not
with the intention of rendering service to a Carmel that
would be willing to receive me, that I would leave all that
is dear to me. No doubt, I would do everything that I possibly could, but I know my incapacity and that even if I did
my best, I would not succeed in doing well. . . . My only aim
would be to accomplish the will of the good Lord, to sacrifice myself for Him in a manner that would please Him." [124]

By such expressions did the young Saint show her burning love for God and her eagerness to make sacrifices for Him.
The reserve she had imposed upon herself in her relations
with her sisters, Therese recommended also to them that they
might continue to practice it after her death. She considered
this necessary to preserve unity and peace in the community.

Finally, so that nothing might be lacking in her martyrdom of the heart, she suffered in regard to her father whom
she loved more than anyone else in the world. For three years
he suffered from a dreadful illness which obscured his mind.
Therese's letters to Celine reveal what she underwent at that
time: "Now we have nothing to hope for here on earth except
suffering and more and more suffering." [125] One day she had
said to her Mistress of Novices, to the latter's great surprise:
"I suffer much, Mother, but I feel that I can bear still greater
trials." When, a few months later, her father became men-
tally ill, she then said that she would no longer have the

courage to repeat those words.[126] And yet, in spite of everything, she thanked God for having given her "that portion and lot that is worthy of envy." [127] "Some day," she wrote in 1895, "when we are in heaven, we shall enjoy speaking together about those dark days of our exile. Yes, the three years of my father's martyrdom seem the most lovable, the most fruitful of our lives. I would not give them in exchange for all the ecstasies and revelations of the saints. My heart overflows with gratitude when I think of that priceless treasure. . . . O my dear Mother! How sweet our great trial has been since from the hearts of all of us sprang sighs of love and gratitude. We no longer walked at that time; we flew along the paths of perfection." [128]

Martyrdom of the Soul

However great the suffering sent us by God, it is not truly complete unless it comprises martyrdom of the soul, and since He wanted Therese to have a full share of suffering, He did not fail to grant her that martyrdom.

There may still be people who believe that Therese's life was spent amidst spiritual consolations. The reality is quite different. Her existence was not often blest with spiritual comfort. True, she did occasionally taste divine love. She had been granted that favor practically from her childhood; and, in fact, her first meeting with Jesus in Holy Communion was truly a fusion of love. Again, during her conversations with Celine in the little summer house (1887), God's presence was so manifest to both sisters that they "felt no longer a need for faith and hope; for love caused them to find on earth Him whom they longed to possess." [129]

In later years, mystical graces gave special light to her soul and wounded her heart with divine darts; however, such sensible, mystical graces were the exception. Her way was rather one of pure faith; "her consolation was that of not having any consolation on earth." [130]

We have described earlier the troubles, fears and scruples which afflicted Therese when she was still a child. These were only the beginning of her soul's martyrdom which was to be her special torment during her life in the cloister. Scarcely had she entered Carmel when trials began to assail her. First came the test of her love, and to some degree, of her faith. Her soul was parched with spiritual dryness; darkness enveloped her. Jesus hid Himself and kept silence. She seemed to walk in an underground in which she was unable to see anything and which seemed to have no exit. Even her retreats made before her reception and profession, were passed in a desert climate.

Next came a torturing trial of her faith and her hope, a testing much more severe than the first. Heaven now seemed to be veiled forever. It was as if a wall rose before her and blocked her road. When doubts entered her mind about the blessed life beyond; if, to reanimate her hope, she tried to cling to the happiness she had formerly foreseen, she seemed to hear a diabolical voice shouting that this was an empty dream and that annihilation was the lot of her destiny. If at times there was a gleam of light, it was but for one moment, and her martyrdom began anew with increased intensity.

For one who had longed for heaven from her most tender years and had received a foretaste of that happiness, this was a severe blow; this trial was to afflict her from a short time after Easter, 1896, to the end of the Saint's life on earth. However crucifying we may consider each of these martyrdoms taken singly, we shall not realize the extent of her sufferings unless we recall that Therese endured them throughout her life and that, often and especially at the end, all three martyrdoms tortured her simultaneously. She suffered most intensely in body and in soul during the last months of her life, her pain increasing horribly as she drew nearer to the end. For proof of their severity we need only recall that though Therese had ardently desired that triple martyrdom in order to give all her love to Jesus and save souls, she had to confess in the end that she could no longer bear it and that her cup was filled to overflowing.[131]

During the course of the month of August, she remained several days, as it were, beside herself and in a state of inexpressible anguish; [132] for, at that time, the trial of her faith was extreme. The veil grew thicker as her death came nearer.[133] Furthermore, the demon was prowling around her. One night, she asked the infirmarian to throw holy water on her bed. "I don't see him," she said, "but I feel he is there. He torments me, he holds me in an iron grip. . . . He increases my ills so as to make me yield to despair . . . and I am unable to pray! I can only look at the Blessed Virgin and say: 'Jesus!' I am experiencing something mysterious. I am not suffering for myself but for another soul . . . and the demon seeks to prevent it." [134]

As a climax to her sufferings, Therese, who was so eager to receive Jesus in Holy Communion and would have drawn so much comfort from the Blessed Sacrament during that painful crisis, was deprived of it from the nineteenth of August on, because she was hemorrhaging so frequently. But, "all is grace" and we should adore God's will whatever it may be.[135]

THERESE'S DEATH OF LOVE

Therese had desired to die of love. God had always caused her to desire what He Himself wished to give to her; so she had the hope and even felt certain that her prayer would be heard. Two months before her death, quoting the words of St. John of the Cross, "break the web of this sweet meeting," she said: "I have always applied these words to the death of love which I would like to have. Love will not wear out the

fabric of my life; it will rupture it all at once." [136] Returning
to the same thought one month later, she exclaimed: "It is
unbelievable how well all my hopes are being realized. When
I used to read St. John of the Cross, I would beg the good
Lord to accomplish in me what St. John describes; that is,
to sanctify me as much in a few years, as I might have
been sanctified had I reached a ripe old age, so that I
might be quickly consumed in love, and my prayer has been
granted." [137]

On the very evening of her death she said: "My least
desires have been fulfilled; hence, the greatest of all, to die
of love, will also be accomplished." [138]

These words are confirmed by the testimony of her sisters
at the Process of Information: "She always preserved the
hope or, rather, assurance," said Mother Agnes, "that she
would die 'a death of love.' " [139] She was willing to live a long
life, added Sister Genevieve, and to be ill during the whole
course of her earthly existence. The only grace she desired
was that (the thread of) her life should be broken by love.[140]
Finally, in a note to Sister Marie of the Trinity, Therese
declared: "I do not rely on illness (to put an end to my life),
for it is a too-slow-moving guide. I count only on love. Ask
the good Lord that all the prayers that are said for me may
serve to increase the fire that must consume me." [141]

Therese had prepared herself for a death of love. Knowing
the greater her charity, the more quickly she would be consumed, she had applied herself most fervently to love: "With
what longing and consolation did I not repeat, from the
beginning of my religious life, these words of St. John of the
Cross: 'It is most important to apply ourselves in this life
to acts of love so that our souls, being quickly consumed,
may not have to wait long here or hereafter for the vision
of God.' " [142]

According to St. John of the Cross, a death of love is the
consummation of the mystical life, by the introduction of

the soul into the beatific life. Hence, it is accompanied by the impetuosity and the sweet embraces of love.[143] It is possible that Therese, who considered St. John of the Cross to be a great master of the spiritual life, believed at first that her death would be accompanied by such transports of love. But later, seeing what actually happened, and enlightened by heaven, she understood that God, without denying her a death of love, reserved for her an end that would not give external signs of her happiness. "Don't grieve," she told her sisters when saying goodbye to them, "if you see I am in great suffering and show no signs of happiness at the hour of my death. Our Lord died truly as a victim of love and yet, behold how much He suffered in His agony!" [144]

On July 4, she returned to the same thought: "Our Lord died in anguish on the Cross and yet, He had the most beautiful death of love that ever was! To die of love does not mean dying amidst transports (of love). I openly confess to you that, as it seems to me, this is what is taking place in me."

At the most, she tasted some deep but, no doubt, passing joy. To Mother Agnes, who spoke to her of the transports that accompany the death of those who are consummated in charity, Therese answered with a sigh: "We will have to say that it is only in the depths of my soul that joy and transports are to be found." [145]

From the words we have quoted there follows a twofold conclusion. First, it is evident that Therese believed, that she felt certain, that she would die a death of love. Secondly, she foresaw that her death would be unaccompanied by the signs which, according to St. John of the Cross, characterize the end of those who have attained transforming union. The validity of our first conclusion gains additional proof from the fact that the words that testify in its favor were spoken at a later date than the others in which Therese reveals that she foresaw a death that would be deprived of all external signs of joy and happiness.

We shall see that, in reality, Therese did die a death of love. On the other hand, we know that she suffered and was tried in her faith to the very last moment of her earthly life. A death of love then, as Therese herself affirmed, is not necessarily accompanied by sweet transports, but what essentially constitutes this kind of death is the flame that consumes the soul; it is a divine assault of divine love that ruptures the web of life and carries the soul away to the Heart of Eternal Charity. That there be accompanying favors is something accidental. Because St. John of the Cross says that these ordinarily manifest themselves, we are not justified in concluding that they must inevitably be present. God is the master of His gifts. He distributes them according to His good pleasure. He does not bind Himself in regard to the particular method of distributing His graces. Therese was a true mystic in the authentic sense of that term. From her childhood she had been under the dominion of the Holy Ghost. Everything in her life shows us that she remained in that state throughout its course. If her death did not resemble that of most mystics; if it took place amidst darkness and suffering, it is because she had offered herself for souls and also because her life was to serve as an example for others.

When Therese was still quite young, she felt called to cooperate with Jesus in the salvation of sinners. She exerted herself in this task with absolute devotedness. On the day of her death she still affirmed that she could not explain why she suffered such horrible tortures, except by the fact that she had such an ardent desire to save souls. To obtain their salvation she had even aspired after martyrdom. Hence, we need not be astonished that her death was marked with suffering.

Secondly, Therese was also to serve as an example for us. She had the mission of teaching us the way of spiritual childhood. She had to show to those who are called to follow her that it is possible to reach the summit of love and to die of love, by walking in the path of pure faith and through the loving performance of ordinary actions. She herself, therefore, had to be the first to start upon this road. Had she died a death that was accompanied by evident transports of ecstatic love, that would not have been in harmony with such a plan.

Death is ordinarily painful. While it is true that the thought of heaven, of which it is the gate, may serve to alleviate the pains and anguish of the dying, nevertheless, death remains a separation of soul from body [146] and a bodily separation from those whom we love, a last expiation for sin. Therefore, if Therese's death were similar to that of ordinary mortals, it would naturally be a great encouragement to souls. That is why, when her "little mother" had spoken to her of the death full of consolation of souls that have attained union, she replied: "That sort of thing would not encourage souls as much as the recollection that I also had to suffer greatly (at my death.)" [147]

Finally, knowing the heart of Therese, it is safe to suppose that, having contemplated in Jesus the most beautiful of all deaths of love, a death so evidently accompanied by the most severe sufferings, she desired to resemble Him by dying of love amidst the trial of her faith.

However, in spite of what we have said, we would fail in our description of the last moments of Therese, if we maintained that her death had none of the signs that ordinarily accompany the departure from this world of souls that are perfect in charity. Here are the facts.

Therese's death agony had begun and, according to the prevision of the Mother Prioress, it seemed probable that it was to last for some time. Mother Marie de Gonzaga had just told this to the patient. Our Saint replied with her accustomed generosity that she had no desire to suffer less. Looking at the Crucifix with ardent love, she said: "Oh! I love Him, my God . . . I . . . love . . . You!" She had scarcely pronounced those words when she gently fell back, her head inclining to the right side. The sisters having been called, they hastily pressed around her. They thought she had died, but she suddenly sat up, opened her eyes, and for a few minutes, the time it takes to say slowly one Credo, she looked upward, a light of intense happiness shining from her eyes. Sister Marie of the Holy Eucharist, wishing to see this beatific look more clearly, moved a light back and forth close to Therese's eyes, but there was no evidence that she saw it. Several times Therese gently moved her head. She then closed her eyes again and gave up her beautiful spirit to God. Love, as she had foretold, had suddenly ruptured the web of her life.[148]

Such a victim which succumbs under a divine assault, uttering a cry of love, a soul which, after an ecstasy, takes its flight to the Heart of Eternal Charity, surely fulfills to perfection the death of souls that are consummated in love.

Therese had accomplished her mission. She had ended her life in suffering and been tempted against faith. God, at that supreme moment, rewarded her with the favor He has in store for His saints.

COROLLARY: THE ROLE OF SUFFERING—THE WAY TO SUFFER.

The record of Therese's trials loudly proclaims that she was not in the least the little Saint whom everybody tried to please and who walked comfortably on a path strewn with roses. This record Therese wanted others to know, so that souls might not misunderstand the meaning and value of her life and her Spiritual Way. "Certainly," she said, "I have found joy and happiness on earth, but I found it only in suffering, for I have suffered much here below. This should be made known to souls. . . . Many will be astonished at the end of the world when they see the road that my soul had to follow." [149]

All the saints have suffered; St. Therese of the Child Jesus had a particular thirst for suffering. In her writings we come constantly across passages which express her burning love, her desire and her joy in regard to suffering: "It is precisely suffering that gives me pleasure in the present life." [150] And the greater the suffering, the greater her happiness.[151] She considered a day lost that had not been marked with the cross.[152]

She rejoiced especially when her suffering was unaccompanied by spiritual comfort. "I know one spring," she said, "and having drunk from it you are still thirsty, but it is not a panting, gasping sort of thirst; on the contrary, it is very sweet, for it is satiating. This spring is suffering, a suffering known to Jesus alone." [153] "Happiness," she wrote to Mother Agnes, "is found only in suffering, and in suffering, moreover, that is unaccompanied by any consolation whatsoever." [154] Speaking to her on another occasion, she emphasized this view: "I am glad that I am suffering alone. As soon as I am pitied and flooded with attentions, I no longer have joy." Elsewhere she said similarly: "The more intimate the suffering, the less it appears to the eyes of others, the more it gladdens You (oh my God) and if—what is clearly impossible —You happened not to know that I am suffering, I would still be happy." [155]

The source of Therese's thirst for suffering.

The chief source was her intense love of God. This is so because nothing, outside abandonment to God, so well expresses our love for Him as sacrifices under every form and for the complete immolation of ourselves to Him. It was thus that Jesus loved His Father, and it is in this way, also, that He has loved us.

At a later date Therese understood that abandonment to God is a greater proof of love of God than any desire, even the desire for suffering. But until she grasped this truth, she longed to give to God, to Jesus, all the suffering of which she was capable. She felt so much more obliged to desire it because she realized how greatly God loved her. It seemed to her that she heard the voice of the Crucified complaining because He is not loved, in spite of His own excessive love for us. Another reason for her desire for suffering was that she knew she had been called by our Lord to cooperate in His work of redemption, a work that is realized specially through suffering.

Finally, she believed that suffering, that all trials whatever their nature or origin, were willed by God, were a part of His plan for her soul. On several occasions she declared that "He alone (Jesus) disposes the events of our life of exile. . . . Creatures are like stepping stones, instruments, but it is the hand of Jesus that guides everything." [156] "Jesus is our Spouse of blood. He wants for Himself all the blood of our heart. . . . Far from complaining to Jesus because of the cross He sends us, I cannot understand the infinite love that prompted Him to treat me in this manner. . . . Is it still possible to have doubts about the designs that Jesus has regarding our souls?" [157]

Having gained an understanding of this divine plan, she adjusted herself to it with all the ardor of her loving heart. Nevertheless, the love for suffering does not do away with its painfulness; neither is it because we desire it that the cross weighs less heavily upon us and that we carry it with greater joy. Therese, in spite of her love and desires, did not always carry her cross with joy. If, by dint of effort and prayer, and especially through the grace of Jesus, she learned to suffer with joy, to embrace suffering with a smile on her lips, she at first bore her crosses feebly and with tears. "Let us not believe," she wrote to her sister Celine, "that we can love without suffering, and without suffering a great deal. It is our human nature that suffers, our poor God-given human nature which, however, is so precious, that Jesus came on purpose to our earth to clothe Himself with it. Let us suffer without bitterness, that is, without feeling courage. Jesus suffered with sadness. Could we say that a soul was suffering if it did not experience sadness? And could we then claim that we are suffering generously, nobly . . . Celine . . . what an illusion that would be!" [158]

Another time she wrote to the same: "Jesus is there on His Cross. Since you have the privilege of receiving His love, He also wants to make you resemble Him. Why fear that you might not be able to carry that cross without growing weak? Didn't Jesus fall three times on His way to Calvary and you, poor little child, should you not resemble your Bridegroom? Would you want to refuse to fall a hundred times, if that were necessary to prove your love to Him, and to rise each time with renewed strength? [159] What a happiness to realize that suffering does cost us something! What an ineffable joy to carry our crosses in weakness!" [160]

These are most comforting and encouraging words. Weak as we are, we are often unable to bear our crosses without sighs and tears. This is human. The cross is painful and nature rebels against suffering. Hence, however much we may desire to give to Jesus a proof of our love and to souls the benefits of our sufferings, when the cross is actually afflicting us, we often greet it with fear and bear it with sadness. Our nature groans under its weight. God knows our weakness and takes it into account. If suffering were not repugnant to us, how could it still be called suffering and how, then, could it be an expression of our love?

Let us not bewail the fact that we weakly bear the cross and fall under its weight. That very weakness is for us "a gain." It shows Jesus what we can and cannot do. Hence, He feels obliged to come to our assistance. We have only to appeal to Him with humility and confidence. All the same, however consoling these utterances of Therese, we must not think that in them she proposes the ideal she wants us to pursue. She would remind us of this if that were necessary and her own life itself gives the lie to softness.

These words of Therese, which we have just quoted, show us how well she understood human weakness and how earnestly she desired to console and encourage feeble souls. But in reality, a generous acceptance of suffering, the happiness of being able to suffer, remain always the goal to which we should tend. Therese ardently pursued that ideal and she succeeded in attaining it. "I have always endeavored to love suffering," she wrote, "and welcome it. When I suffer much, when painful, disagreeable things happen to me, instead of looking sad, I try to smile. I was not always successful in this at the start, but it has now become a habit.[161] I have suffered much since I am on earth, but if, in my childhood, I suffered with sadness . . . I now suffer with joy and peace. I am truly happy to suffer." [162]

Towards the end of her life, she said: "My life, in the eyes of others must have seemed to be filled with the most pleasant colors. . . . To them I seemed to be drinking an exquisite draft, but in reality it was bitterness. I say bitterness and yet my life has not been bitter, for I have been able to find joy and sweetness in all bitterness." [163]

She maintained that she was happier in the convent, even in the midst of interior and exterior trials, than she had been in the world where nothing was wanting to her, especially since she was able to enjoy there the sweetness of an ideal home.[164] Hence, she no longer grieved because she had to suffer: "My Mother," she told Mother Agnes, who grieved over Therese's sufferings, "do not worry on my account. I have reached the point where I suffer no longer, for suffering has become sweet to me ." [165] And to Celine she wrote: "Here below, all is tiresome to me; I find only one joy, that of suffering for Jesus. . . . But that joy which is not felt surpasses all joy." [166] For in a joy that is felt, there is still a human element. Almost inevitably there creeps in an element of self-love, which spoils the purity of joy. "If you wish to feel and to have an attraction for suffering," she said to Sister Marie of the Sacred Heart, "you are in search of your own consolation, for when we love anything, pain disappears."[167] On the contrary, a joy that is not felt, is one that is entirely for God.

Therese has just told us that she suffered in peace and with joy. What did she mean by *suffering in peace?*

She has explained this in regard to the illness of her father: "I confess that this word peace seemed rather strong but, the other day, reflecting on it, I found the secret of being able to suffer in peace. To say that we suffer in peace does not mean that we suffer with joy, at least with a joy that is felt. In order to suffer in peace, it is enough to will truly all that Jesus wills." [168]

What is meant by *suffering with joy?* It means to transcend the bitterness we naturally experience so that we place all our contentment in pleasing God Who sends us suffering; to place our happiness in sacrificing ourselves for Jesus and in imitation of Jesus, in spite of our natural repugnance for it. That is the "joy that surpasses all joy," a joy in which all creatures—which are truly nothing—give place to the Uncreated who is Reality.[169] How was she able to derive such happiness from what is so repugnant to our nature? She herself tells us: "It is impossible to create such sentiments in ourselves. It is the Holy Ghost who imparts them to us." [170]

Therese was accustomed to suffering; it had become so much a part of her that, as she wrote, "she found it hard to conceive how, in heaven, she would be able to be happy without suffering; how it would be possible for her to become acclimatized in a land where joy reigns without any admixture of sorrow. No doubt, Jesus will change my nature; otherwise, I would pine for the sufferings of this valley of tears." [171]

Therese knew, of course, that the absence of suffering could not be an obstacle to celestial happiness, but by these

words she expressed in an unusual way the important role
which suffering played in her life.

We must all suffer; it is the lot of human kind and, at
the same time, it is a grace which Jesus bestows on every
Christian. How could we claim to be true members of the
Mystical Body of Christ, disciples of the divine Crucified, if
we did not resemble Him by our sufferings and if, by means
of it, and in union with Him, we did not help in the salvation
of souls. We are not all called to suffer as much as Therese.
To every one his own cross and his own cup! God knows how
to apportion them according to our strength and our love,
and He adapts them to His particular designs for each individual soul. "Jesus," wrote Therese, "prepares for us a chalice
having the degree of bitterness which our feeble nature is
able to bear. . . . He never asks of us a sacrifice that is beyond
our strength. . . ." [172] Sometimes, no doubt, our divine Savior
makes us taste fully the bitterness of the cup He offers to us,
but "He helps us that we may be able to drink it." [173] What,
then, ought we to do that we may bear our crosses properly
and merit Christ's help?

Love and Pray!

Love, and love alone, has the power to enable us to bear
generously and to the end, the sacrifices and sufferings of our
life. It was in her love of Jesus that Therese found the strength
to follow Him to Calvary. Suffering becomes lovable, and
hence also less burdensome, according to the degree of our
love of Christ.

We should also learn to suffer from moment to moment,
for the cross is less heavy when we carry only what is actually laid on our shoulder. "We can bear much suffering, when
we suffer it from moment to moment" said Therese.[174] Moreover, we receive grace only for the present moment. To stop
and recall the sufferings we have already endured; to try to

foresee what might happen to us, is a vain pursuit and merely serves to increase our burden of crosses. "Jesus gives me at every moment what I am able to bear," she wrote, "and nothing more, and if the next moment He increases my suffering, He also increases my strength. . . . Suffering may reach extreme limits (of endurance) but I am sure that the good Lord will never abandon me." She often repeated this same thought: "I suffer only from instant to instant . . . from minute to minute. . . . It is because we reflect on the past and think of the future that we get discouraged and despair." [175]

Let us, then, endeavor to accept our sufferings in the proper spirit, to carry valiantly the crosses God sends us, and beg Him to grant us the necessary grace. On the other hand, let us not have the presumption to ask for crosses unless we are sure God wills to give them.

If St. Therese of the Child Jesus desired sufferings, it was because they were a means of corresponding to God's designs. "Jesus made me understand that it is by the cross that He would give me souls, and my attraction for suffering grew in the same measure that my sufferings increased." [176] But she never asked Him to send her greater ones, and she gives us the reason for it: "I never want to ask God for greater sufferings, for these, then, would be *my* sufferings. I would have to bear them alone and I have never succeeded in doing anything unaided." [177]

If we accept the sacrifices God sends us, and are faithful in bearing the crosses of each day, God, if He judges it good, can, in His love, give us heavier ones. In the meantime, let us simply offer to suffer everything that will please Him. He will, thus, be free to grant us the sacrifices of His own choice.

Therese understood, as few souls have done, the greatness and effectiveness of suffering. Being preeminently God's gift to men, it is also, at least after abandonment to God, the best proof we can give of our love for God. More than any other work, it sanctifies us and increases our capacity for happiness and our measure of glory. More than any other, it is the instrument of the salvation of souls. For it serves to identify us with the suffering Christ and makes us His co-workers in the plan of Redemption.

Therese, in one of her poems, adds that man has, by that fact, a certain advantage over the angels. True enough, an angel, because of his purity, constantly enjoys the vision of God; nevertheless, he is unable to suffer or die for God, whereas men can be pure and can also immolate their whole substance out of love for God.

Like Therese, let us, then, give to suffering the welcome it deserves. "When we suffer out of love and to prove our love," says Father Combes, "we shall also die through love and to prove our love. To die is then a most happy event. And since it is the last thing we experience here below, every suffering prepares us for it and the total of all our immolated joys becomes the most beautiful offering that can be presented by us to the divine Crucified." [178]

CHAPTER XIII

Therese's Contemplative Life

BEFORE THERESE'S ENTRANCE INTO CARMEL

ST. THERESE of the Child Jesus was essentially a contemplative. Moreover, everything predisposed her for it. She was endowed with a very keen intelligence, a perfect judgment, an exquisite sensibility, and in her tender and delicate heart there burned from her childhood a most generous love. Add to this the spiritual atmosphere that greeted her from her birth, the lessons so devotedly given to her and the wonderful examples she witnessed; all these helped her to develop her natural gifts.

A soul thus gifted was a wonderful field for the action of the Holy Spirit, and since she had been chosen by God to teach us a new way of perfection, the Paraclete took hold of her soul from her early childhood. Surrendering completely to Him, docile to His guidance, she resolutely entered the way of love and sacrifice. She herself testified later on that she had never refused God anything since she was three years old.

But a soul matures and perfects itself only through sufferings. God desired that Therese should belong to Him alone, and He made her walk very early in the way of the cross: "I had to pass through the crucible of trials and suffer from my childhood, so that I could be offered very early to Jesus." [1]

We might think that these words refer only to the bonds she contracted through her religious profession; but we believe that they also refer to those early sufferings which were to dispose her for the mystical betrothal with which she was to be favored.

In Chapter XII we recalled the early trials of Therese: the death of her mother; her own mysterious illness; her sorrow and mental suffering caused by the departure of her sisters for Carmel; her scruples; the oppositions to her entrance into Carmel. According to Therese herself, as we have seen, these sufferings must be considered as trials that were to prepare her for her union with Jesus.

BEGINNING AND DEVELOPMENT OF THERESE'S CONTEMPLATIVE LIFE

Her contemplation developed in line with her gradual purification. She tells us that, from the age of four, she felt enraptured by the beauty of nature. Sometimes when her father went fishing on the banks of the Touques, she would sit at some distance from him and listen to distant sounds, to whispering breezes, to military music vaguely floating on the air, and her heart was filled with a sweet melancholy . . . the earth seemed indeed a place of exile and she dreamt of heaven.[2] She acknowledged later (1895) that "without knowing the meaning of 'meditation,' she was already then absorbed in true mental prayer." [3]

One day she saw lightning fall on a meadow that lay close by. Far from being frightened, she was enthralled by it; the good Lord seemed very close.[4] When she was about six or seven years old, she beheld the ocean for the very first time. It enraptured her; instinctively her thoughts rose Godwards and her mind was in ectasy at the contemplation of the greatness and power of God. In the evening, she looked a long time at the sun as it slowly sank in the waves leaving after it a luminous path, the image of grace which traces the golden way the small boat with its white sail must follow.

She resolved that she would never keep Jesus out of her sight so that she might peacefully reach the heavenly shore.[5]

Later, when traveling through Switzerland, her heart was filled with similar sentiments, and she resolved to remember them as a means of raising her mind to God once she had entered the convent.[6]

Knowing that she liked books and pictures, her sisters gave her just the kind she wanted. Both awakened in her thoughts that betray the action of the Holy Spirit. It was thus that a picture of "The Little Flower of the Divine Prisoner" gave her the idea of offering herself to be cultivated and then plucked by Jesus to give Him consolation.

Reading the life of St. Joan of Arc, she came to realize that her own glory would consist in being hidden and in practicing virtue.[7] When she was about nine years old, she played hermit with her cousin Marie Guerin, constructed a hut and tried to practice contemplation; [8] but above all she showed an ardent love for Jesus present in the Holy Eucharist. When still very small she loved to pay visits to her Eucharistic Lord in the company of her father, and longed for the day when she would be able to receive Him.

Her First Communion.

On May 8, 1884, Therese received her Lord for the first time and it made her inexpressibly happy. As she listened to her sister Marie who instructed her, the child sensed the increasing fire of love in her heart and, wishing to receive Jesus as worthily as possible, she multiplied her acts of love and her sacrifices. On the day itself, so great was her joy that "her eyes were flooded with most sweet tears," for she felt that the Lord truly loved her and she in turn gave herself to Jesus forever. That First Communion, she tells us, was not a mere meeting with the good Lord; it was a "fusion" with Him and from that time on Jesus alone was capable of satisfying her heart. Her second Communion, which took place in the feast of the Ascension was not less fervent. Her tears flowed once more and she constantly said to herself: "It is now no longer I that live; but Christ lives in me." [9]

Some time after that, Marie, while preparing her for Communion, had spoken to Therese about suffering, saying she did not think that God would lead her little sister by that road. Contrary to this, Therese herself writes, "the very day after my Communion I felt that there was born in my heart a great desire for suffering, and I felt certain, at the same time, that Jesus had a great number of crosses in store for me. I was flooded with such extraordinary consolation that I look upon it as one of the greatest graces of my life. Suffering had become like a magnet attracting me. It had ravishing charms, although I then failed to understand it properly. Until that time I had suffered without loving suffering. From that day on I had a veritable love for it. I also felt the desire of loving no one but the good Lord and finding my joy in Him alone. During my communions I often repeated the words of the Imitation: 'O Jesus, ineffable sweetness, change for me into bitterness all the consolations of earth.' " [10] Not being able to receive Jesus every day—for daily Communion was not practiced at that time—she at least desired to communicate as often as possible.

After she had left boarding school at the age of thirteen, she returned there twice a week. She did the work assigned to her in silence and then withdrew to the chapel for a colloquy with Jesus: "Jesus was my one and only Friend. It was only to Him that I felt able to talk. Conversations with creatures, even with the devout, tired my soul." [11]

Therese's Confirmation.

She was confirmed one month after her First Communion (June 14, 1884). She had prepared herself for it with extraordinary fervor, for she realized the importance of this sacrament for a vigorous spiritual life. She listened with rapt attention to what her sisters taught her about its effects and the gifts of the Holy Spirit. In her turn she spoke about the subject to Celine in such a tone of ardent love and fervor that the latter was profoundly moved.

On the day of her Confirmation Therese received strength and courage to suffer, for her soul's martyrdom was soon to begin.[12] The Holy Eucharist made her share Christ's own sentiments. Confirmation intensified the action of the Holy Spirit in her soul and thus invigorated her interior life. She spoke with so much familiarity to the Divine Persons dwelling in her, that she found it hard to engage in vocal prayers. Her fellow-pupils in the boarding school thought that Therese was not following the Mass as she should have done. The chaplain at first seemed to think likewise, for she appeared absent-minded. In reality she was absorbed in Christ. When told to use her missal, she smiled, directed her eyes to the book but could not help returning to her thoughts.[13]

The grace she received on Christmas night, 1886, not only cured her of her extreme sensitiveness, but it also was instrumental in increasing her love. That day, in fact, charity entered her heart, together with the urge for forgetting herself so as to give pleasure to others.

Apart from her connections with her family, all relations with others were painful to her. At the abbey, while her companions amused themselves in their games, Therese often stayed aside and, while looking at them in their sports, she was absorbed in serious reflections.[14]

Therese's Reading.

From her earliest years, Therese, as we have seen, had begun reading spiritual books. Her taste for this type of reading had increased with the years. Even before her First Communion, she was reading the *Imitation of Christ*. She had relished this work so much that, according to her associates, she almost knew it by heart.[15] At the age of fourteen, she got hold of the lectures of Father Arminjon on *The End of the Present Time and the Mysteries of the Future Life*. This book gave her "transports of joy" and a happiness that was not of this earth. She copied several passages from it and constantly repeated the words that had inflamed her heart. She had a presentiment of what God has in store for those whom He loves and of the manner in which He rewards the small sacrifices that are made for Him. Hence she wished to love Jesus passionately and give Him a thousand tokens of her love.[16]

Therese's Mental Prayer.

At the same time there developed in her a love for mental prayer. We have mentioned already her reflections when she was contemplating nature. This tendency to contemplation had grown with age. It had even aroused the attention of those with whom she came in contact. One of her teachers was eager to find out more about it, so she questioned Therese about what she was doing on free days. "Madam," Therese answered timidly, "I very often hide in a little corner of my room which I can easily close off with the curtains of my bed, and there I reflect." "But what do you think about," asked the religious smiling. "I think of the good Lord; I think of how quickly this life is passing; I think of eternity; well . . . *I think*." [17]

This does not mean that she already knew the method of mental prayer, but she was eager to learn it. With this in mind she approached the president of the Children of Mary, but this lady, much embarrassed, did not know what to answer. She then had recourse to a lay Benedictine, Sister Henriette. This religious replied that all she did was to talk to God as to a father, while making herself very little; that she spoke to Him of her joys, her sorrows and all the rest; that she made mental prayer *with the heart*. Of this Therese retained especially those last words "prayer with the heart," but she did not dare to content herself with this until she had spoken about it to Mother Agnes. So the latter asked her: "Well, my little Therese, what do you yourself think about that?" "I think," the child replied, "that it is not difficult to meditate." "If so, act in that way and do it with your heart, if that satisfies you," was Mother Agnes's reply.

It would be difficult to claim that Therese from that time on engaged regularly in the practice of meditation of the heart, for she herself tells us that she had asked her sister Marie's permission to practice mental prayer, were it only for one half-hour or even for a quarter of an hour; but Marie considered that Therese "was getting too pious" and, being afraid that God might take her to Himself, she did not allow Therese to make use of anything except vocal prayers.

In any case, Therese "was thinking." [18] Though this is a vague term in itself, in Therese's case it certainly meant genuine mental prayer. Therese herself affirms this. When, in later years, she was at work on her first manuscript, she wrote: "I now understand that I was then practicing mental prayer without knowing it, and that the good Lord was already instructing me in secret." [19]

What were the subjects of her thinking? First, Jesus. She realized that He loved her, and in turn she desired to love Him alone and love Him with all her heart; and she also desired to make sinners love Him. Secondly, she thought about heaven. From early childhood, Therese had been struck by the ephemeral character of earthly satisfactions. Her mother's untimely death and her own numerous disappointments had contributed not a little to that view. On the other hand, her mother's departure for heaven, wither she would have liked to accompany her, and later, the reading of the lectures of Father Arminjon had given her a great longing for the home of the blessed. The passage in which that author describes heavenly bliss, the eternal participation of the blessed in the life and beatitude of God, had made a strong impression on Therese, and she wanted to give herself entirely to divine love and thus share in the greatest measure possible the divine life of the Blessed Trinity. Jesus enlightened her and infused love in her heart during her mental prayer: "Because she was so little and so feeble, He stooped down to her and secretly instructed her in the things that pertain to His love." [20]

A very close union had been formed between Celine and Therese. They shared both their joys and their sorrows. Therese recalled that she considered the day of her sister's First Communion (May 18, 1880) as one of the most beautiful in her own life, for she felt that on that day she also had received special graces.[21] Other common favors were granted to those two sisters at a later date, during their colloquies in the summer house. "How sweet," writes the Saint, "those conversations we had every evening in the summer house! Everything served to elevate our souls and raise them to heaven . . . although as yet we contemplated only its transparent side . . . I believe that we then received graces as great as those that are given to great saints. As we read in the *Imitation*, the good Lord sometimes manifests himself amidst glorious splendor; at other times, under shadows and in figures. It was in the latter way that He deigned to manifest Himself to our souls, but how thin and transparent the veil behind which Jesus hid Himself from our eyes. . . . Doubt was impossible. Faith and hope were no longer necessary. Love revealed to us on earth the One whom our hearts were seeking. We had found Him and He had kissed us and no one in the future could despise us." [22]

Quite naturally from that time she grew rapidly in the love of God: "The practice of virtue became sweet and natural. Renunciation offered no difficulty even from the first moment." [23] She was then fourteen years old. She received similar graces again and again: "I sometimes experience great ardor . . . true transports of love." [24]

One evening, being unable to express to Jesus how much she loved Him and how much she wanted Him to be loved and glorified everywhere, she exclaimed that she was willing to be plunged into hell so that He might be loved eternally. She knew that these were foolish thoughts but as she said, "When we love, we are inclined to say a thousand foolish things. My heaven, then, was nothing but love and in my ardor I felt that there was nothing that could separate me from the divine Object that ravished my heart." [25]

Nine years later (1895), she recalled with gratitude the graces she had received in her youth: "If learned men who have spent their lives in study had come to question me, they would, no doubt, have been astonished to find that a fourteen-year-old girl understood the secrets of perfection, secrets hidden from their vast science, a knowledge which requires poverty of spirit." [26]

THERESE'S CONTEMPLATIVE LIFE IN CARMEL

Things took on a new aspect with Therese's entrance into Carmel. The sufferings of her childhood as we have noted were to serve as an introduction to passive purifications. From now on, trials would constitute her daily food, and increasingly severe purifications would finish the task. Suffering would gnaw deeper and deeper into her soul; it would cleanse it more and more until Therese attained the degree of perfection when Christ would mystically transform her into Himself.

Passive Purifications

It is possible to discern two periods in these trials: a *first* one during which Therese was particularly tried and tested in her love; a *second,* and the more painful, during which there was a special *trial of her faith and her hope.*

She had scarcely entered the cloister of Carmel when her soul became parched by spiritual aridity and wrapped in darkness: "Jesus hid Himself." [27] Hence, during her retreat before receiving the habit, she wrote: "I feel nothing on the part of Jesus. There is aridity . . . there is sleep; but if Jesus wants to sleep, why hinder Him? I am very glad because He is at perfect ease with me. He thus shows me that He does not look upon me as on a stranger, and I can assure you that He makes no effort to speak to me." [28]

During that retreat, her notes to Mother Agnes repeatedly mentioned that same condition of aridity and darkness: "It is my belief that what Jesus did during that retreat was to try to detach me from everything that was not Himself. . . . If only you knew how great is my joy because I can please Jesus by having none. . . . This is a most subtle sort of joy and one that is not felt in any way." [29] "I thank Jesus because He considers this good for my soul. Perhaps, if He were to console me, I would cling to such sweetness; but He wants everything for Himself alone. Well! I will give Him everything, everything! Even when I feel I have nothing to offer, I will give Him that 'nothing.' " [30]

How encouraging those words for us who are so keenly aware of our extreme poverty!

In a letter addressed to Celine at a later date, Therese explains in greater detail what are some of these "nothings" which we can offer to Jesus in times of spiritual dryness: "You spoke the truth, Celine. The 'fresh mornings' (an expression that reminds us of St. John of the Cross who thus designates sentiments of love) are for us a thing of the past! There are no more flowers for us to pick. Jesus has taken them all for Himself. Maybe some day He will make new ones to spring up, but in the meantime what should we do? Well, I think I received some light on this matter. St. Teresa of Avila says that we must keep the fire of our love going. We have no wood when we are in the state of aridity and darkness, but must we not at least cast in a few small straws? Surely Jesus can keep that fire going all by Himself! Nevertheless, He likes to see us feeding it a little. Such a gesture gives Him pleasure. He then throws in much wood. We don't see it but we feel the vehement heat of love. This I have personally experienced; when I am as it were without feeling, seem unable to pray or practice virtue, that is the time when I must look around for little opportunities, for "nothings" which please Jesus more than if I gave Him complete dominion over the world, or suffered martyrdom; for example a smile, a kind word, when I would prefer saying nothing or might wish to show a sad countenance. . . . And when I see no opportunities for such things, I at least wish to tell Him repeatedly that I love Him. Even if it seemed to me that the fire of love had gone out, I still would want to cast something in it, and I know for sure that Jesus would revive it." [31]

After she had received the habit her spiritual dryness became even worse; she found consolation neither in heaven nor on earth: "dryness was my daily bread and although I had no consolation of any kind I was the happiest of creatures, for all my desires (for suffering) were fulfilled." [32]

Even her communions failed to comfort her: "I cannot say I often received consolations during my acts of thanksgiving. On the contrary these may be just the times when I have least consolation. I find this quite natural for I have offered myself to Jesus, not like one who wishes to receive a visit for her own satisfaction, but for the pleasure of Him who gives Himself to me." [33]

One year had elapsed and Therese was now making her retreat for profession. The climate had not changed. As she wrote to Mother Agnes: "Jesus has taken me by the hand and led me into a tunnel, where there is neither heat nor cold, nor sunshine either, and there I see only a half-veiled

light, a light coming from the downcast eyes of my Bridegroom. He says nothing to me and I say nothing to Him
except that I love Him more than myself. . . . I don't see
that we are advancing towards the end of the mountain, for
we are traveling underground; and yet I feel that we are
approaching the end, although I don't know how. The way
I am following brings me no consolation and yet it gives
me all consolations, for it is Jesus who has chosen it and all
I want is to please Him alone, yes, Him alone! [34] Oh! ask our
Lord . . . not to permit that souls, because of me, should be
deprived of the lights they need, but ask that my darkness
may serve to enlighten them. Ask Him that I may make a
good retreat and may give Him the maximum of pleasure.
I shall then be satisfied and, if it be His will, I consent to
walk in the darkness that now envelops me during my
whole life." [35]

So thick was the veil of darkness that covered her on the
eve of her profession that she was seized with a vivid thought
that she had no religious vocation and that it was her duty to
leave Carmel.[36] For one who had given herself so wholeheartedly to God, this was a most grievous trial; but Therese
accepted it with a willing spirit. She even found joy in it.
Enlightened by the Spirit of wisdom and love which was
leading her throughout, she understood Christ acted thus
because he desired to purify her love; He withdrew the
pleasure of His palpable presence in order that she might
love Him alone and without any consideration of His gifts.
"He does not want us to love Him for His gifts," she tells us,
"but for Himself alone. . . . He is so beautiful, so ravishing,
even when He remains silent, even when He hides Himself." [37] Moreover, He is never far from us. "He is even so
much closer when He hides Himself."

A second reason was that the less she benefited herself by
her relations with our Lord, the more she herself would give
to Him: "He hides to be able to beg for our love. Jesus does

not want us to find our repose in His adorable presence. If He hides and clothes Himself in darkness, if He keeps silence, it is that we may practice charity towards Him as to one who is in want. He puts Himself at our mercy. He does not want to accept anything from us unless we give it with a good heart. He stretches out His hand to us to receive a little love." Jesus gives consolations to souls whose love is weak. When, on the contrary, they have made progress in charity, He is silent and waits for their gifts.[38]

Therese had prepared herself for her spiritual nuptials by suffering. It is not strange then that on the morning of September 8, 1890, she experienced a peace that surpasses all understanding and in that peace pronounced her sacred vows.

Other than this, there was no respite in Therese's trials, no alternations of dryness and consolation as usually happens. This, as we have said, was chiefly a test and trial of her love; but it was also a purification of her faith, for Therese repeatedly spoke of the darkness into which she was plunged, as "a dark night"; and she declared that she was "traveling in a tunnel." Despite all this, her real ordeal was just beginning. Once during this period she remarked: "I really have no great external sufferings, and if the good Lord wants me to suffer interior ones, He will have to change my way. I don't think He will do that. Nevertheless I cannot live forever in this state of repose. I wonder what means He is going to discover?"

She was soon to learn that her Beloved is never short of means. Without changing "her way," He sent her the great *trial of her faith.*[39] This attack burst upon her in the midst of the Paschal season of 1896 (April 5) and proved to be a cross that she would bear until her death.

From her tenderest years Therese's heart had longed for the blessedness of heaven, and the thought of union with God had filled her with enthusiasm. Father Arminjon's lectures on the future life and her conversations with Celine in the summer house had greatly increased her eager expectations; but now, just as she felt herself ready to reach the blessed shore, heaven seemed to become unreal. Doubts about the very existence of a blessed eternity invaded her mind. She tried to recall her former thoughts about heavenly bliss to give comfort to her heart, but it was all in vain. She even seemed to hear a voice coming from the surrounding darkness and sneeringly cyring out to her:"You dream of light, of eternal possession of the Creator . . . come forward; death is not going to give you what you expect, but (it will give you) an even darker night, the night of annihilation." [40]

Therese told Mother Agnes that she understood a little of what our Lord suffered in His agony by what she herself was undergoing. If now and then a ray of hope shone through the darkness it immediately disappeared, leaving behind an even darker night.[41] "Look," she said one day, "at that dark hole in which you cannot discern anything. Well, it is in such a hole that I am living in body and soul. . . . What a darkness! Nevertheless I live in peace." [42] And she continued to sing of the blessedness of heaven; but, as she confessed, this was rather by sheer force of will than by anything she actually felt; she experienced no joy. She hymned the praise of heaven because she willed to believe it.[43]

Apart from Mother Agnes, and Mother Marie de Gonzaga to whom she opened her mind in her manuscript, the nuns were unaware of Therese's struggles and sufferings, so well did she manage to hide them. Relating that great trial to Mother Marie de Gonzaga she said: "I must tell you the sentiments of my soul; otherwise these pages might make you smile. It might seem that no soul is so little tried as my own; but in reality, if the martyrdom I have suffered during the last year were revealed to others, they would be filled with astonishment."[44] Her confessor, not knowing the nature of her trial, considered her to be in a state that endangered her salvation.[45]

The Role of Passive Purification.

Trials of this kind belong to the mystical order. Every soul that is called to divine union has to pass through them. God is a pure Spirit and infinite Holiness; and it is only by being in accord with divine purity, as far as this is humanly attainable, that it can be united to God and transformed into Him. Now this requires a complete renunciation. By means of mortification, absolute detachment from creatures and especially from itself, and through purification of its faculties, the soul must become capable of undergoing the divine action and dispose itself for union. But, however generous its efforts may be, they cannot produce that purity, that sort of "connaturality" which is necessary that the soul might become one spirit with God. Our self-love is most subtle and it mingles itself unobtrusively with all that we do. Again, our evil tendencies are so deeply rooted in us that we fail to recognize them properly or eradicate them. What we need is God's own action. He alone can make the necessary adjustments. He does this by means of "passive purifications." We call them passive because God is their agent, while the soul submits to His action and endeavors to be in accord with it.

St. John of the Cross also used the term "nights" to designate these purifications. There is in reality only one night, but it has two aspects according as it affects the senses or the mind.[46] The night first affects the senses to make them become subject to the mind. After that comes the night of the mind or spirit.

Mystical authors are not agreed as to the delimitation of these nights. According to St. John of the Cross, *the night of the senses* extends over the period of the spiritual life that elapses between the purgative life and the illuminative life; or, to use his terminology, between the state of "beginners who still practice meditation," and the state of the "advanced" who are already initiated in contemplation. It is when they emerge from the first night that the latter are said to be "the advanced."

The night of the spirit usually comes several years after the soul has entered contemplation, which is the state of the advanced. It seems to take place at the moment when the soul enters the unitive way.[47] However, it sometimes begins before the night of the senses is over.

These nights vary in intensity and duration, according to the need for purification of individual souls and the degree of union to which God desires to raise them. They are of various kinds: temporal trials, physical and moral sufferings, temptations against the theological and moral virtues; but it is their common purpose to purify the soul and to dispose it for the reception of divine favors.

Although these trials may be called "nights," light issues from their darkness. The Holy Spirit is there enlightening the soul by His gifts of understanding and wisdom. Now, because that gift of understanding shines too brightly on the soul whose eyes are but imperfectly purified, it inevitably produces darkness in it, just as the sun blinds those who gaze at it. Aided by this vivid light the soul discovers its numerous imperfections. Until then, however low the opinion it had of itself, it did not really know its great misery; now on the contrary it beholds its true condition. The same light also gives the soul a higher idea of the divine Being. Finally, through it God communicates to the soul the secrets of His love and reveals the way the soul must act to correspond with His designs.

It was necessary to recall briefly the role of passive purifications that we might understand the trials of St. Therese of the Child Jesus. So much suffering in body, heart and soul was not given her merely to fulfill her desire of proving her love to Jesus and in order to permit her to resemble Him in His passion; those sufferings were also the result of her entrance into the mystical way. God used them to transform her into Himself by complete union.

Therese recognized the meaning of these purifications. God, she wrote, desired to test her faith and her hope, by taking away from her all natural satisfaction in her longing for heaven. He wanted to purify her faith and make her hope more supernatural.[48]

However, we must not think that her trial was solely for the purification of her soul. Therese herself attributed to it an apostolic purpose. She offered it to God to obtain the light of divine faith for unbelievers and to make reparation for the faults committed against that virtue. That she might merit these graces for sinners "she accepted to eat nothing but the bread of affliction, until the time when it would please Jesus to introduce her into His glorious kingdom." [49] Her trials, as we have seen, lasted until the end of her life. Even on the very morning of her death her suffering forced her to say: "This is pure agony without any admixture of consolation."

Therese expressed gratitude to God because He had sent this trial at a time when she was able to bear it. She believed that if it had been sent at an earlier date, it would have led her to discouragement. She bore it admirably, constantly making acts of faith. She said that she had made a greater number of such acts in one year than during all the rest of her life. When the devil attacked her, she flouted him and turned to Jesus declaring her faith and hope in Him. Hence, though deprived of any sentiment of joy, she had the courage to say: "Lord, you overwhelm me with joy by everything you do to me; for, is there a greater joy than to suffer for love of You? The more intimate that suffering is, and the less it appears to the eyes of men, the more joy it gives You, O my God! And if You were unaware of that suffering—which of course is impossible—I would still rejoice in bearing it, if by it I were able to prevent, or make reparation for, a single fault committed against faith." [50]

THERESE'S MENTAL PRAYER DURING HER TRIALS

In spite of aridity, frequent distractions, and a constant drowsiness which afflicted her during prayer, even during her thanksgiving after Holy Communion, Therese remained faithful to the practice of mental prayer and made use of every means to make it as well as possible. Because others realized how much she suffered at such times, they sometimes advised her to omit, or at least to shorten, that exercise, but she never consented to it. "The hours set apart by the Constitutions," she said, "are God's own time, and it is not right to rob Him of it." [51] When she felt unable to tell Jesus that she loved Him, she then "threw a few shavings into the fire which was still smoldering under the ashes, with the hope that it would be re-kindled." When she had nothing to offer Him, she gave Him that "nothing," or recited slowly one Our Father and one Hail Mary: "These prayers alone ravish me. They nourish my soul with a divine food." [52]

To awaken or stimulate her love for Jesus, she kept in her pew an image of the Holy Face, which was her "favorite devotion." The Face of Jesus was for her a mirror from which she learned the science of love; it enkindled her desire for suffering and her zeal for souls; it was also an object lesson in humility.[53] To throw off her drowsiness, she had recourse to reading, and considered it proper to use a book during mental prayer when one feels a need for it. During her novitiate she read Father Surin's *Foundations of the Spiritual Life*. When she was seventeen and eighteen, her only spiritual food was the works of the mystical doctor, St. John of the Cross; in them she found abundant light.[54] But as aridity increased, spiritual books, with the exception of the Gospel and the *Imitation*, ceased to be of any help to her. "When I open a book," she said, "I read without being able to understand or, if I do understand, my mind comes to a halt and it is unable to meditate." [55] The Gospel then became her "bedside book"; in it she found "always new lights, hidden and mysterious meanings." That term "always" seems a little strong, for she wrote sometime later that "the vast field of the Scriptures where the heart would like to find nourishment . . . seems to be a dry desert without water. We even become lost and do not know where we are. Instead of peace and light, we find nothing but trouble or at least darkness." [56]

Reading did not always prove a remedy against falling asleep, but this did not worry Therese. She preserved her peace and abandonment, and resumed the service of love the moment she awoke. "(You think) that I ought to feel sad because I fall asleep (a thing that has been going on for seven years) during my meditation and my acts of thanksgiving? Well, I don't grieve over that!" [57] She knew that Jesus knows our weakness perfectly well. She also felt certain that "little children please their parents as much while they sleep as when they are awake," that Jesus can act just as well during our sleep as during our prayers. She said to herself that "doctors put patients to sleep when they want to perform an operation on them." [58] Moreover—as she also said about her communions—she engaged in mental prayer, not so much for her own benefits, as to please Jesus. What she had been unable to give Him during the hours set apart for the exercises of prayer, she gave to Him throughout the day.

GRACES OF MENTAL PRAYER

Therese suffered from aridity and darkness during the greater part of her life in Carmel; but, on the other hand, she received, on several occasions, spiritual favors and graces of mental prayer of a high order. She was even raised to the summit of the mystical state. Having been asked by Mother

Agnes to reveal these graces of mental prayer, she told her that she had learned from experience during her contemplations on summer evenings in the garden what is meant by the "flight of the spirit" mentioned by St. Teresa of Jesus.[59]

She received a similar grace in July 1889, in the grotto of St. Mary Magdalen; and it was followed by the state of quietude which lasted several days: "It was as if a veil had been thrown over all earthly things. I felt entirely hidden under the veil of the Blessed Mother. . . . At that time I had charge of the refectory, and I recall that I was doing things as not doing them myself; I seemed to be acting with a borrowed body. I remained in this state for a whole week. It is a supernatural state which I find hard to describe. The good Lord alone can place us in such a condition and an experience of that sort is sometimes sufficient to detach us forever from the things of earth." [60]

She seems to refer to a similar experience in a letter to Celine of July 7, 1894: "We sometimes seem to have been abandoned . . . but Jesus . . . sees our sorrow and His sweet voice is suddenly heard, a voice sweeter than the rustle of spring, and it says to us 'Return, return, my Sulamitess; return that we may look at thee!' He wishes to look at us at His leisure, but He is not alone; with Him are the two other Persons of the Blessed Trinity who have come to take possession of our soul. . . . This Jesus promised when He was ready to ascend once more to His Father and our Father. He said then with unspeakable tenderness: 'If any one love me, he will keep my word, and my Father will love him and we shall come to him and shall take up our abode in him.' "

But the principal grace of that kind with which Therese was favored was the *wound of love*. This was given to her on the Friday which followed upon her Act of Oblation to Merciful Love. She was making the Stations of the Cross when she suddenly felt pierced by a dart of fire so ardent that she thought she was going to die: "I cannot explain it; it was as if an invisible hand had plunged me into a fire; and what a fire, burning, yet full of sweetness! I was burning and I thought that if this were to last one minute, one second longer, I would not be able to bear such ardor without expiring. I then understood what the saints have said about those states which they so frequently experienced. . . . I experienced this just once and only for one moment, but immediately after that I fell back into my habitual aridity." [61]

St. Teresa of Jesus, in her autobiography, speaks at length about that wound of love.[62] St. John of the Cross deals with it in his *Living Flame of Love*, but his description seems to have been borrowed from St. Teresa of Jesus. He attributes that wound to the Spirit of love, and claims that not many souls are granted this favor. God gives it principally to those who have followers to whom they ought to transmit their virtue and spirit.[63]

Those special graces which Therese of the Child Jesus received over a period of nine years, appear to be few, and according to her own words they were of a transitory nature. But there was one thing that persisted throughout, namely, *her love*, a love not always felt, but which, nevertheless, was constantly alive within her.

Therese had also the *feeling of the presence of Jesus in her*. Jesus dwelt in her soul, enlightening her and uniting her ever more closely to Himself, even in the midst of aridity and darkness. She told Celine that "the Well-Beloved instructs my soul in silence, in darkness." [64] Elsewhere she said: "The retreat I made before my profession was far from bringing me consolation. A most complete dryness and a feeling that I was almost abandoned (by God), these were my portion. Jesus was asleep, as usual. . . . However, the good Lord showed me clearly—though I took no particular notice of it, how to please Him and practice the most sublime virtue. I have often come to the conclusion that Jesus does not wish to give me provisions for the future. He feeds me from moment to moment, with a food that is entirely new. I find it in me not knowing how it came to be there. I simply believe that it is Jesus, hidden in the depths of my poor little heart, who operates in me through grace, and causes me to think of everything He wants me to do at each moment." [65]

Jesus also gave her an understanding of the Scriptures and, little by little, showed her her Little Way: "I understand and know by experience that the kingdom of heaven is within us. Jesus does not need books nor doctors to teach souls. He, the Doctor of doctors, teaches without the noise of words. I have never heard Him speak and yet I know He is in me. At every moment, He guides me and inspires me with what He wants me to say or do. I find, just at the time when I need them, lights which I had not seen before. It is not most frequently during my meditation that they are given to me in greater abundance, but rather during the occupations of my daily life." [66]

Therese ordinarily uses the term "to feel" to designate the lights she received during her meditation or at other times. This is important, for "to feel" in this context does not mean a sensible impression but, as we shall see, it is a knowledge that springs from love. This seems even to have been her habitual way of knowing supernatural things. To Mother Agnes who had asked her whether she had an intuition of the approach of her death, Therese replied: "O Mother (do you speak of), *intuition?* I only guess what I believe and what *I feel.*" [67] On another occasion she said: "How very much I would tell you if I could find the words to express to you what I think, or what I don't think, but *feel.*" [68] And to Celine: "Life is very mysterious. We know nothing, see nothing, and yet Jesus has already shown to our souls what no eye of man has even seen. Yes, our heart has a presentiment of that which the heart cannot understand, for we are sometimes at a loss for thoughts to judge I-know-not-what which we *feel* in our soul." [69]

It is in this way that, from her childhood, she *felt* sure that she would go to heaven. She did not merely believe it ... because of what others told her, but "she *felt* in her heart aspirations that were directed to a better country." [70] It was also by means of such a knowledge of love that Jesus made known to her her Little Way. Numerous passages in her writings allude to that fact.

To give one example: "Dear Sister (Marie of the Sacred Heart): How can you say that my desires are a sign of my love? Oh! I *feel* truly that it is not that at all which pleases the good Lord, as He looks in my little soul. What pleases Him is to find that I love my littleness and my poverty; that I have a blind hope in His mercy. . . . Oh! How much I wish I could make you understand what I feel. . . . It is confidence and confidence alone that ought to lead us to Love." [71] She *feels* that even if she were guilty of all the sins that men can commit, she would still preserve her confidence in God.[72]

It was this same "light" and "feeling" that told her that the practice of spiritual childhood leads to the summit of Love; "I *feel* that if you could find a soul that is more feeble, more insignificant than mine, You (my God) would desire to shower it with even greater favors, if that soul abandoned itself to your infinite mercy with entire confidence.[73] If all souls that are weak and imperfect could feel what your little Therese, the most insignificant of souls, feels, not one would despair of reaching the top of the mountain of Love." [74]

This kind of knowledge had convinced her more and more that her Way was right and true. To one who asked her who had taught her that doctrine, she replied: "Jesus alone! No book, no theologian taught this Way to me, and yet I *feel* in the depths of my heart that I possess the truth." [75] Finally, it was this light and "feeling" that gave her the assurance that she was giving the right direction to her novices: "I *feel*," she told them, "that when I am telling you these things, I am not mistaken and that Jesus is speaking through my mouth." [76]

These lights and "feelings" are then the fruits of love; they are something perceived by way of the heart; for when a soul gives itself entirely to God, He draws and unites it to Himself in charity and the Holy Spirit. He makes Himself known and the soul relishes Him through the gift of wisdom. This affective experience produces in the soul a new knowledge of God and of His divine secrets, a living and instinctive love. There are no distinct and particular concepts that can express that kind of love. It is obscure and yet surpasses particular knowledge, and produces practical certitude.[77] It is of this knowledge that St. John of the Cross speaks in the Canticle which he explains in the *Ascent of Carmel:*

"In that blessed night . . . (I was) *without any other light* or guide *than that which burned within my heart.*

> More surely than the noonday sun
> There, waiting for me, was He
> Whom I knew so well!"

It is precisely this passage which Therese quotes in order to indicate the nature of her own knowledge.

SPIRITUAL DIRECTION

Enlightened by this knowledge of love, Therese advanced with sure steps. The Holy Spirit had taken her under His guidance, from her most tender years, and, as she grew in love, He poured more and more light into her soul; in fact He reserved the direction of Therese to Himself.

Speaking of her dispositions when she was about fourteen years old, she wrote: "I never said a word to anyone about my interior sentiments. The road I traveled was so straight and bright that I had no need of any one but Jesus to guide me. Spiritual directors looked to me like faithful mirrors which reflect Jesus, but as for myself, the good Lord used no intermediary but acted directly in me. . . ." [78]

She repeatedly mentions these lights she received from Jesus; [79] nevertheless she consulted priests whom God placed on her way, and even asked them to direct her. It was thus that she addressed herself to Father Pichon, S.J., who was the spiritual director of the nuns.[80] Two months after her entrance into Carmel (end of May, 1888), she made a general confession. At its close the priest told her: "My child, may our Lord be always your superior and your novice-master." This He truly was, remarks Therese and he "was also my director." [81]

During the year which followed her profession, being overwhelmed by interior sufferings, she opened her heart to Father Alexis Prou, O.F.M., who was giving a retreat at the convent. This Father understood her perfectly and "he sent her out with full sails on the waters of confidence and love, for which she felt so great an attraction, but on which she had not dared to navigate (without the counsel of others)." [82] At a later date she wrote every month to Father Pichon who had been sent to Canada. He replied to her only once a year and for that reason she considered it useless to continue to follow his direction. Jesus, from that time on was indeed her one and only spiritual director: [83] "It was Jesus, the Director of directors, who instructed me in the science which is hidden from scholars and the wise, but which He deigns to reveal to little ones." [84] On the other hand, in her relations with her superiors she "always tried to be to them like an open book."

DID THERESE ATTAIN TO TRANSFORMING UNION?

Basing ourselves on Therese's own testimony we have recalled the mystical graces she received from God. Beyond that she has not left us any explicit statement that she had also received the grace of "transforming union" which is the apex of the mystical state. Hence we ask whether this favor was likewise granted to her.

Before we answer that question, let us recall what the Carmelite Doctor in the spiritual life, St. John of the Cross, and St. Teresa of Jesus understand by that union.

In his description of the state of those who have reached that sublime stage in the spiritual life, St. John tells us that the passions which formerly disturbed the soul are then overcome. Faith sheds great light, and a purified love penetrates deeply into and consumes the soul. The latter is flooded with peace and, however severe the pains and crosses, the soul remains serene. The Holy Spirit now reigns supreme and rules that abode of peace. He directs all its activity so that the person's actions are more divine than human. The Spirit of God also infuses in the soul exquisite lights and discloses to it divine secrets. Finally, reaching the climax of His love, God draws the soul to Himself and unites it to Him. So complete is the transformation of the soul in God, that though He and the soul remain what they are, they now seem both to be God.[85]

St. Teresa of Jesus also deals at length with the effects of that ineffable union: "The soul, or rather the spirit of the soul, has become one being with God; for He unites Himself so intimately to His creatures that, after the example of those who on earth are united forever, He no longer desires to be separated from her. . . . The soul in that condition is in such great self-forgetfulness that she seems no longer to have any being. She seems to be and to will nothing any more, in anything. She is detached from everything. She no longer asks herself whether there is to be a heaven for her, life, or happiness. She no longer desires to die. She does not long for the glory of the saints. Her whole life is spent in the remembrance of our Lord and in tender love for Him. Sometimes her sentiments are so strong that they make her utter words that are full of the fire of love. She cares for nothing except the glory of God. If she were given the assurance that she could enjoy God immediately, she would prefer to continue to live for many more years suffering the most horrible torments, for she wants to give Him that small amount of glory and in some way assist the divine Crucified whom she contemplates as He receives numerous insults. She has a most ardent desire for suffering. She realizes that the life of the divine Master was one continuous suffering; hence at this stage she wants to resemble Him, or at least she wants to have the desire to resemble Him in that respect."

So perfect is such a soul's conformity with the divine will that she considers whatever God sends to be good, whether it be suffering or something else. Sometimes the thought of the glory of God becomes less vivid and there reappears a desire to go to God and enjoy Him; but the soul soon recovers from this passing sentiment. Realizing that God is always with her, she recovers her disposition of perfect abandonment to Him.

Lastly, the saintly reformer, Teresa of Jesus, says that, in that condition, the soul no longer, or rarely, suffers interior afflictions and aridity. She enjoys a profound peace,[86] and is almost always in a state of quietude. This state is usually accompanied by external phenomena of divine love such as the wound of love, sentiments of intimate contact with God and the like.[87]

We are now in a position to answer the question with which we began. It is our opinion that Therese did attain transforming union. Everything points to this fact: she suffered passive purifications; she was favored with special graces of mental prayer that prepare for such a union, and she enjoyed the fruits of such a union. Her sisters have testified that her virtues developed in a way that was unique.[88] Her love, especially, burned with a singular intensity. Therese herself confessed that she was unable to fathom its depth.

From this sprang those glowing expressions which fell from her lips on certain occasions. "I don't see very well what more I shall possess in heaven than here on earth," she told a sister; "of course in heaven I shall see the good Lord, but when it comes to being with Him, I already have this entirely." [89] And to Mother Agnes: "How wise God is to veil Himself from my eyes and to show Himself but rarely to me and, as it were, through the bars of His mercy; [90] for I feel that I could not bear its sweetness." [91]

She has also recorded for us that, from the day of her oblation to merciful Love, love surrounded and permeated her, renewed and purified her at every moment, leaving no trace of sin in her.[92] And in spite of the sharpness of her pains, "her peace of heart remained entire, and her abandonment to God complete." So great was this abandonment that she no longer desired to suffer or to die, or even to go to heaven. The will of God, and the ardent desire to love Him, were her only aspirations. Moreover, suffering had become so sweet to her, that she no longer suffered but felt she was the happiest of creatures.[93] She said she knew from experience that the kingdom of God is within us and that Jesus Himself, hidden at the bottom of her heart, was acting in her in a mysterious way.[94]

Finally, she boldly affirmed that no praise bestowed on her could produce in her even the shadow of vanity; that she then understood what is meant by humility of heart and knew that she was a little saint.[95] "God," says St. John of the Cross, "reveals to souls that have reached perfect love, and are about to enter His kingdom, how beautiful they are and makes them conscious of the favors and virtues He has imparted to them. For in such souls everything is transformed into love and thanksgiving and they are no longer moved by presumption and vanity; neither is there any longer in them any leaven that could corrupt the whole mass." [96] All this seems to prove conclusively that Therese did reach the pinnacle of the mystical state.

Some have objected to this that Therese underwent the trial of her hope and her faith even until her death. That trial, they claim, is a passive purification and is therefore incompatible with transforming union. For St. Teresa of Jesus states that the soul which is in that state is in peace and no longer undergoes interior trials.

Let us remark first of all that St. Teresa of Jesus is not as categorical as it might at first appear, regarding the incompatibility of the spiritual marriage and interior suffering. If in the text we have quoted, Teresa of Jesus says that such suffering is no longer undergone when souls are in that condition, she writes elsewhere that the soul "almost" never suffers dryness or interior trouble in this state, so that the soul is "almost always in repose." [97] And she adds that those who have attained this stage, may still have to "fight against the poisonous beasts which are then banded together against the soul"; [98] and that such persons sometimes even commit venial sins though these are sins of weakness (non-voluntary).[99] She also affirms that God does not grant that favor to fill us with delight but to strengthen us who are so weak, and enable us to endure much suffering. And she cites the example of the Blessed Virgin and St. Paul.[100]

St. John of the Cross says likewise that, although souls in the state of transforming union, ordinarily suffer no longer, there can be exceptions and God could permit a soul to suffer, to enable her to merit more and become inflamed with love. God chose to act in this way in the case of His Blessed Mother and St. Paul.[101]

To these two examples we may add the more recent one of St. Therese Marguerite Redi. The Trinitarian character of this Saint's contemplations, the ardor of her love, the excellence of her virtue during the last years of her life, clearly showed that she had been favored with the spiritual espousals. And yet she suffered terribly until her death because the tendencies in her lower nature were so contrary to the aspirations of her mind. God wished by this means to make her grow in love.[102]

It follows then that if the trial of faith or that of the senses is a sign of purification, it does not necessarily mean that they prove the presence of passive purification. We know why St. Therese of the Child Jesus continued to suffer trials in her faith, after she had attained union. She herself has told us the reason; that trial had an apostolic purpose. It was an expiation of the faults that are committed against the faith and it was a providential means for the conversion of unbelievers. For it was just at the moment when the Saint found it difficult to realize that there could be impious people who refused to believe, that the trial of faith began to afflict her. Instructed by God, she offered her sufferings so that those unbelievers might receive the light of faith.[103]

We believe also that there is another explanation of her trial. When, on June 4, 1897, Therese said goodbye to her own sisters, she wished to prevent the sorrow they might feel when they saw her dying amidst sufferings and without any sign of happiness. So she recalled to them how Jesus Himself had died: At the moment when He expired, Jesus gave to His Father the greatest proof of love that was possible. He was therefore more than ever united to Him and yet His anguish was so great that He cried out: "My God, my God, why hast Thou forsaken me?"

Since it is most probable that God had inspired Therese's desire to reproduce the death of Christ, does it seem rash to hold that by continuing to suffer the trial of her faith even in the midst of transforming union, and to her very last breath, she did in fact imitate the divine Savior?

It seems therefore that Therese did attain the summit of the mystical state. Her soul had endured the purifications and acquired the virtues that are required for that state, and the

fruits which such a transforming union produces were manifestly realized in her. Hence the trial of her faith which lasted
to the end of her life, in no way invalidates that conclusion.

Let us keep in mind that Therese became a great saint.
She was favored with the wound of love, a grace which,
according to St. John of the Cross, is rarely granted to souls.
She had been chosen to teach souls a simple way of holiness. How then could we consider it possible that she herself
did not realize holiness in its perfection? Moreover, when
our Saint wished to characterize the particular state of her
soul at the time when she was finishing her first manuscript
(January 1896), she borrowed from the mystical doctor, St.
John of the Cross, the verses of the Spiritual Canticle in which
he describes the life of the soul that is transformed in its twofold phase: the phase in which the soul enjoys high transports, and the ordinary phase in which all life is love, and
when all the soul's faculties act solely for God under the
motion of the Holy Spirit.[104]

Characteristics of the Theresian Mystical Way

Whoever studies the mystical life of St. Therese of the
Child Jesus cannot help recognizing that it has special characteristics. She was a fervent disciple of St. John of the Cross
and knew whole passages of his works by heart. Certain texts
on the subject of love had so struck her that she had adopted
them as guiding principles of her spiritual life. And yet, her
mystical life differs considerably from the description which
St. John of the Cross gives of that kind of life. Therese's Way
is much simpler; it is much less favored with mystical graces
than that of souls about whom the holy doctor speaks in his
works. Again, classification of the states of prayer described
by St. Teresa of Jesus are not found in Therese of the Child
Jesus. We know that she received mystical graces of a high
order, but these were rare.

Regarding extraordinary graces such as visions, revelations, ecstasies, prophecies and miracles, they are almost completely absent. The only favors which Therese received were: the smile of the Virgin who cured her of her illness; the prophetic vision of the malady that would afflict her father; the knowledge of the mission she was called to fulfill and of the diffusion of her manuscript. But when we compare these extraordinary graces which Therese received with the phenomena that made glorious the lives of so many Saints, we realize how few of these favors were granted to her.

Another particularity of her mystical life was the fact that her ordinary conduct was in no way affected by even the most elevated graces of prayer that were given to her. As her sisters have testified, the action of the Holy Ghost did not rob her of her interior freedom nor of her "naturalness." On many occasions she still had to put up a fight to remain faithful to the practice of little sacrifices, renunciations, and the exercise of fraternal charity; but at the same time there was always perfect harmony and union between the dominion of the Holy Spirit over her and her ordinary conduct.

One day a theologian had asked Sister Genevieve whether the graces which Therese had received in the summer house had not produced in her a state of soul that differed greatly from her usual condition, and whether, on that account, she had not shown more indifference towards external things and acted as if she were possessed by God throughout all the hours of the day. Sister Genevieve replied: "I never noticed in my saintly sister, during, before, or after, the summer of 1887, a state of mind that was in the least singular, a state of recollection that was in any way peculiar. Everything in her was simple and ordinary." [105] After all, Therese herself has stated that after she had received the wound of love, she had immediately fallen back into her habitual state of aridity.[106]

To summarize: if it be true that Therese passed through severe trials of passive purifications, which are a necessary preparation for mystical graces of a high order; if she some-times enjoyed graces of mental prayer, her way usually con-sisted of what essentially constitutes the contemplative life namely, a life of faith, complete self-forgetfulness, generous love, boundless confidence in merciful Love, conformity to Christ in her life of suffering and perfect abandonment to the divine will, under the influence of the Holy Spirit. It was because she fulfilled these dispositions that lead to perfec-tion that she was able to attain sanctity.

LITTLE SOULS AND THE MYSTICAL LIFE

Therese has been given to us by God to teach us a new way of holiness. She was destined to be the mother of a legion of "little souls." Are we permitted to conclude that all those who follow her in that Way, will also traverse the mystical way and attain to transforming union?

This is a delicate question. Let us note first of all that it is possible to reach sanctity without passing through the mys-tical way. St. Teresa of Jesus is explicit on that point.[107] On the other hand, to walk in the mystical way is not something that lies within our own powers. It is a gratuitous gift of God, and He raises to that state whomsoever He pleases. All our efforts to attain it will be of no avail without that gift from God. No doubt, our efforts may incline God to grant it to us, and in fact that is what ordinarily happens. He rewards gen-erous persons and permits them to drink at least a little of the "fountain of life" that is, He gives them mystical graces.[108] But it is rarer for Him to grant graces of prayer of a higher order. Regarding such graces, the mystical doctor (St. John of the Cross) writes: "God does not raise to contemplation all that exercise themselves in the way of the spirit. He does not even choose half of them (for such a favor). Why this is so is known to Him alone." [109]

Having recalled all this, it is our opinion that if the divine

Spirit saw fit to simplify the mystical way of Therese, it was not merely for her personal benefit. It was also to enable those who were to follow after her to realize that way in its essential elements. Because Therese reached that summit, it is not lawful for us to conclude that all who engage in the mystical way will likewise attain that pinnacle of love. God always grants higher graces to those who have received the mission of drawing others after them.

It is true enough that Therese declared that "all that she did, 'little souls' would also be able to do; that it was necessary that such souls should not have to feel envy towards her for anything"; but these words do not refer to mystical graces. Therese merely wanted to say that the Way of Childhood implies only very ordinary actions, actions which all can imitate.

Nevertheless, since God, by means of the Way of Childhood, desires to facilitate our union with Himself, and since Therese begged Him to choose for Himself a legion of souls who, through their abandonment, will merit to be victims of His love, it is not presumptuous to believe that if we practice that way of perfection, we too shall be able to reach the summit of love; for she said that "if all feeble and imperfect souls felt as she did, not one would despair of reaching the top of the mountain of love."

THE PRACTICE OF MENTAL PRAYER ACCORDING TO ST. THERESE

Methods of Mental Prayer.

We have described the contemplative life of St. Therese of the Child Jesus in its broad outlines. One question remains which deserves particular attention because of its importance that is, mental prayer as the Saint herself conceived it. Since she was chosen by God as a guide for souls, let us see how she practiced it, for it is universally recognized that mental prayer is one of the chief means for progress in spiritual life. Therese herself called it the lever by which we must lift up the world, and "the furnace which should inflame everything with the fire of love." [110]

Unfortunately she has not left us any substantial text in which she gives a complete teaching on the subject. We have to collect its elements from scattered passages in which the Saint makes allusion to her mental prayer. Even then we must be careful to interpret them rightly, for since these were casual expressions they lend themselves to a wrong interpretation. We must especially keep in mind the personality of Therese, as well as the particular dispositions of her soul at the time when she wrote or spoke those words.

One thing to be remembered from the start is that Therese was by nature, and later also by grace, a truly contemplative soul. As we have already recalled, even in her tender years she took ecstatic delight in the beauty of nature and it helped her to raise her mind to God; she shut herself up in a corner of her room "to think"; during Mass she had a tendency to become absorbed in contemplation, instead of following the text of the missal. Under the guidance of the Holy Spirit, she practiced the kind of prayer which St. Teresa of Jesus defined as "a friendly intercourse in which we talk familiarly with Him who, we know, loves us." However, since she did not at first realize that she was engaged in genuine mental prayer, she sought advice without at first receiving practical help.

When spiritual dryness and darkness began to afflict her, she had recourse to books, with the hope of obtaining light and of drawing from them some sentiments of love; "she tried also to arouse herself by means of affections"; [111] but, apart from the Gospel, which ordinarily continued to instruct her, books were of no assistance to her.

It does not seem that Therese ever made use of any specific method, or that she practiced mental prayer by means of "discourse." She sometimes did say that she "meditated," but this expression signifies rather a thoughtful reading than a true discursive prayer, in which a sort of reasoning is employed. Especially in the beginning, she "was occupied with thinking and loving." She thought of God, of Jesus and their infinite love. She thought about heaven and the blessedness God has in store for us. She thought of souls to be saved. And she loved! She loved with all her heart, and gave herself without reservation. She was disposed to forget herself in everything, to do all she could to please God and save souls. But very early that prayer was transformed into contemplation; her mental prayer was inspired by the principles of the Little Way.[112] This continued until the time when she was plunged into darkness and spiritual dryness; and yet, throughout, love was waking at the bottom of her heart.

Are we permitted to conclude from such facts that Therese "has" freed us from the various methods of mental prayer, and her canonization sealed their doom?" It is our opinion that such a conclusion is not justified. Therese never said or wrote anything that expressed disapproval of such methods or her desire to free us from using them. We know even that she asked information regarding the methods of mental prayer. Moreover she knew that her Carmelite predecessors had taught a method for engaging in mental prayer.

It is true, however, that she would have been opposed to complicated methods, but we do not think that she would have rejected all methods, especially when a particular method was found to be useful for a particular soul. Hence, we should not advise anyone to cast away all methods, or to neglect all methods from the beginning of the spiritual life under the pretext of imitating Therese. Not all souls possess the intellectual dispositions of Therese. They were not, like her, favored from childhood with special divine graces. In general, they have to be initiated in mental prayer, for it does not consist merely in telling God that we love Him. Mental prayer must animate our conduct: at the beginning of the spiritual life, it should instruct us, inflame our will, cause us to become completely detached from creatures and from ourselves, and prompt us to give ourselves entirely to God. Now this requires reflection and resolutions. Mental prayer, however, is not brain work; it is not a labor of the intellect. It remains an intercourse with God. As we progress, our prayer will become more simple, more affective; and finally we may attain to a prayer that resembles that of Therese, in which contemplation is predominant.

Those who are enemies of all methods are glad to be able to invoke the passage in which Therese tells us: "As for myself, prayer is a lifting up of the heart. It is a simple glance towards heaven, a cry of gratitude and love in the midst of trials as well as joys. Finally, it is something great, something supernatural, which dilates the soul and unites it to Jesus." [113] Obviously, we have but to read the context of these words, to realize that in this passage Therese is speaking about prayer in general and not of mental prayer properly so-called.

CHAPTER XIV

Jesus' Place in the Life
and Spiritual Life of Therese

JESUS held a dominant place in the life and spirituality of St. Therese. An unpublished document of the Carmel of Lisieux declares that her spiritual life was "centered" in Jesus. An attentive study of the words of our Saint and of the facts known about her confirms the correctness of this testimony. The name of Jesus or its equivalent appears on every page of her writings and she uses it much more frequently than the terms "God," or "Father"; but we have better evidence than that to show what place Jesus occupied in her life.[1]

When Mother Agnes asked her sister, Therese, to write down what she remembered about her childhood, the latter said she would be glad to write the story of "the little flower which was plucked by Jesus, and to publish the totally gratuitous favors which Jesus had granted her." [2] Hence, that it was principally to Jesus that she felt indebted for the graces she had received seems likely.

Therese's First Communion marks an all-important date in her life. On that day she realized that Jesus loved her, and hence she was prompted to give herself to Him forever. As she tells us, "for a long time Jesus and Therese had known and understood each other, but on that occasion their meeting was a fusion. They were no longer two. Therese had disappeared . . . Jesus alone remained" and He alone would henceforth be able to satisfy her heart.[3] Jesus was her "first Friend, the only All of her soul, the one whom alone she wanted to please, whom alone she wanted to find in all things.

. . . Jesus alone IS; all the rest IS NOT." [4] She desired to "love Him unto folly" and "more than He had ever been loved." [5]

> "When in my youthful heart was kindled
> The fire which we call love,
> You came then, Lord, to claim it;
> And You alone, O Jesus, could fill my soul;
> For boundless was the need I felt of loving You." [6]

Therese's love of Jesus was marked by a most exquisite delicacy although it also was full of the greatest tenderness. She loved to repeat "that we should get hold of Jesus through His heart and smother Him with caresses." It is not difficult to understand such familiarity when we recall what kind of union our Lord wishes to establish between Himself and our souls. Is not our supernatural life a participation in the life which Jesus received from His Father, and is not Holy Communion designed to transform us mystically into Himself?

Animated by this love Therese strove to live more and more "in Jesus" and through Jesus, whom she knew to be present in herself: "To be with You, and in You," she prayed, "this is my one and only desire." And to Celine she wrote: "Let us be one with Jesus. . . ." [7] Let us make our life a continual sacrifice, a martyrdom of love to console Jesus. . . . May all the moments of our life be for Him alone. . . . We have only one task during the night of the present life . . . to love Jesus." [8] Spiritual aridity and darkness were unable to weaken her faith and her love, for Jesus was present and was acting in her: "I know that Jesus is in me. . . ." [9] He it is who does everything in me; I do nothing." [10] He guided her, taught her everything she needed to know: "He guides and inspires me at every moment. . . . He teaches me without the sound of words. . . . Most of the time, He does this not during the hours of prayer . . . but in the midst of my daily occupations. . . . It is Jesus hidden within my wretched heart who does me the favor of acting in me." [11]

Among other things, our Lord revealed to her the meaning of Holy Scripture and, little by little, He showed her her Little Way.[12] She considered that sanctity consists in this sort of intimate union with Jesus: "If we wish to be holy, we have merely to unite ourselves to Jesus, endeavoring to please Him"; [13] or, as she expresses it elsewhere, we have merely to "gaze at Him," but we must keep our eyes always fixed on Him. Jesus will then look at us and "when Jesus looks at a soul, He immediately gives to it a divine resemblance; but it is necessary that it constantly keep its eyes focused on Him alone." [14]

It happens sometimes that the thought of our wretchedness makes us afraid of approaching Our Lord. We should then recall the mercy of His Sacred Heart and the truth that Jesus is "everything for us." [15]Therese sang of this in her poem:

> "The nothingness of me is strangely loved;
>   Sustaining ever
> The All of love, my need, is strangely here;
>   Departing never." [16]

To Marie Guerin she wrote: "We must love our nothingness in His Infinite All, and think only of this All which is infinitely lovable." [17] When Therese wished to do good to others, she always relied on Jesus, for she realized that the practice of charity is difficult because of the faults and imperfections we notice in our neighbor. But knowing that, despite these difficulties, the divine Master commands us to love our neighbor, as He Himself loves him, she strove for an ever closer union with Jesus, feeling that the more complete her union with Him, the more Jesus, abiding in her soul, would love her neighbor. She also tried most earnestly to see only Jesus in others.[18]

To the novices who had shown surprise because she divined their intimate sentiments, she replied that all her lights came from Jesus: "I am astonished at the things I am teaching to you. While telling you these things, I have a feeling that I am not mistaken and that it is Jesus who is speaking through my mouth." [19]

Knowing that nothing comes to pass without God's permission, the young Saint refused to see anything in her trials but the kind hands of Jesus.[20] Finally, it was also Jesus who revealed to her her particular place and role in His Mystical Body.

We know that Jesus is the Mediator, the Pontiff, Bridge-Builder between men and God. "You are Christ's and Christ is God's," said St. Paul.[21] Therese knew this well: "It is by loving You (Jesus) that I draw the Father to me; my poor heart clings to Him and holds Him and will not let Him go. O Trinity, You are the prisoner of my love!" [22]

Jesus was "The Elevator" that should raise her to the bosom of God. He was the "Adorable Eagle who, after feeding her with His own substance, would carry her into the bosom of the Trinity and plunge her for all eternity into the fiery furnace of divine love."

These texts reveal *Therese's devotion to the heavenly Father,* whom she loved tenderly and approached with the simplicity and confidence of a child, even to calling Him "Papa, the good Lord."

She also greatly adored the Most Holy Trinity, though this became evident somewhat later. It was to the Blessed Trinity that she offered herself as a victim of holocaust, and in return, the Blessed Three visited her. In a letter to Celine, she speaks of a grace which, it seems, made her feel and enjoy the presence of the Blessed Trinity in her soul.[23] It remains true nevertheless that Jesus remained the object of her favorite devotion.

UNDER WHAT ASPECTS DID THERESE HONOR JESUS?

Therese loved Jesus in every phase of His life, but she was drawn more strongly to certain mysteries.

The Child Jesus.

At the beginning of her religious life, she had a special love for the Child Jesus. Having been told before she entered Carmel that she would be called Sister Therese of the Child Jesus, she quite naturally offered herself to Him as His "little plaything" with which He could amuse Himself as He pleased. Furthermore, her doctrine of spiritual childhood was one which in the spiritual order required only the simple ordinary actions of daily life and the "gathering of flowers" of small daily sacrifices. It was natural, therefore, that the example of the Child Jesus should present itself to her for her loving imitation.

The Holy Face.

Very soon, however, her devotion to the Holy Face came to take precedence over that of the Holy Childhood. It was her "little mother" who, from the first months of her life in Carmel, revealed to her the depths of the treasures hidden in the Holy Face of Jesus. This devotion was greatly loved by the nuns of Lisieux, having been transmitted to them by the Carmel of Tours. Therese in her turn eagerly adopted it. Writing about what she had learned concerning it from Mother Agnes she said: "She who took first place among my sisters, 'my little mother,' had penetrated deeply into the mysteries hidden in the Face of our Bridegroom. She revealed them to me and I understood. . . . How merciful the way in which the good Lord has always guided me!" [24]

The devotion to the Holy Face was, in fact, to be most helpful to Therese in her spiritual life. When, in 1889, she received the habit of Carmel, she asked and was granted permission to add that title to her name.[25] In February of the same year her father, Mr. Martin, suffering from a disease that affected his brain, was placed in a rest home. After his death in 1894, Therese understood the prophetic meaning of the vision she had seen as a child in the garden of "Les Buissonnets" (August, 1879). At that time she had seen her father as a stoopshouldered old man, his head hidden by a thick veil. Now, because Mr. Martin had offered himself as a victim, Therese saw a relation between her father in his illness and the "servant of Jahweh" whose distorted features are described by Isaias.

During the years 1889 and 1890 Therese makes frequent allusions to the Face of Jesus. Thus in 1890 she wrote to Celine: "I am sending you a leaflet which says a great deal to my soul. It seems to me that your soul will be equally moved by it. Celine, it is a long time since the soul of Isaias the prophet, like ours at this time, was steeped in the 'hidden beauty of Jesus.'" This leaflet quoted among other texts the words of Isaias: "There is no beauty in him, nor comeliness: and we have seen him, and there was no sightliness, that we should be desirous of him: Despised and the most abject of men, a man of sorrows, and acquainted with infirmity: and his look was as it were hidden and despised, whereupon we esteemed him not." [26]

A few weeks before her death, she said that all her devotion had been inspired by these words of Isaias.[27] Behind the downcast eyes of Jesus, Therese saw the beauty of His soul; His swollen and bloodstained Face revealed His love. "Jesus," she wrote to Celine, "burns with love for us. Contemplate His adorable Face; behold His eyes which have lost their lustre and are downcast. . . . Contemplate His wounds. Look at the Face of Jesus! There you will recognize how much He loves us." [28] "The King of kings humbled Himself to such a degree that His Face was hidden and He could no longer be recognized. I too desire to hide my face; I desire that only my Well-Beloved should see it, that He alone should be able to number my tears, so that He may rest His head at least in my heart and feel that in it He is known and understood." [29]

To Mother Agnes she said: "The poor little bride of Jesus feels that she loves Jesus for Himself alone and she desires to gaze at the face of her Beloved merely that she may collect the tears that are flowing from those eyes that have ravished her by their hidden charms." [30]

The contemplation of the Holy Face was for her a lesson in humility: "I understand better than ever what true glory is. He whose kingdom is not of this world shows me that there is only one kind of royalty that we should envy and desire: our royalty should consist of a willingness to be forgotten, to be considered as nothing and to find our joy in despising ourselves. Oh! how I wish that my face, like that of Jesus, were hidden from all eyes, and that, on this earth, no one would recognize me." [31] This was a favorite expression of St. Therese.[32]

The disfigured face of the divine Savior also inspired her with a love for suffering and zeal for souls. Recalling to Celine the trials that had assailed her father, she wrote: "Jesus has sent us the best cross that His immense love could have invented. . . . How can we complain, when He Himself was thought of "as a man struck by God and humiliated?" Hence Therese thirsted for sufferings and eagerly desired to be forgotten.[33]

In regard to souls she wished to save, she notes that "the grain of sand desires to save souls at any price. It is necessary that Jesus should grant her this grace. Ask the radiant Face of Jesus to give it to her." [34]

She drew Celine along the same road: "I am sending you a beautiful picture of the Holy Face which our Mother gave me some time ago. I think it ought to be in the hands of Marie-of-the-Holy-Face, and I must not keep it for myself. I thought for a long time of giving it to my dear Celine. May Marie-of-the-Holy-Face [35] be another Veronica who wipes away the blood and tears of Jesus, her only Beloved. May she gain many souls for Him, especially the souls she loves (that is, souls of priests)!" [36]

The Holy Face of Jesus was to her like a beacon [37] guiding her and sustaining her courage during her times of darkness and aridity. Transplanted on the Mountain of Carmel, the "little flower" unfolded in the shadow of the cross, bedewed with the tears and the blood of the divine Savior and warmed by the radiant sun of the adorable Face of Jesus: "Having entered the underground passage where there is neither heat nor cold nor sunshine, she walks, following a light half-veiled, a light shed by the downcast eyes of the Face of her Bridegroom." [38] And thus, in spite of all her suffering, Therese was happy. She kept a picture of the Holy Face in her pew during mental prayer; she asked that one should be hung from one of the curtains of her bed during her illness. As an outpouring of her love, she composed a Consecration to the Holy Face, and towards the end of her life wrote a hymn in its honor. For her day of special honor to it she chose the feast of the Transfiguration.

Therese's love for the Holy Eucharist.

We know with what ardor she longed to receive the Eucharistic Bread; we recall her visits to the Blessed Sacrament as a child, in the company of her father; we admire her solitary adorations while she was at boarding school; we are edified by the care with which she prepared for her first Holy Communion, and are awed by the favors with which she was blessed by our Eucharistic Lord. It was through contact with the Eucharist Christ that she received her most outstanding graces: during her first Communions she received both an attraction for suffering and great consolation; it was during her Christmas Communion in 1886 that the grace of "conversion" was given to her. However, she did not always find consolation in this Sacrament. In Carmel, her acts of thanksgiving were often made in the midst of aridity and sleepiness; but this did not grieve her, for she considered that she was receiving Jesus in order to give Him pleasure rather than for her own satisfaction.[39]

At that time, daily communion was not commonly practiced and the rules of religious Institutes specified the days on which it was permissible to receive. Hence, though Therese could not receive communion daily, as she would have liked to do, she did use every opportunity that was given her to approach the Holy Table. During her illness, in spite of her state of exhaustion, she dragged herself to the Chapel to assist at Mass and unite herself to her only Friend.

Similarly, she made every effort to promote daily communion among the nuns. To Mother Marie de Gonzaga who did not share her views, she foretold that, after her own death, Therese would make Mother de Gonzaga change her opinion in this respect. Likewise she foretold what actually did happen, that a chaplain who was favorable to the practice of daily communion would replace the present one.[40]

Therese had learned that there is no more efficacious means of transforming ourselves into Jesus than the worthy reception of Christ's Sacred Body.

Therese and the Mystical Body of Christ.

Although Therese never mentioned the Mystical Body of Christ by name, it is evident that she was well acquainted with this truth and appreciated its great riches, for on several occasions she referred to the doctrine of the transfer of merits. She knew that by virtue of our union with Jesus, Head of the Mystical Body, whatever is His is also ours.[41] It is primarily this, which, despite the spiritual poverty she attributed to herself, gave her that audacious confidence which was so characteristic of her. She wanted to become holy, to reach the degree of glory which God had in store for her; she desired to rise to the highest summits of heaven, but she did not count on her own merits to achieve such high goals. She wanted to rely only on the merits of Jesus Christ. She would enter heaven vested only with the justice and holiness of the divine Savior.

Though Therese desired to save souls with Christ, she realized that all she could offer Him were the flowers of her small sacrifices; even so, she gave those little "nothings" to the triumphant Church, hoping that the saints would pass them on with a smile to the divine hands. The Lord would then endow them with infinite value and pour them out over the Church militant, and the Church suffering.[42]

To persons who could not adapt themselves to poverty and yet desired to give to God acts that would console Him, she advised to offer the works of others: "When we grieve because of our incapacity to do good, our only resource is to offer the works of others. Herein lies the advantage of the Communion of Saints." [43] Therese herself loved to rely on the help of others: "I greatly love prayers said in common, for Jesus has promised to be in the midst of those who are assembled in His Name. I then feel that the fervor of my sisters is added to my own.[44] It is God's will that those who are still in this world should communicate heavenly gifts to one another by means of prayers, so that, when they have entered their heavenly country, they may love one another, with a grateful love, a love much greater than any that could ever be found among the members of the most ideal family of earth. . . . How often have I not reflected that perhaps all the graces that I have received in abundance have come through the prayers of some little soul whom I shall know only in heaven!" [45]

She acknowledged that since the good Lord had filled her with graces for others as well as for herself, her only desire was to distribute them to others: [46] "All that is mine belongs to each (of my brother-missionaries). I feel that God is too good, too generous to give His favors meagerly."

It is clear then from all that has been said that Therese's spirituality was centered in Jesus. This caused her to be inspired by the purest spirit of the Gospel and makes her virtually a disciple of that Apostle who desired to "know nothing but Christ." [47] In this she is also faithful to the principles of her spiritual Father, St. John of the Cross, who wants us to imitate Christ in all things. Guided by the Holy Spirit who was sent to teach us all things and remind us of all that Jesus had said,[48] Therese held that the Son should be everything to us, since the Father has given Him to us; for God made Him "our wisdom, our justice, our sanctification." [49] It is in Him that we know the Father, for "we can go to the Father only through Him." Moreover, "we are in Him and He is in us." [50] Our supernatural life is His life in us, and our ideal consists in reproducing Him.

It follows that we should strive, with all our strength, to be one in mind and heart with Christ, making all our thoughts, sentiments and volitions coincide with His, and reproducing in ourselves His conduct and His virtues. We shall be pleasing to the Father to the extent that we re-live Christ; we shall be saints when we shall have attained the degree of resemblance to Christ to which we have been predestined by God.

CHAPTER XV

Mary's Place in the Life of St. Therese

IN late years much has been written about Therese's devotion to the Blessed Virgin. These studies have been generally successful in showing that Mary held an important place in the life and the spirituality of our Saint; nevertheless, since this matter was treated as an isolated subject and by writers who were most devoted clients of Our Lady, there may at times have been given the impression that Mary occupied the principal place in Therese's life. We believe we have proved in the preceding chapter that, on the contrary, her devotion was centered in Jesus.

It remains true, nevertheless, that the Blessed Mother occupied a place in Therese's devotion that can hardly be exaggerated. Moreover it would be difficult to conceive a life of spiritual childhood in which Mary would not have a part. J. H. Nicolas has well said that "the way of spiritual childhood requires, for its full development, an intense devotion to the Blessed Virgin; for a child feels the need of a mother and, on the other hand, it is on thinking of his mother that a man becomes a child again in the depths of his heart. If the love of God for us contains a note of motherly tenderness, our love of Him in return, must be marked by something like that which marks the affection we have for our mother. And just as the person of Mary incarnates in some manner that aspect of divine love, so it is through her that our filial love must pass, in order that it may reach the secret fibres of God's Heart. The Blessed Virgin does not hide God from us; on the contrary, she manifests Him in that which in Him is most lovable and sweet. And the love we have for Him ascends through her, straight to the Heart of God." [1]

UNDER WHAT ASPECT DID THERESE CONSIDER MARY?

All the Saints have honored and loved our Lady. It could not be otherwise. Having entered the way of holiness which is a way of light and truth, they could not help recognizing the role of Christ's Mother in the work of salvation and sanctification of souls, and the relation which God's Mother has to us. But each saint considers Mary according to his or her own temperament, mentality or particular attraction. Hence their devotion to her is marked with a character and coloring that is proper to each.

Therese saw above all in Mary, the Mother, the Mother of Jesus and our mother. Without neglecting the other aspects of Mary's life, she admired also in a particular way, Mary's simplicity, her spirit of faith, her silence and recollection in God, for these were in harmony with her personal attraction and with the way of spiritual childhood which it was her mission to teach. Her inclination in that direction was also furthered because Mary's virtues were those that flourished in her own family circle.

Therese's devotion to Mary before her entrance into Carmel.

Since most of the facts that illustrate Therese's devotion to Mary within her own family are well known, we shall confine ourselves to the more salient ones.

When she was about three-and-a-half years old, every evening, before retiring, she asked whether the good Lord was pleased with her. When the answer was in the affirmative, she asked then whether the Blessed Virgin was likewise satisfied.

At the age of five-and-a-half, she made her first confession. The confessor spoke to her about the Mother of Jesus. She recalls in her autobiography that although the Blessed Virgin had already occupied a prominent place in her heart, she promised then, because of that exhortation, to increase her tender love towards Mary. At the age of seven, she wrote in one of her copybooks: "The Blessed Virgin is my mother and little children ordinarily resemble their mama." [2]

In the afternoon of her First Communion Day, she pronounced the Act of Consecration to the Blessed Virgin, putting all her heart into the act and asking the Holy Virgin, Mother of God, to watch over her. Recalling this later on, she added "that it seemed to her that Mary looked with love at her little flower and smiled at her."

But the most striking event of her youth is the smile the Immaculate Virgin granted her as she lay on her bed of suffering (May 13, 1883). The details of that event are sufficiently known, but we should like to show how greatly Therese was influenced by the grace she then received, for most authors have not given sufficient attention to this fact. [3] That vision and the smile of our Lady produced an effect on Therese that went far beyond procuring her a bodily cure. As she tells us, the statue became as it were alive, and it acquired an inexpressible beauty. Mary's face breathed a sweetness and a tenderness which human words cannot describe. Her smile, says our Saint, penetrated to the very depths of her soul. It is not an exaggeration on our part to claim that that miraculous smile of God's Mother imprinted on Therese's soul those exquisite dispositions which were to develop constantly during her life and make her, what she felicitously calls "a miniature of the Blessed Virgin."

Since she had been refused the permission of her Bishop to enter Carmel at the age of fifteen, she went to Rome to implore the Holy Father. At the beginning of her journey to the Holy City, she stopped to pay a visit to Our Lady of Victories in Paris. About this she wrote afterwards: "I find it impossible to describe what I felt in that sanctuary. The grace which Our Lady granted me there resembled those I had received at my First Communion. The Blessed Virgin made me feel that it was truly she herself who had smiled at me and had cured me. Oh! how great the fervor with which I begged her to be always my protector and to help me realize my dream, hiding me in the shadow of her virginal mantle!" [4]

She also visited the shrine of Loretto and it was with intense emotion that she entered the "Holy House" where Mary had borne Jesus close to her heart and where she had for many long years dwelt with this Son of God who was also her son. She was anxious to be able to receive Him in Holy Communion in Mary's own house and, in spite of a contrary custom, that permission was granted to her.[5]

Therese's devotion to Mary during her life in Carmel.

Carmel is truly the Order of Mary, and Carmelites honor her especially as a mother. On the other hand, since the life in a Carmelite convent is one of solitude, silence, and prayer, it is a reproduction of the life of Nazareth. Hence Therese found there a favorable climate for the development of her devotion to Our Lady.

She entered the Carmel of Lisieux on April 9, 1888, which happened to be the feast of the Annunciation (having been transferred to that date because that year, it would otherwise have fallen during Holy Week). She received her habit on the feast of Our Lady of Mercy (24th of September, 1888). On September 8, 1890, the feast of Mary's Nativity, she made her profession: "It was the little one-day-old Blessed Virgin who presented her little flower to the little Jesus." [6] Now let us follow Therese in what "her life revealed" about her devotion to Mary.

We say "what her life revealed" because she has not left us any special doctrine concerning Our Lady and no special system of Marian spirituality. Apart from some remarks and her hymn *Why I love Thee, O Mary*—of which she said that it expressed all that she thought and would preach about the Blessed Virgin, if she were a priest—all we know about her Marian spirituality is what we can gather from her conduct.

Now, her conduct was directed by the doctrines of faith and the Gospel. Therese learned nothing from theological or spiritual treatises and she received nothing from preachers. A short time before her death, she told Mother Agnes that all the sermons she had ever heard had left her cold,[7] and what she herself thought about Mary was quite different from what she usually heard in sermons. "How much I should have liked to be a priest," she said, "so that I might have preached about the Virgin Mary. It seems to me that one occasion would have been sufficient to make clear what I think on that subject." And she goes on to explain with characteristic charm how she conceived the life of Mary: "I would show how little the life of the Blessed Virgin is known. We should refrain from saying improbable things about her or things we know nothing about. . . . If we wish a sermon on the Blessed Virgin to bear fruit, we ought to show what sort of life Mary actually led, as it is indicated in the Gospel, and not as fabricated by our imagination. It is easy to deduce that her life both in Nazareth and later on, was quite ordinary. . . . Everything took place as things occur in our own lives. The Blessed Virgin is sometimes pictured as if she were unapproachable. We should realize on the contrary that it is possible to imitate her by practicing her hidden virtues. She lived a life of faith common to all of us and we should prove this from what we are told in the pages of the Gospel. The Blessed Virgin is the Queen of heaven and earth, quite true, but she is more mother than queen. . . . It is proper to speak of her prerogatives, but we must not content ourselves with that. We must do all we can to make her beloved of souls." [8]

Here is good common sense, and in these words is found

the complete doctrine of Therese concerning Our Lady. Mary, to her mind, is above all a mother, the Mother of Jesus and our mother. She is a mother with a tenderly maternal heart who "loved us truly as Jesus loves us." [9] Mary's life, like ours, was a "life of common faith," "quite ordinary," and "made up, above all, of hidden virtues." Hence Mary is imitable. Our devotion to her then, while giving her the homage which her dignity commands, should consist above all in loving her with a childlike love and trying to follow her example.

In the hymn *Why I love Thee, O Mary,* we find the same teaching, though in greater detail. In it she reviews the life of Mary and finds there a wonderful inspiration for imitating Our Lady's virtues: the love of virginity; humility so profound that it draws to itself the Most Holy Trinity; material and spiritual poverty; being deprived of extraordinary graces as well as of the goods of this world; ardent charity that is eager to serve the neighbor; confidence in God which awaits help from Him alone; silence which keeps within and adores the divine mysteries; a living faith, the only light in the night of the spirit and anguish of heart; a love that gives all and itself also, in a complete sacrifice.

Briefly, a life of admirable perfection, although it was the common road in which Mary was pleased "to walk, showing us the way to heaven."

Reading Therese's description of Mary's life, we cannot help noticing how well that life corresponds with her own, and how well the Little Way of spiritual childhood resembles the life of the Mother of God. This is so true that we are tempted to ask ourselves whether the Saint did not interpret Mary's life according to her own life and her Way of Childhood, until we realize that the traits she describes are taken from the Gospel. It is well to note that the texts we have quoted date from the last months of Therese's life (May and August of 1897); the hymn was her last poetical composition (May). Those words are therefore truly significant, since they give us the fruit of mature consideration.

Therese practiced "what she preached." She approached Mary like a child: "I felt that the Blessed Virgin was watching over me, that I was her child. Hence I found it necessary to call her "Mama," for this name seemed even more tender than that of mother." [10]

She had perfect confidence in Mary not only because of Mary's power over the heart of her Son, but also because she realized that Mary's spiritual motherhood embraces with love all her children who are still in this valley of tears. Hence she felt certain that Mary never disappoints anyone who has recourse to her. "When we address ourselves to (other) saints," she said, "they make us wait a while. We feel that they have to go and present their request (to God), but when we ask a grace from the Blessed Virgin, we receive immediate help. Have you not experienced this? Well, try it and you will see." [11] "The Blessed Virgin never fails to protect me as soon as I invoke her. In my troubles and anxieties I very quickly turn towards her and, like the most tender of mothers, she always takes care of my interests." [12]

Therese even presented to Mary the requests which she did not like to address to God, because she feared that they might not be agreeable to Him. This is the way she explains it: "To ask something of the Blessed Virgin is not the same thing as asking it of the good Lord. She knows very well what to do with my little wishes, whether to transmit them (to God) or not. Finally, it belongs to her to see to it that the good Lord be not (as it were) forced to hear me." [13] "If, after that, we obtain nothing, it is because what we asked for, is not in accordance with God's designs. We must abandon ourselves (to Him); when we have prayed to the Blessed Virgin and she has not given us what we asked for, we should let her do what she pleases, without insisting on our request; and after that let us not worry any more about it." [14]

So childlike was her love that she never undertook anything without first having recourse to Mary. In this she was
like a child who asks advice from its mother and will not let
go her hand. Therese entrusted to her the most insignificant
as well as the most important things. She invoked Mary for
the guidance of her soul. For example she asked Mary to prepare her for a proper reception of Jesus in Holy Communion.
Since Mary had borne Jesus in the temple of her body, no
one could better "remove from her own soul, the debris of
imperfections that encumbered it." [15]

However, it was especially during her illness that Therese's recourse to Mary manifested itself. She knew how
much Mary herself had suffered, hence she made Christ's
Mother her confidante, her support, and asked her that she
might teach her how to benefit more from her sufferings. She
candidly confessed to one of her novices: "I like to hide my
pains from the good Lord, because I want to give Him the
impression that I am always happy; but I hide nothing from
the Blessed Virgin; to her I tell everything." [16]

Knowing that the sight of her physical dejection caused
grief to her own sisters, she said: "I have asked the Blessed
Mother to put an end to the drowsiness and dejection that
has afflicted me during the last days. I felt I was causing you
pain; today she heard me." [17]

On another occasion she asked Our Lady to take her head
into her hands to enable her to hold it up; [18] another time
Therese asked her to stop her cough, and so to give her sister,
Genevieve, a chance to sleep.[19]

Since her sisters were afraid that Therese might die during the night, and they might thus miss assisting at her beautiful death, Therese told Mary "that she would like to die
during the day and have a beautiful death, and thus give joy
to her sisters." [20] This, at the same time, is an example of how
she could make an exception to her sacrifice of indifference
to all things, for the sake of giving pleasure to her neighbor.

One day, when she was suffering more than usual, she told Mother Agnes: "I have ... a great desire to depart (this was on June 6, 1897) and yet I entrust this to the Blessed Virgin. She will do with my desire what she sees fit." [21] Having been asked, in the midst of her spiritual trials, whether Mary was also hidden from her, she replied: "No, the Blessed Virgin will never be hidden from me, for I love her too much." [22] When she no longer beheld the good Lord, she charged the Blessed Virgin to transmit her wishes to Him. She asked her especially to tell Him that He ought not to be afraid of sending her trials: "All He has given to me, Jesus may take back again. O tell Him not to be shy with me. Let Him hide if He wishes; I am willing to wait until the day which has no setting sun, and when my darksome faith will vanish at His sight." [23]

One night, having a feeling that the demon was roaming close to her, she asked that Holy Water should be sprinkled on her bed, and then she said: "Think of it, I am unable to pray! I can merely gaze at the Blessed Virgin and say 'Jesus.'" [24]

Likewise, when she wanted to help those around her, Therese had recourse to our Lady. Familiar to us are the truths that Mary gave us Jesus and cooperated in the work of our salvation; that she is the mediatrix of all graces and forms Jesus in us.

Our Saint too was inspired by these principles. Having been put in charge of the novices, (she inspired them with a tender, childlike devotion towards the Mother of Jesus. She had placed the statue of the "Virgin of the smile" in a small oratory that was next to her cell, and often led her pupils there to counsel them. If one or the other had some difficulty, it was in the presence of Mary that Therese asked her to explain her trouble or to offer up her sacrifice.[25]

She recommended to her brother-missionaries that they entrust their apostolate to our Lady. Finally, when ordered to recount the memories of her childhood, she knelt before the statue of the Virgin, asking that she might be prevented from writing even one line that would not be pleasing to our Lady.

All this goes to show that Therese led a truly "Marian life," in the full sense of this term. She lived in Mary's company and acted only in union with her: "During this sorrowful exile, O my beloved Mother; I want to live with you, and then follow you to heaven some day."

The tenderness of her love for Mary and her trust in the Mother of God were extraordinary, prompting a familiarity that is truly childlike: "I sometimes find myself saying," she wrote to her sister Celine, " 'But my good Holy Virgin, I see that I am happier than you, for I have you for a mother, but you have no blessed virgin whom you can love.' " [26]

There are also those charming words which she wrote with a trembling hand (September 8, 1897) on the back of a picture of Our Lady of Victories. She had pasted on it a flower which her father had presented to her the day he gave her permission to enter Carmel. "O Mary," it reads, "if I were Queen of heaven and you were Therese, I would rather become Therese, that you might be the Queen of heaven." These are the last lines she penned on earth!

All through her life, Mary had surrounded Therese with motherly tenderness, granting her a transforming smile in the springtime of her life and a mystical favor in the grotto of St. Mary Magdalen, in July 1889. About this she told Mother Agnes: "It was as if a veil were cast over the things of this earth . . . I felt entirely hidden under the veil of the Blessed Virgin. . . . At that time I had charge of the refectory and I recall that I was doing things as if not doing them. It was as if I were acting with a borrowed body. I remained in that state for an entire week." [27]

Finally, it is only natural for us to believe that Mary, who had shown so much kindness to her during her life, also came to meet her with a smile at her last hour, for Therese, in a song, had asked for this favor: "You came to smile at me in the morning of my life; come and smile at me again . . . Mother, now that it is eventide."

During her last moments, her mind was filled with the thought of the Blessed Virgin. On the morning of September 20, exhausted and breathing heavily, Therese joined her hands and looking at the miraculous statue of the Virgin, she sighed: "Oh! I have prayed to her with fervor, but this (which I suffer) is pure agony, without any admixture of consolation." Later she murmured: "O my good Blessed Virgin, come to my assistance!"

Towards three o'clock, Therese stretched out her arms, as if on the cross. The Prioress placed on her knees a picture of Our Lady of Mount Carmel. She looked at it for one instant and then asked: "Mother, present me quickly to the Blessed Virgin, help me to die a good death." At six, hearing the Angelus bell, she raised her suppliant eyes towards the statue of the Blessed Virgin; she had already entered into her death agony. One hour later, she ended her life of victim, in a last act of love. Because she had gently fallen backwards, it was believed that she had died, but she suddenly lifted up her head; her eyes gazed fixedly at the statue of Mary and then above her in an ecstatic look. They then closed, but an inexpressible smile lit up her countenance. May we not see in it a last reflection of a smile of the Mother of Jesus?

Therese loved Mary and lived in the closest union with her, following the purest traditions of Carmel; but in addition, she also lived her life in such a manner that it was to serve as a model for souls who were to walk in her Little Way. It was a life patterned after that of the Blessed Virgin, a life quite ordinary and simple. No doubt, Jesus remains always the divine model to which we must conform according to the will of the heavenly Father.[28] Mary herself, the perfect reproduction of this model, holds for us the grace to help us to reproduce Christ's life in our own. Without this help we should know that it is impossible to re-live Christ's life, that is, to be truly Christian.

Though Mary has sublime prerogatives and is the highest of God's saints in heaven, yet she remains always our mother, whose great role is to give to Jesus a multitude of brothers and sisters, other Christs. That is why, like Therese, we must constantly go to Mary, giving ourselves completely to her, that she may form Jesus in us. The closer our union with Mary, the more quickly also will that transformation be accomplished.

CHAPTER XVI

Complimentary Traits of the Physiognomy of Therese

THERESE'S FIRMNESS

IN the course of our study, we have pointed out the natural qualities of our Saint and have also dealt at length with her virtues. In order to be complete we shall bring out certain traits of Therese's physiognomy which we have not shown sufficiently thus far.

Therese's maturity of judgment
her experience and her firmness.

Maturity of mind is a rare quality. It presupposes good judgment and reflection. Experience is ordinarily acquired with age and is the fruit of attentive observation.

St. Therese of the Child Jesus had maturity and experience beyond her age. Without a doubt, she had exceptional natural gifts, but so precocious a maturity as was found in her can be fully explained only by the action of grace. She herself affirmed that during the night of Christmas, 1886, Jesus brought her forth from her swaddling bands and the imperfections of childhood, and so transformed her that she was unable to recognize herself.

Aware of her own maturity, Therese spoke of it to others. One day, in reply to her sisters' anxiety regarding her health, "God is a Father," she told them, "allow Him to act as He pleases. He knows well what His very small baby needs." "Are you a baby then?" asked Sister Marie of the Sacred

Heart. "Yes," replied Therese, with all seriousness, "but a baby who knows a great deal, a baby who is an old man." [1] And to Mother Marie de Gonzaga she wrote concerning the direction of the novices of whom she had charge: "My youth, and my lack of experience have not made you afraid. Perhaps you have recalled that the Lord is often pleased to give wisdom to little ones." And she went on citing the example of David who sang in his youth (Psalm 118, 100): "I have had understanding above ancients; because I have sought thy commandments." [2]

In fact, her Mother Prioress did recognize that the divine Master enlightened Therese's soul in a special way and gave her the experience of years. [3] The manner in which the young nun directed the novitiate proves to what extent the judgment of the Prioress was right in this.

In her dealing with those inexperienced souls, Therese gave proof of great understanding and indulgence. It is not in one day that a novice adapts herself to Carmelite observances and austerities, nor does she immediately learn how to benefit from mental prayer and overcome its difficulties. Thanks to her psychological insight and the lights she received from heaven, Therese quickly found out what was hidden in each soul. Indulgent in the presence of weakness, she nevertheless wanted her novices to become strong and generous. Since they had entered religion to give themselves to God, their mistress wanted them to make their gift as perfect as possible.

Because she had a natural amiability and an ever-welcoming smile, it would be a great mistake to represent Therese as easy-going and uncritical. When necessary, she knew how to speak frankly and energetically. To a novice who found it difficult to acknowledge her faults and who had argued with Therese, the latter said: "I have fought much; I am very tired but I am not afraid of battle. I am as much at peace there as during mental prayer. It is God's will that I should fight to the finish. When we are directing souls we must be truth-

ful and say what we think. This is what I always do. If they
don't like me, that does not matter. I am not seeking popularity. Let them not come to see me if they don't want to
know the whole truth." [4] "The Lord," she wrote also, "has
given me the grace of not fearing combat. I must do my
duty at any price. More than once I have heard this: 'If you
want to get something from me, you must approach me with
mildness. You will not get anything from me through force.'
But I know that no one is a good judge in his own cause and
that a child whom the surgeon has subjected to a painful
operation, will not fail to cry to high heaven and say that
the remedy is worse than the evil. But he finds himself cured
after a few days, and he is very happy to be able to play
and run. So is it with souls. They soon recognize that a bit
of bitterness is preferable to sugar and they do not fear to
acknowledge it." [5]

This opinion she confirmed in the following words: "In
order that a reprimand may bear fruit, we must give it dis-
passionately. When we have scolded a person, within the
bounds of justice, let us stop there and not become soft-
hearted, tormenting ourselves because we realize we have
inflicted pain on someone. To run after the one we have thus
afflicted, to console her, is to do her more harm than good.
But when we leave her to herself, we force her to expect
nothing from the human side, but to have recourse to the
good Lord, recognize her faults, and humble herself. Otherwise we shall make her accustomed to being consoled after
we have administered a deserved reproof, and she will then
act like a spoiled child which jumps with rage and cries,
knowing that this will make his mother come to him and wipe
away his tears." [6]

Therese also refused to yield to discouragement when she
saw the apparent futility of her efforts. It is God who changes
and enlightens souls in His own good time: "When we have
to deal with a disagreeable character, let us not lose heart

and let us never give her up. Let us always have the sword of the spirit to reprove such a person for her faults. We should not allow things to go their own way, so that we may preserve our tranquility. Let us fight without respite, but also without hope of winning the battle. Success is not important. We must always go on, however burdensome the struggle. Let us not say, 'I shall not get anywhere with that person, she does not understand; she should be abandoned.' That would be cowardice on our part. We must do our duty to the end." [7] "There are souls with whom God is endlessly long-suffering; to whom He gives His light only by degrees. That is why I was very much on my guard against advancing His hour, but I waited patiently until it would please Him to make her obey His designs." [8]

In her own community, some nuns thought that Therese was at times too severe towards her novices. Sister Genevieve spoke about such an opinion during the Process of Canonization. The promoter of the Cause, being astonished to hear nothing but praises of the Servant of God, urged the sisters to make known at least some small tendency that could be called defective. It was then that Sister Genevieve replied: "Sometimes Therese showed severity in the guidance of her novices; but I cannot truthfully affirm that it was a fault. It was a holy anger and it did not cause her to lose her self-possession nor her peace." [9] She herself wrote about this: "I know, my Mother, that your little lambs consider me severe. . . . The little lambs may say what they please. Fundamentally they feel that I love them with a genuine love." [10]

Finally, an unpublished fragment gives us her own reflections concerning the government of novices: "The time I have spent in working for the novices has been a time of war, of struggle. I labored for God. He worked for me, and my soul never advanced more rapidly than at that time. I did not seek to be loved. I merely sought to do my duty and to please the good Lord without desiring that my efforts should bear fruit. We must serve our Lord; sow what is good around us without worrying about its growth. For us the labors; for Jesus, success! We should never fear the battle when the good of our neighbor is involved. We must reprove others at the cost of our personal tranquility and we must do this much less in order to open the eyes of our subjects, than to serve God. He will take care of the results." [11]

The reason for Therese's firmness in her guidance of novices is that she realized that she had been made responsible for them. But Therese also showed firmness in her relations with others.

We know how much she esteemed fraternal charity, peace and union, and how she hated disputes: "We should not be justices of the peace" she said, "but angels of peace." [12] However, there are limits to the love of peace and silence. Pushed too far, they become faults. To remain silent in the presence of evident errors or abuses, to yield always to excessive vanities, to advocate conciliation on all occasions, would lead us to do harm to souls, to introduce looseness in religious observances, to favor the demands of those who have poor judgment or who are arrogant in their demands.

"There exists," writes Father Petitot, "even in monastic and religious life, a certain conciliatory pacifism which, from many points of view, is worse than passing faults or even than divisions and battle. By being excessively tolerant in their mutual relations—a thing that should rather be called tacit complicity—religious who owe fraternal correction to one another, arrive at taking liberties with the rule so that a community or even an Order are led to laxity." [13]

Therese knew this to be so. Hence, in certain circumstances when the common good required it, or when charity and justice were not observed, she did not fear to speak her mind openly. For example she respectfully let it be known—subject always to obedience—that the sufferings endured by the sisters in winter time, because they had insufficient cov-

erings during the night, were not willed by God, and that it
would be well to give them some alleviation. She believed
that not to take account of differences of climate and the
diversities of temperaments, under the plea of observing
customs, was in reality tempting God and committing a sin
against prudence.[14]

She did not even fear to speak out, when she foresaw that
her intervention might cause the Prioress to become ill-dis-
posed towards her. She recalled with her customary simplicity, in a letter to Mother Marie de Gonzaga, the case to
which we have alluded. Therese at that time was not yet in
charge of the novices, but she had permission to converse
with one of them for the good of the latter's soul. This novice
happened to have a too natural affection for her Prioress (the
same Mother de Gonzaga). Therese had noticed it; but if
she were to reprove the conduct of that novice, she would
run the risk of indirectly offending her Prioress. This consideration, however, did not stop Therese: she prayed and
then, judging that the favorable moment had come, she
approached the novice. After some affectionate words by
way of introduction, she explained to her that this affection
for her Prioress constituted an obstacle to her perfection. She
ended with this suggestion: "If our Mother (Prioress) notices
that you grieve (because of what I have said to you), you
may tell her all; I prefer being sent away from the monastery,
if she so desires, than to be wanting in my duty and failing
to warn you for the good of your soul." The novice accepted
that lesson, and twenty years later, during the Process of
Canonization, she still recounted it with deep emotion.[15]

On another occasion, Therese's intervention was more
direct. Towards the end of the priorate of Mother Agnes,
Mother Marie de Gonzaga, who was then in charge of the
novitiate, and foresaw that she would be elected Prioress,
desired to postpone the profession of the two novices, Sister
Genevieve of St. Teresa (later called "of the Holy Face"),

and Sister Marie of the Trinity, because she wanted to have the honor of receiving their vows. On one occasion, a sister who upheld the claims of Mother de Gonzaga, had argued in favor of the rights of the Mistress of novices. Therese suddenly replied with firmness: "there are trials which a Mistress of novices has no right to impose on her novices." [16]

Nevertheless, Therese ordinarily preferred to stand aside, and her interventions in community affairs were the exception. When Mother Agnes paid a visit to her in the infirmary, a few weeks before Therese's death, she said jokingly: "Well, our warrior is down!" "I am not a warrior who has fought with earthly weapons," replied Therese, "but I have fought with the sword of the spirit which is the word of God. That is why illness has not been able to cast me down. Not later than yesterday I used my sword against a novice. I said, 'I shall die bearing arms.'" [17]

In one of her poems she had previously sung:

"Smiling I brave the fire;
And in Your arms, O my divine Bridegroom,
With a song on my lips, I shall die on the field of battle,
My weapons in my hand." [18]

Therese, then, knew how to combine an all-embracing charity and mildness with firmness and holy indignation. The latter virtue is sometimes imperative. "Without anger," wrote St. John Chrysostom, "virtue fails to progress, laws cease and faults remain unpunished." And St. Thomas quoting these words, adds that "one may sin by not having used a holy anger, when it was proper or necessary to do so." [19]

We may remark here, however, that one should not attempt to imitate indiscreetly interventions like those we have mentioned in regard to St. Therese. Besides the fact that they demand a just motive, they also presuppose good judgment and self-possession on the part of the critic. Now, blind passion easily makes us believe we have a sufficient motive to intervene, or it makes us go beyond the limits of prudence. That is why such interventions must remain the exception.

Therese possessed harmony and balance in her virtues. This was a source of admiration for those who knew her. One of her confessors, who was best able to judge this, declared: "I have never noticed in her anything that was imprudent or inconsiderate. There was no trace of exaggeration or natural impetuosity. In all her words and even in the expression of her countenance there was found a marvelous maturity." Therese's oldest sister says likewise: "Sister Therese of the Child Jesus was so well-balanced in everything that it seemed something inborn in her. She was not excessive in anything." [20]

Such an equilibrium is the combined result of natural gifts and the action of the Holy Spirit. Saints are masterpieces of this divine Artist.

It may be well to close this chapter with what Therese's sister, Marie of the Sacred Heart, said about our Saint: "I often relive in thought the days when Therese was in our midst, and I find that there is nothing that can resuscitate for us what we have seen. . . . What a perfection in everything and yet what simplicity! How often, when I saw her walking through the cloisters, simple, modest, and recollected. I said to myself, 'Think of it that it will never be known here below how much that soul loves the good Lord!' Whatever may be said or written about her, nothing can give me her true portrait. One must have known her. I myself would be unable to retrace it. But it is engraved in the depths of my heart like a heavenly vision which nothing can alter."

CHAPTER XVII

Resume

POPE BENEDICT XV proclaimed that St. Therese had brought to men "the secret of sanctity." In his turn Pius XI declared that she is "a word of God descended from heaven to reveal to us the way of spiritual childhood," and that she "traced for us a sure way of salvation." [1]

Therese did not reveal new truths, nor did she teach new means for attaining perfection. As Stanislas Fumet so well expressed it,[2] her doctrine was not a "revelation of a new kind of sanctity, but merely a new way of revealing sanctity to us." What she teaches flows from the knowledge of God as He stands revealed in The Gospel, and the consideration of the creature's dependence on Him. God is the infinite Being, He who IS. He is Love infinitely merciful; "God is Charity," infinite Love. The creature is that which IS NOT, and of itself it cannot accomplish anything for eternal life.

Therese had a deep conviction of our spiritual poverty and our fundamental incapacity in the supernatural order. She realized fully that it is God who sanctifies us,[3] and not we ourselves (I Cor., 15:28; Eph., 2:7); that our labor, however necessary, is but a preparation for the work which God Himself desires to do in us. Her whole doctrine, and her Way of Childhood in particular, rest on these principles. That is why she placed as its foundation, *humility, the spirit of spiritual poverty;* and, on the other hand, faithful recourse to God, and *a blind confidence in His merciful Love.*

Therese wants us to acknowledge our imperfection and incapacity; to be content to remain always in that condition; not to be astonished at our falls; to go to God with the heart of a beggar. At the same time, because it is God who accomplishes things, and because He is infinite Love, she wants us to have recourse to Him with boundless confidence, expecting everything from His grace.

Blind confidence is such a striking characteristic of her Little Way that some have seen in it the principal element of her spirituality; but this is not so; it must be affirmed that its chief object is Love.

LOVE IS THE OF THERESIAN SPIRITUALITY

Love is its root principle, the motive power that sustains its activity; love is also its end. Therese tells us that love "preceded her in her childhood"; and that her love increased with the years. After her entrance into Carmel she learned from St. John of the Cross that if we want to hasten our meeting with God here or hereafter, we should multiply our acts of love, and also that the smallest act of love is more useful than the sum of all works.

Moreover, she told Celine, that her Director, who was none other than Jesus, had taught her to do everything for love. This sufficed to make her apply herself to this practice with the utmost ardor. Desiring to love Jesus "passionately," to "love Him as He has loved us," but conscious of her own incapacity, she sought enlightenment from the Holy Spirit. Thus aided she conceived the thought of offering herself as a holocaust to merciful Love, that she might attract God's love into herself and thus love Him with His own love (June 9, 1895).[4] God responded to her generous offering. Therese tells us she felt within her such a fire of love that she could not conceive a love more immense than that which then filled her heart.

Loving God with His own love, she quite naturally was inflamed with apostolic zeal. She desired to love Jesus as much as the martyrs, and the missionaries, as much as all those who are engaged in all the various holy vocations. But how could such a thing be realized? Holy Scripture revealed to her that the Church has a heart. She found there the answer she had been looking for; as she said: "She would be LOVE in the heart of the Church!" When love is sufficiently strong, it can give to God as much as all other vocations. Hence, from that moment, Therese had but one aspiration: "To love, and cause others to love (Him who is) LOVE." This objective she even promised to pursue until the end of the world and to return to earth, after her death, to fulfill it. She also begged Jesus to give her "a legion of little souls" who would cooperate with her.

It is perfectly clear, therefore, that *Therese's fundamental aspiration and the ultimate end of her message can be expressed in that one word: LOVE.* That is why, on the eve of her death, when Sister Genevieve asked her for a parting word, she had replied: "It is LOVE ALONE that counts."

Let us add, however, that *Therese's love was especially directed to Jesus.* She loved the heavenly Father with filial love and extreme tenderness but she loved Jesus in a very special way. Even before entering Carmel she had written: "Jesus! I want to give myself completely to Him! I want to live only for Him . . .[5] to be one with Him." [6] She realized also that "Jesus was in her"; [7] that He "acted in her . . ." and that "it is He who does everything." [8] Jesus is "the divine Elevator who lifts (her) up in His arms and carries (her) to the Heart of God to make (her) holy." [9] He is the "adorable Eagle" whom she loves, and who draws her to Himself.

He is the Word of God who came to this land of exile to suffer and die and draw the souls He has redeemed to the eternal Furnace of the Blessed Trinity. He dwells in inaccessible Light and there at the centre of the Sun of Love she contemplated Him, and kept her eyes fixed on Him to be enraptured by that divine glance; to become a prey of His love that He might imprint on her His divine likeness; [10] and she hoped that one day He would come for her and re-ascend with her to the fiery Centre of Love and plunge her forever in that flaming abyss.[11]

Words like these reveal the ardor of Therese's love and the sublimity of her thought, an aspect of Theresian spirituality which has not received the attention it deserves.

It is through Christ then that she went to the Blessed Trinity, to the Furnace of merciful Love, to God who is Charity. Christ is "our holiness," [12] our model.[13] He is in us and we live by His life; we must allow Him to captivate our faculties so completely that our actions are no longer purely human but are become divine, inspired by the Spirit of love who wants to make us like to Himself.[14]

TO SUM UP: Therese's spirituality, her doctrine of the Way of Childhood can be reduced to three fundamental principles:

1. We must fully recognize our spiritual poverty, our incapacity, and accept this condition.
2. We must have recourse to God with blind and filial confidence, in order that He may accomplish in us what we cannot do by our own powers; for God is our Father; He is Love infinitely merciful.
3. We must believe in Love and apply ourselves to the practice of love.

Love prompted God to create us that we might live His own life and share His eternal blessedness. Love made the Father give us His Son who would restore to us the supernatural goods which we had lost. Love made Jesus, the Son, humble Himself for us, immolate Himself; make us members of His Body, give Himself to us as our food. Love makes the Holy Spirit dwell in our soul, to guide us and form Jesus in us. This we believe.

But to prove our belief we must apply ourselves like

Therese to loving the Triune God in return, loving as Christ loves, as He loves the Father, as He loves His brethren; and we must eagerly desire that others would love Him.

Therese endeavored to act always by practical love; to act every moment under the influence of the Spirit of Jesus; to act no longer prompted by nature or by her own mind and will; and hence she lived a life of abnegation and renunciation. Her doctrine, therefore, was not one of minimal effort; by the very fact that it was the doctrine of the Gospel it had to demand renunciation.

After all, for Therese, "to love means to give everything, and most of all, to give oneself; it is ONLY THE ENTIRE IMMOLATION OF SELF THAT CAN BE CALLED LOVE."

Therese's entire life was a vivid illustration of these words.

References

ABBREVIATIONS OF TITLES FOR THE NOTES

The numbers found throughout the present work refer to notes printed in the back of the book and arranged according to the successive chapters. Our references are identical with those that appear in the French original of which we offer a translation and which was published under the title: FRAN-COIS DE L' IMMACULEE CONCEPTION, O.C.D.: Mieux connaitre Sainte Thérèse de Lisieux, Librairie Saint Paul, 6, rue Cassette, Paris, 1958.

Sum: Summarium des Procès canoniques, edition, S.C. of Rites. Rome, 1920.

Proc. dioc.: Diocesan Process.

Proc. ap.: Apostolic Process.

Proc. ap. Ag.: Deposition of Mother Agnes.

Proc. ap. Gen.: Deposition of Sr. Genevieve.

Proc. dioc. M.S.Cr.: Deposition of Sr. Marie du S. Coeur.

Proc. dioc. M. Trin.: Deposition of Sr. Marie de la Trinité.

M.A.: Manuscript addressed to Mother Agnes: Chapter 1 to 8 of Histoire d' une âme.

M.B.: Manuscript addressed to Sr. Marie du S. Coeur: Chapter 11 of Histoire d' une âme.

M.C.: Manuscript addressed to Mother Marie de Gonzague: Chapter 9 and 10 of Hist. d.a.

f.1.: folio 1.

f.1. v: folio 1 verso.

H.A.: Histoire d' une âme (The Story of a Soul).

C.S.: Conseils et Souvenirs dans H.A. (as found in The Story of a Soul).

C.S. Gen.: Conseils et Souvenirs publiés par Sr. Géneviève. Editions St. Paul.

D.C.L.:   Documentation of The Carmel of Lisieux.

Esp.:   Esprit de Sainte Thérèse de l'Enfant-Jésus.

N.V.:   Novissima Verba.

Souv. ined.:   Souvenirs inédits.

Circ. M. Trin.:   Circulaire nécrologique de S. Marie de la Trinité.

L.:   Letters of St. Therese of the Child Jesus.

Ag. August 1890:   Letter addressed to Mother Agnes on that date.

M.S.C.:   Letter addressed to Sr. Genevieve.

Cel.:   Letter addressed to Celine.

M.G.:   Letter addressed to Marie Guerin.

Mad. G.:   Letter addressed to Mrs. Guerin.

Leon.:   Letter addressed to Sr. Leonie.

Bel.:   Letter addressed to Abbe Belliere.

Roul.:   Letter addressed to Father Rouland.

St. John of the Cross: Works.

St. Teresa of Jesus: Works.

Mgr. Martin: La Petite voie d' enfance spirituelle.

Combes: Intr.:   "Introduction à la spiritualité de S. Thérèse de l'Enfant-Jésus." 2nd ed. Paris, Vrin, 1948.

Combes: Cont. apost.:   Contemplation et apostolat. Paris. Bonne Presse, 1950.

Combes: Le Problème de l'Histoire d'une âme et des oeuvres complètes de sainte Thérèse de Lisieux. Paris. Edit. St. Paul 1950.

Combes: Amour de Jésus chez sainte Thérèse de Lisieux.

Lav.: Laveille: Sainte Thérèse de l'Enfant-Jésus.

Phil: Philipon, O.P.:   Sainte Thérèse de Lisieux. Une voie toute nouvelle.

Pet.: Petitot, O.P.:   Sainte Thérèse de Lisieux. Une renaissance spirituelle. Editions de la Revue des Jeunes. Paris. Desclée.

A.N.: André Noche, S.J. in: La Petite Sainte de Max. Vandermeersch devant la critique et devant les textes. Editions St. Paul, 1950.

INTRODUCTION

1 H.A., I, 5; XI, 217; M.A., f. 2; M.B., f. 3.
2 N.V., July 17.
3 H.A., V, 57; M.A., f. 45 v.
4 H.A., 75; M.A., 45 v.-46 v.
5 H.A., IX, 158; M.C., f. 6.
6 H.A., IX, 158; M.C., f. 5 v.
7 H.V., July 17.
8 M.A., f. 45 v. These lines were omitted in H.A.
9 H.A., VI, 74; M.A., f. 56.
10 H.A., VIII, 118; M.A., f. 69 v.
11 Cel., August 15, 1892.
12 H.A., VI, 59; M.A., f. 56.
13 N.V., July 17. Cf. Combes. Int., 225.
14 N.V., July 17.
15 N.V., July 11.

CHAPTER I

1 N.V., August 3, 1897.
2 Proc. Ap., M. Agnes.
3 H.A., I, 11; M.A., f. 4 v.
4 Lav., 54.
5 Proc. ap. M.S.C.
6 H.A. III, 44; M.A., f. 27.
7 Proc. ap., Agnes or, according to N.V., August 1st: "If you act otherwise, the devil will try to ensnare you in many ways to prevent or spoil the work of God. This is a very important work."
8 N.V., July 17.
9 N.V., August 1st.
10 Proc. ap., Agn.
11 N.V., July 11.
12 H.A., XII, 246.
13 On the same occasion Our Lord said to Mother Prioress: "My daughter, Little Therese is the joy of my heart." Testimony according to a letter of M. Agnes.
14 N.V., September 25.
15 N.V., June 9.
16 N.V., July 12 and August 1st.
17 N.V., July 12.
18 She had already expressed these last words to Father Pichon before her entrance into Carmel. Cf. Combes: S. Thérèse de l'Enfant-Jésus: Contemplation et apostolat, p. 50.
19 N.V., July 17.
20 N.V., July 18.
21 N.V., July 18.
22 C.S., 305; Bel., Febr. 24, 1897.
23 M. Ag., May 28, 1897.
24 N.V., July 12; C.S., 303.
25 N.V., August 1st.
26 N.V., July 27.
27 Vie spir., May 1924.
28 Petitot., p. 125.
29 N.V., September 14.

30 N.V., August 7-Sept. 30.
31 *Living Flame:* Str. I, v. 6.
32 Discourse of February 11, 1923. Autograph Letter to Cardinal Vico (1923).
33 Same Discourse.
34 Same Discourse. Homily for the Canonization Mass, May 17, 1925.
35 Same Homily and Brief of Beatification.
36 Same Homily. Discourse to the pilgrims of Lisieux.
37 Letter to Mgr. Picaud, on the occasion of the Theresian Congress.
38 Discourse of Cardinal Pacelli in Lisieux, July 11, 1937.
39 Pius XII.
40 Combes, Intr., 35.
41 N.V., July 17.
42 N.V., July 17.
43 N.V., August 6.
44 It seems that it was Mgr. Martin who first pointed out the characteristics of spiritual childhood in his book: *La Petite Voie d'enfance spirituelle.* We have drawn inspiration from this work.
45 N.V., July 12 and 17; H.A., 269.
46 D.C.L.
47 Discourse on the heroic nature of the virtues.
48 Circ. M. de la Trinité.
49 N.V., August 20 and 23; C.S., 288.
50 H.A., IX, 153; M.C., f. 2 v.
51 H.A., IX, 153; M.C., f. 2 v.
52 H.A., IV, 55; M.A., f. 32; M.C., f. 3
53 H.A., IX, 154; M.C., f. 2.
54 D.C.L.; N.V.
55 H.A., I, 4; M.A., f. 2.
56 H.A., VIII, 147; MA.A., f. 83. Cf. a text of the Summa of St. Thomas which shows the depth of St. Therese's thought: "In God it is mercy that is supreme, for it is mercy that bestows gifts and supplies for what is wanting in others. Now this belongs especially to a higher being. This is the reason for saying that mercifulness is proper to God; and it is especially in this that He manifests His almighty power. (2, 2; q. 30, a. 4).

CHAPTER II

1 Littleness and humility are synonymous terms; and yet when littleness is mentioned we add to it a note of simplicity, a nuance of sweet self-effacement. A.N., 466.
2 N.V., August 6.
3 H.A., 15; M.A., f. 2 v.; H.A., XI, 217; M.B., f. 3 v.
4 Poem: *J'ai soif d'amour* (I thrist for love).
5 H.A., IX, 153, 154; M.C., f. 2 v.
6 H.A., VII, 121; M.A., f. 71; H.A., VIII, 142; M.A., f. 81 v.
7 Poem: *I thirst for love.*
8 M. du S.-C., May 1888; Ag. end of April, or May 1890 and May 1890.
9 H.A., VII, 128; M.A., f. 74 v.; N.V., August 1st.
10 H.A., IX, 174; M.C., f. 15.
11 N.V., August 13.
12 H.A., IX, 156; M.C., f. 4.
13 H.A., VIII, 141; M.A., f. 80.
14 N.V., August 7.
15 N.V., July 5.
16 Cel., April 26, 1889.
17 N.V., August 7.
18 C.S., 264.
19 Ag. August 1890.
20 N.V., July 5.
21 Ag., August 1890.

22 Bel., July 26, 1897.
23 Ag., May 1897.
24 M.G., July 1890.
25 Proc. Dioc. Gen.
26 Esp., 137; C.S.; 268.
27 N.V., August 7; Poem: *Ma paix et ma joie.*
28 N.V., July 29.
29 Cel., April 25, 1893.
30 Bel., July 26, 1897.
31 Ag., May 1889.
32 Cel., April, 1894.
33 C. Ibid.
34 M. du S.C., Sept. 17, 1896.
35 Bel., Feb. 24, 1897.
36 Gen., June 7, 1897.
37 M.V., July, 1890.
38 Cel., July 6, 1893.
39 M.G., July, 1890.
40 H.A., 312.
41 H.A., XII, 229.
42 C.S., 282.
43 H.A. X, 190; M.C., f. 27.
44 N.V., July 29.
45 Cf. texts mentioned above. Ag., end April or May 1890.
46 C.S., 261; Cel., Feb. 28, 1889.
47 Cel., June 7, 1897.
48 C.S., 275; N.V., August 3.
49 N.V., Sept. 25; H.A., XII, 251.
50 N.V., August 4-Sept. 30.

CHAPTER III

1 N.V., August 6.
2 H.A., XI, 217; M.B., f. 3 v.; M.S.C., Sept. 17, 1896.
3 M.S.C., Sept., 1896.
4 N.V., August 6.
5 Sum. of 1919.
6 H.A., IV, 55; M.A., f. 32.
7 Esp., 203.
8 H.A., VIII, 132; M.A., f. 76.
9 N.V., May 15.
10 N.V., July 12-August 18.
11 C.S., 268.
12 M.G., July, 1890.
13 Souv. ined.
14 Cel., July 6, 1893.
15 H.A., X, 178; M.C., f. 18 v. Poem: *Pourquoi je t'aime, o Marie.*
16 Man. A., f. 32 v.
17 H.A., IX, 170; M.C., f. 16 v.

CHAPTER IV

1 H.A., VIII, 147; M.A., f. 83 v.
2 Rom., VIII, 32.
3 H.A., VIII, 147; M.A., f. 83 v.
4 Roul., May 9, 1897.
5 Ps. 102.
6 Proc. Dioc.-Ag.

7 Roul., May 9, 1897.
8 Proc. M. Trin.
9 M.G., May 3-10, 1889.
10 Proc. M. Trin.
11 M.S.C., Sept. 14, 1896.
12 H.A., IV, 55; M.A., f. 32.
13 H.A., XI, 209; M.B., f. 1 v.
14 H.A., X, 181; M.C., f. 21.
15 H.A., X, 204; M.C., f. 36. These last lines leave the thought in suspense. They were written in pencil on the bed of sickness, but this gives them additional value.
16 Proc. ap., M. Trin.
17 Esp., 81.
18 Proc. ap., M. Trin.
19 Ag., August, 1890.
20 Bel., June 21, 1897.
21 H.A., VIII, 146; M.A., f. 83; H.A., X, 196; M.C., f. 31; Cel., July 18, 1893.
22 C.S., 280; Cel., Oct. 20, 1888; C.S.G., 98.
23 Souv. ined., Esp., 144.
24 Leon., July 12, 1896; Bel., July 18, 1897.
25 C.S., 280.
26 H.A., XII, 246.
27 Cel., July 18, 1893.
28 Ag., April or May, 1890.
29 H.A., VIII, 132; M.A., f. 75 v.
30 Poem: *Pourquoi je t'aime, o Marie.*
31 H.A., XI, 217; M.B., f. 4.
32 Souv. ined., Esp. 145.
33 Ag., August, 1890.
34 Cel., July 6, 1893.
35 II Cor., XII, 10.
36 II Cor., III, 5.
37 Eph., II, 8-9.
38 C.S., 261.
39 Souv. ined., Esp. 17.
40 Cel., April 26, 1894.
41 N.V., June 23.
42 C.S., 300.
43 H.A., V, 74-75; M.A., f. 45.
44 N.V., August 3.
45 II Tim., I, 12.
46 Bel., April 25, 1897. Cel., Oct. 20, 1890. Cf. also: St. Francis de Sales: Sermon for the Purification.
47 Bel., April, 1896.
48 Proc. dioc., Gen.; H.A., X, 192. M.B., f. 1 v.
49 H.A., X, 192; M.C., f. 28.

CHAPTER V

1 M.S.C., Sept. 17, 1896.
2 *The Living Flame,* Str. I. 15, 6. She had written that motto at the bottom of her coat of arms. H.A., 313; M.A., f. 86.
3 I John, IV, 16.
4 H.A., I, 5; M.A., f. 2 v.; H.A., XI, 217; M.B., f. 3 v.
5 H.A., VIII, 147; M.A., f. 83 v.
6 H.A., XI, 208; M.B., f. 1.
7 M.G., July, 1890.
8 Leonie, July 12, 1896.
9 Celine, July 6, 93.

10 This expression is repeated sixteen times in her writings. Etudes et Documents, 6th Year, p. 22.

11 Esprit, p. 9-12.

12 Celine, July 6, 1893.

13 Leon., July 17, 1897.

14 Cel., July 6, 1893.

15 N.V., July 16.

16 Poem: *Un lys au milieu des épines.*

17 H.A., IV, 65; M.A., f. 39.

18 H.A., XI, 210; M.B., f. 1 v.; N.V., August 7; *The Eternal Canticle*; Ag., Jan. 8, 1889.

19 H.A., II, 26; IV, 70; V, 87; M.A., f. 15 v.; 44 v.; f. 52 v.

20 H.A., V, 87; M.A., f. 52.

21 H.A., X, 201; M.C., f. 35.

22 *Canticle of Canticles*, II, 9.

23 N.V., June 7.

24 S.M., du S.C., Sept. 14, 1896.

25 H.A., XII, 226; N.V., May 15.

26 H.A., XI, 219; M.B., f. 4.

27 H.A., IV, 62; M.A., f. 36 v.

28 Cel., Dec. 31, 1889; M.S.C., Sept. 14, 1896; H.A., XI, 219; M.B., f. 4 v.

29 Poem: *Jésus seul.*

30 Ag., March, 1888.

31 Ag., Jan. 7-8, 1889.

32 H.A., VIII, 134; M.A., f. 76 bis.

33 Cel., April 26, 1889.

34 Ag., Sept., 1890; May, 1889.

35 Act of Offering.

36 Proc. ap., Ag.

37 N.V., August 18.

38 Act of Offering.

39 Ag., March, 1888; May, 1890; Cel., July 14, 1889; August 19, 1894.

40 Cel., July 18, 1893; H.A., XI, 218; M.B., f. 4; Proc. dioc., There., S., Aug.; Proc. ap., M. Trin.

41 C.S., 289.

42 H.A., V, 79; M.A., f. 47 v.

43 Cel., August, 1893.

44 Ag., August, 1890.

45 Cel., May, 1890; Jan., 1889.

46 Cel., July 14, 1889.

47 Souv. ined.; Esp. 39.

48 Cel., July 7, 1894.

49 C.S., 296. Thought of St. John of the Cross.

50 Ag., Oct. 8, 1887; Cel., April 26, 1889; Poem: *Vivre d' amour.*

51 Cel., July 6, 1893.

52 Cel., July 23, 1888.

53 Cel., Feb. 28, 1889.

54 Cel., Oct., 1889.

55 Poem: *Pourquoi je t'aime o Marie.*

56 N.V., July 6; H.A., XII, 237.

57 C.S., 266.

58 H.A., I, 15; M.A., f. 2 v.; Proc. ap., Gen.; Agn., Jan. 8, 1889; Leon., April 28, 1895; Bel., July 18, 1897.

59 H.A., IX, 164; M.C., f. 11.

60 H.A., X, 196; M.C., f. 39.

61 H.A., XI 210; M.B., f. 1 v.; Cel., Oct. 20, 1888.

62 Proc. ap., Ag.; M.S.C. Circulaire nécrologique.

63 A.N., 421.
64 A.N., 421.
65 A.N., 513; Proc. ap., Ag., Gen.
66 Proc. M. de la Tr.
67 Proc. ap., Gen.
68 Pet., 43-44.
69 Cel., July 6, 1893.
70 Bel., Dec. 26, 1896.
71 N.V., August 30-Sept. 4.
72 N.V., August 10.
73 Bel., June 9, 1897.
74 Bel., July 18, 1897.
75 Roul., July 14, 1897.
76 C.S., 296.
77 Esp., 47.
78 *La mélodie de Sainte Cécile.*
79 Lav., 253.
80 Doc. Lis.
81 Leon., July 12, 1896; Bel., July 18, 1897; H.A., XII, 246; C.S., 289; Poem: *Jésus seul.*

CHAPTER VI

1 Souv. ined.
2 H.A., IX, 166-168; M.C., f. 12, 13; H.A., X, 191; M.C., f. 27 v.; C.S.
3 C.S., 263.
4 C.S., 274.
5 H.A., IX, 168-170; M.C., f. 15 v.
6 Cel., July 7, 1894.
7 Lettres, Note, p. 370.
8 Lav., 269-271.
9 Proc. dioc., Gen.
10 Sum.
11 H.A., IX, 171; M.C., f. 18 v.
12 H.A., X, 192; N.V., May 9.
13 Matt., V, 42; H.A., IX, 170; M.C., f. 18.
14 H.A., X, 191; M.C., f. 27 v.; 28 v.; H.A., IX, 172; M.C., f. 13 v.-14.
15 Sum., 1919, Lav.
16 C.S., 299.
17 Souv. ined., Esp., 83.
18 Inedit; Proc. ap., Gen.
19 A.N., 308; C.S., 288.
20 H.A., X, 193; M.C., f. 28 v.-29 v.
21 H.A., IX, 169, 173; M.C., f. 16 v.; f. 14 v.-15.
22 N.V., Sept. 6.
23 N.V., August 25.
24 N.V., July 30.
25 Poem: *Vivre d'amour,* Febr., 1896.
26 H.A., IX, 165-167; M.C., f. 11 v.-12 v.
27 H.A., IX, 173; M.C., f. 14; H.A., X, 195; M.C., f. 30
28 H.A., 171; M.C., f. 18.
29 Idem.
30 Sum. Ag.
31 S. Thom. 1, 2, Q. 28, 3-4.
32 H.A.V., 75; M.A., f. 45 v.; Doc. Lis.
33 H.A.V., 75; M.A., f. 45 v.
34 Combes, Introd., 219.
35 She wrote that she made use of every imaginable spiritual means to obtain that

favor. Nevertheless, knowing that she was unable to attain anything by herself alone, she offered the infinite merits of Our Lord Jesus Christ and the treasures of Holy Church. She even had a Mass said for that intention.

36 Souv. ined. Esp. 27; Proc. dioc. Gen.; Lav., 140.
37 H.A., VIII, 118.
38 H.A., VIII, 118; M.A., f. 69 v.
39 Cel., March 12, 1889; August 15, 1892.
40 N.V., July 12-August 18; C.S., 281.
41 H.A., X, 199; M.C., f. 33 v.
42 N.V., June 4.
43 H.A., IX, 158-160; M.C., f. 6-7; Espr., 87. Concerning her works and sacrifices for souls, Cf. also: *Spiritual Poverty* and *Disinterested Love.*
44 Cel., August 15, 1892.
45 Bel., Oct. 21, 1896.
46 Bel., Dec. 26, 1896.
47 N.V., July 12, 17, 18; Roul., July 14, 1897.
48 N.V., August 28.
49 Bel., Feb. 24, 1897.
50 Bel., July 13, 1897.
51 H.A., VI, 95; M.A., f. 56; N.V., August 7; Cel., July 14, 1889; July 18, 1890; August 15, 1892; Oct. 14, 1890; Cel., Oct. 15, 1889; Cel., Dec. 31, 1889.
52 Cel., Oct. 15, 1889.

CHAPTER VII

1 C.S., 266.
2 H.A., I, 10.
3 H.A., I, 14; M.A., f. 8; II, 27; M.A., f. 15 v.
4 H.A., I, 13; M.A., f. 8 v.
5 H.A., V, 75; M.A., f. 45 v.; H.A., VI 113; M.A., f. 68 v.
6 H.A., V, 80; M.A., f. 48 v.
7 M.S.C., Feb. 21, 1888.
8 H.A., VI, 97; M.A., f. 58; Proc. Apost., Ag.
9 H.A., I, 15; M.A., f. 10
10 C.S., 273; Proc. M.S.C.
11 H.A., XII, 230.
12 H.A., VI, 113; M.A., f. 68 v.; H.A., VII, 121; M.A., f. 71; H.A., VIII, 142; M.A., f. 81 v., Ag., Jan. 8, 1889; Cel., March 12, 1889.
13 C.S., 278.
14 H.A., VIII, 134; M.A., f. 77 suppl.
15 "Alpargates" are foot-coverings which were worn by the poor in Spain in the time of St. Therese of Avila; they are still used by Carmelites.
16 H.A., XII, 230; A.N., 379, 390, 339.
17 Proc. ap., M. de la Trin.
18 H.A., XII, 231.
19 Sum.
20 Pet.
21 H.A., VII, 130; M.A., f. 74 v.
22 D.C.L.
23 D.C.L.
24 D.C.L.; Lav., 246; Proc. ap., Gen.
25 H.A., X, 195; M.C., f. 30
26 H.A., X, 196; M.C., f. 30.
27 N.V., July 20.
28 H.A., X, 184; M.C., f. 32 v.
29 Souv. ined., Esp., 39.
30 C.S., 296.
31 Bel., June 9, 1897.

32 Souv. ined., Esp., 50.
33 H.A., VII, 116; M.A., f. 69 v.
34 Cel., Feb. 28, 1889.
35 A.N., 427.
36 H.A., IX, 174; M.C., f. 15.
37 N.V., July 12.
38 H.A., X, 178, 179; M.C., f. 19.
39 C.S., 275.
40 C.S., 276.
41 C.S., 266; N.V., Aug. 8.
42 C.S., 282.
43 N.V., May 28.
44 C.S., 274.
45 H.A., XI, 218; M.B., f. 4 v.

CHAPTER VIII

1 Combes, Intr. à la Spir., 2nd edit., p. 243.
2 H.A., VIII, 145; M.A., f. 81; 82 v.-83; *Spir. Cant.* Str. 28.
3 N.V., Sept. 25.
4 N.V., June 15.
5 Bel., June 21, 1897.
6 Cel., Sept. 23, 1890; Roul., Nov. 1, 1896.
7 Cel., 1893.
8 N.V., June 10; July 12; August 14.
9 N.V., July 6.
10 Ag., March, 1888.
11 Roul., Nov. 1, 1896.
12 N.V., July 7.
13 H.A., XI, 209; M.B., f. 1.
14 H.A., XII, 236; H.A., IX, 164; M.C., f. 10.
15 H.A., IX, 161; M.C., f. 7 v.; Inedit.
16 N.V., Sept. 4.
17 Leon., July 17, 1897.
18 N.V., 21-26; May 28-Sept. 4.
19 H.A., IX, 161; M.C., f. 8.
20 N.V., August 18.
21 N.V., July 29-August 28.
22 N.V., June 4.
23 N.V., June 10.
24 H.A., XII, 235.
25 N.V., July 23.
26 Poem: *Mon Chant d'aujourd'hui.*
27 Matt., VI, 34.

CHAPTER IX

1 N.V., July 4.
2 Roul., May 9, 1897.
3 N.V., August 3.
4 H.A., X, 188; M.C., f. 25.
5 H.A., X, 199; M.C., f. 33 v.
6 H.A., X, 199, 203; M.C., f. 33 v.; 36.
7 N.V., August 4.
8 N.V., August 4.
9 N.V., June 4.
10 C.S., 287.
11 Esp., 200.
12 N.V., July 7-11; C.S., 301.

13 Ag., May, 1890.
14 Espr., 167-168-183; N.V., June 4.
15 N.V., Sept. 24.
16 C.S., 246.
17 N.V., August 13.
18 N.V., June 4, August 10, Sept. 11.
19 *Ascent of Carmel*, II, IX.
20 Esp., 167; Souv. ined.; H.A., XII, 246.
21 H.A., X, 196; M.C., f. 31.
22 Cel., April 25, 1893; Leon., July 12, 1896; H.H., X, 179; M.C., f. 19 v.
23 H.A., IV, 55; M.A., f. 32.
24 Leon., August 13, 1893.
25 Leon., May 22, 1894.
26 Leon., July 12, 1896; H.A., VIII, 142; M.A., f. 41 v.
27 Ag., Jan. 7-8, 1889.
28 C.S., 273.
29 H.A., VII, 128; M.A., f. 74.
30 A.N., 521; The Way of Perf., ch. 43 and 25.
31 H.A., XII, 231.
32 N.V., August 3.
33 Bel., June 21, 1897.
34 N.V., August 3.
35 N.V., August 31; N.V., July 23.
36 N.V., August 1, Proc. dioc. Ag.
37 A.N., 520; Proc. Ag.
38 Lav., 246.
39 *A l'Ecole de Sainte Thérèse*, p. 8.
40 H.A., IX; 161; M.C., f. 7 v.
41 C.S., 248; N.V., August 26.
42 Espr.
43 Leon., July 12, 1896.
44 H.A., XII, 250; C.S., 284; H.A., XI, 218; M.V., f. 4 v.; Sum.
45 H.A., X, 182; M.C., f. 21 v.
46 H.A., IX, 152, 156; M.C., f. 2, 4; Bel., April 25, 1897; H.A., VIII, 142; M.A., f. 81 v.
47 Cel., July 6, 1893.
48 Espr., 32.
49 N.V., Sept. 25
50 H.A., XII, 234.
51 M. Ag. and Sum; A.N., 328, 330, 427.
52 M. Ag., Sum.
53 H.A., VIII, 138.
54 Bel., July 26, 1897.

CHAPTER X

1 Therese wrote these lines in 1895. At the end of the same year, or at the beginning of 1896, she received a new light on that subject. God revealed to her that there are various "families" of souls; some being called to honor one divine perfection, others another. To her God had assigned His infinite mercy and it is through this attribute that she had to consider all the others. H.A., I, 4-7; M.A., f. 1-3.
2 H.A., VIII, 147; M.A., f. 83 v.
3 H.A., VIII, 147; M.A., f. 84.
4 H.A., XII, 226; N.V., July 7.
5 H.A., VIII, 148; A., f. 84.
6 N.V., May 15, 1897.
7 Ag., May 28, 1897.
8 H.A., XI, 219; M.B., f. 4 v.

9 H.A., X, 202; M.C., f. 35.
10 Circ. M. Trin.
11 H.A., XI, 216, 221; M.B., f. 3 v., f. 5 v.
12 C.S., 282.
13 H.A., VIII, 146; M.A., f. 83.
14 H.A., XII, 224.
15 *Spir. Cant.*, Str. 9; *Living Flame*, Str. 1, 2.
16 M. Agnes in the *"Petit Catéchisme de l'Acte d'offrande; Combes, Introduction,* 2nd ed., p. 185. S. Genevieve in *Rivista di vita sp.*, art. of Father Gabriel de Ste. M.-Mad., July 1950; Circ. M. Ag. (43).
17 H.A., XII, 224.

CHAPTER XI

1 H.A., XI, 213, ffw.; M.B., f. 3 v.
2 N.V., July 22.
3 H.A., XI, 219.
4 Let.: M.S.C., Sept. 14, 1896.
5 Ag., August, 1890.
6 Cel., Oct. 15, 1889.
7 N.V., July 27.
8 N.V., Sept. 29.
9 N.V., July 22.

CHAPTER XII

1 Cel., Jan.; Feb. 28, 1889.
2 Cel., July 23, 1888, Souv. ined.
3 Ag., March, 1888; Jan., 1889; Cel., July 14, 1889; July 7, 1894.
4 N.V., July 6.
5 Bel., June 9, 1897.
6 Cel., April 26, 1889; Leon., Jan., 1895. Esp.
7 Cel., Jan.; Feb. 28, 1889; Leon., Jan., 1895, Mad. Guérin, Nov. 18, 1888.
8 Cel., July 14, 1889.
9 H.A., IX, 160; M.C., f. 7.
10 Cel., August 2, 1893; July 7, 1894.
11 Cel., Oct. 15, 1889.
12 Sum.
13 M. du S.C., Jan. 9, 1889.
14 Cel., July 28, 1888; July 18, 1890.
15 Ag., March, 1888.
16 Cel., July 23, 1888.
17 Hebr. IX, 22.
18 Col., I, 24.
19 Cel., July, 1891.
20 Cel., August 15, 1892.
21 Agnes, March, 1888.
22 Souv. ined.; Esp. 27; H.A., IV, 55; M.A., f. 10.
23 Bel., July 13, 1897.
24 H.A., I, 18; M.A., f. 12.
25 H.A., VIII, 145; M.A., f. 83.
26 Combes. Laveille.
27 H.A., III, 41-44; M.A., f. 25 v.; 27.
28 H.A., III, 45-46; M.A., f. 27-30.
29 H.A., III, 50; M.A., f. 30 v.; H.A., VI, 95; M.A., f. 56 v. Cf. also Combes: Intr., 462; Lav.; Piat.
30 H.A., IV, 61; M.A., f. 36.
31 Souv. ined.; Doc. Lis.; H.A., IV, 62; M.A., f. 36.
32 Imit., III, c. 26, 3; H.A., IV, 62; N.V., July 31.

33 H.A., IV, 62; M.A., f. 36.
34 C.S., 267; N.V., July 31.
35 H.A., IV, 65; M.A., f. 39.
36 H.A., IV, 67; M.A., f. 39 v.
37 H.A., IV, 70; M.A., f. 44; Lav. 130.
38 H.A., V, 73; M.A., f. 44 v.
39 N.V., July 31.
40 H.A., V, 73-75; M.A., f. 44-45.
41 H.A., VIII, 137; M.A., f. 80 v.; Combes: Intr.
42 H.A., V, 74; M.A., f. 44 v.
43 H.A., V, 73; M.A., f. 44 v.
44 Proc. dioc.; Sum Cel.; Piat, 265; A.N., 291-292.
45 H.A., V, 75; M.A., f. 45 v.
46 H.A., IV, 70; M.A., f. 43.
47 H.A., I, 12; M.A., f. 6.
48 H.A., III, 42; M.A., f. 26.
49 H.A., V, 81; M.A., f. 49.
50 H.A., V, 85-87; M.A., f. 52.
51 H.A., VI, 107; M.A., f. 64.
52 H.A., VI, 92, 107; M.A., f. 55 v.
53 H.A., VI, 113; M.A., f. 68 v.
54 H.A., VII, 118; M.A., f. 69 v.
55 N.V., July 25; Bel., July 13, 1897; Cel., May 8, 1888.
56 H.A., VIII, 134; M.A., f. 77.
57 Cel., July 18, 1894.
58 N.V., July 12.
59 A.N., 391-393; H.A., IX, 156-157; M.C., f. 4 v.
60 H.A., XII, 233.
61 N.V., May 28.
62 N.V., August 15, 19, 23.
63 N.V., June 15, August 17 and 29.
64 H.A., XII, 240.
65 N.V., July 8, 12.
66 N.V., August 22.
67 Lav., 381.
68 N.V., August 3.
69 N.V., August 18.
70 N.V., August 18.
71 N.V., August 4.
72 N.V., August 3 and 25.
73 Pet. 283.
74 N.V., August 19.
75 N.V., August 22 and 23.
76 N.V., August 24.
77 N.V., August 31.
78 N.V., August 25; Sept. 24, 25.
79 N.V., Sept. 26; C.S., 247.
80 Lav. 387.
81 C.S. 252.
82 N.V., Sept. 29.
83 N.V., Sept. 30.
84 A.N., 401. Concerning the facts that follow, cf. also A.N., 385, 395, 397, 401, 403, 406; H.A., X, 191; M.C., f. 27 v.
85 A.N. 380.
86 Sum.
87 These words are the literary expression of a soldier who was taking part in a military assault.

88 Cf. A.N., 386, 399-400.
89 Sum. Y. de N.
90 N.V., May 18.
91 Sum.-Pet. 85.
92 This was also the opinion of Mgr. Laveille, 300; of Mgr. Martin, in: *La Petite Sainte Thérèse de Max. Vander Meersch*, 183; of Sr. Genevieve in her: *Conseils et souvenirs*, 165.
93 A.N., 389; Pet. 245.
94 H.A., IX, 162; M.C. f. 8 v.
95 Cel. July 18, 1894.
96 Lav. 183.
97 H.A. VII, 117; M.A., f. 70.—Kissing the floor is a penance imposed when one receives a reprimand.—*Alleged* faults.
98 Ag., Jan. 9, 1889.
99 Sum.
100 Archives of the Carmel Convent of Tours.
101 Sum.
102 Sum.
103 H.A., IX, 152-153, 163-164; M.C., f. 2, 10.
104 Sum.
105 N.V., Sept. 22.
106 Circular; Lav. 186.
107 Cf. Lettres 300, note 3.
108 Lav. 235; Pet. 251.
109 H.A., VII, 117; M.A., f. 69 v.
110 Ag., Jan. 8, 1889.
111 Gen., July 22, 1897.
112 Ag., May, 1889.
113 H.A., X, 191-192; M.C., f. 28.
114 A.N., 313; H.A., XII, 229.
115 A.N., 317, 320, 311, 312; H.A., IX (172); M.C., f. 14. Nevertheless, they did not deserve to be branded with the note of meanness which some have attributed to them.
116 A.N., 344-347.
117 Sum. and A.N., 318, 328, 330.
118 H.A., IX, 162; M.C. f. 8 v.
119 Pet. 252.
120 H.A., XII, 225; Lav. 194.
121 Lav. 194.
122 N.V., July 20.
123 Pet. 254. Lettres 153, note.
124 H.A., IX, 163; M.C., f. 10; N.V., May 15.
125 Cel., Feb. 9, 1889.
126 H.A., VII, 126; M.A., f. 73.
127 Cel., Feb. 9, 1889.
128 H.A., VII, 126; M.A., f. 73.
129 H.A., IV, 80; M.A., f. 48.
130 H.A., XI, 208; M.B., f. 1.
131 N.V., 24, 29, and 30th of Sept.
132 H.A., XII, 238.
133 Pet. 280; N.V., August 28; Sept. 24.
134 H.A., XII, 238; N.V., August 25.
135 Lettres 191; Lav. 382.
136 H.A., IX, 161; M.C., f. 7; N.V., July 27.
137 N.V., August 31.
138 N.V., Sept. 30.
139 Proc. dioc. Ag.

140 Proc. apost. Gen.; M.A., f. 85 v.
141 M. Trin., June 6, 1897.
142 *Living Flame*, Str. I, v. 6; N.V., July 27.
143 *Living Flame*, Str. I, v. 6.
144 N.V., June 4. Cf. Confidential words of Sr. Genevieve in *Rivista di vita spirituale*, July, 1950, art. by Father Gabriel de Ste Marie-Madeleine.
145 N.V., August 15.
146 Therese has confessed that she had some apprehension about this. N.V., Sept. 11.
147 N.V., August 15.
148 N.V.; Sum.; C. and S. of Sr. Genevieve.
149 N.V., July 31; M.A., f. 70.
150 N.V., July 25.
151 Esprit, 117, 118; N.V., August 22.
152 Cel., May 8, 1888.
153 M.S.C., January 7 or 8, 1889.
154 Ag., Jan. 8, 1889.
155 N.V., 21-26th of May; H.A., XII, 234; H.A., IX, 160; M.C., f. 7.
156 Cel., 1893.
157 Celine, Feb. 28, 1889.
158 Celine, Apr. 26, 1889.
159 Cel., Jan. 7, 1889.
160 Cel., Feb. 28, 1889.
161 H.A., XII, 247.
162 H.A., IX, 156; M.C., f. 4 v.
163 N.V., July 30.
164 H.A., VI, 109; M.A., f. 65.
165 N.V., May 29.
166 Cel., March 12, 1889.
167 M.S.C., Sept. 17, 1896.
168 Cel., April 4, 1889.
169 Cel., April 4, 1889; S.M.S.C., Sept. 7, 1890.
170 A.N., 482.
171 Roul., July 14, 1897; Bel., July 18, 1897.
172 Cel., Apr., 1889; N.V., August 25.
173 Bel., Dec. 26, 1896.
174 N.V., June 14.
175 H.A., XII, 236; N.V., August 19.
176 H.A., VII, 118; M.A., f. 69 v.
177 N.V., August 11.
178 Combes: Intr. 432.

CHAPTER XIII

1 H.A., I, 18; M.A., f. 12.
2 H.A., I, 17; 24; M.A., f. 11 v.
3 H.A., II, 24; M.A., f. 14 v.
4 H.A., II, 25; M.A., f. 14 v.
5 H.A., II, 35; M.A., f. 22.
6 H.A., VI, 97, 98; M.A., f. 58.
7 H.A., IV, 54; M.A., f. 31 v.-32.
8 H.A., III, 39; M.A., f. 23.
9 Gal., II, 20.
10 H.A., IV, 62; M.A., f. 36 v.
11 H.A., IV, 68; M.A., f. 40 v.
12 Proc. dioc. Gen.; H.A., IV, 62-63; M.A., f. 36 v.-37.
13 Pet. 71. However, the chaplain and Sister St. Francis de Sales understood very soon that Therese was being carried away by her contemplative spirit.
14 H.A., IV, 63; M.A., f. 37.

15 H.A., V, 78; M.A., f. 47. Combes, Intr. 62.

16 H.A., V, 79; M.A., f. 47.

17 At that time, Therese was not yet eleven years old. Combes: *Saint Therese of the Child-Jesus;* Cont. et apost. 24.

18 The exact sequence of the events we have recorded is not certain. Cf. Combes: Intr. 241 ffw.; Lav., 107, 118; Pet., 68; H.A., IV, 57.

19 H.A., IV, 57; M.A. f. 33.

20 H.A., V, 81; M.A., f. 49.

21 H.A., III, 41; M.A., f. 25 v.

22 H.A., V, 79-80; M.A., f. 48.

23 H.A., V, 79-80; M.A., f. 48.

24 H.A., V, 87; M.A., f. 52.

25 H.A., V, 87; M.A., f. 52. Similar thoughts are found in the life of St. Therese-Marguerite Redi.

26 D.L. and M.A., f. 48 v.

27 H.A., VII, 117; M.A., f. 69 v.-70; Cel., July 1888.

28 Ag., Jan. 8, 1889.

29 Ag., Jan. 9, 1889.

30 Ag., Jan. 7-8, 1889.

31 Cel., July 18, 1893.

32 H.A., VII, 127; M.A., f. 73 v.

33 H.A., VIII, 140; M.A., f. 79 v.

34 Ag., Sept., 1890.

35 Ibid.

36 H.A., VIII, 133; M.A., f. 76.

37 M.S.C., Sept. 3, 1890; Cel., August 2, 1893.

38 Cel., August 2, 1893.

39 H.A., X, 1896; M.C., f. 31.

40 H.A., IX, 159; M.C., f. 6 v.-7; N.V., August 8.

41 H.A., IX, 161; M.C., f. 7 v. One such light was the apparition, in a dream, of Venerable Mother Ann of Jesus. Therese said that when she awoke she felt that there was a heaven and that it was inhabited by souls that loved her.

42 N.V., August 28.

43 H.A., IX, 161; M.C., f. 7 v.

44 H.A., IX, 156; M.C., f. 4 v.

45 Pet. 268.

46 According to the terminology of St. John of the Cross, the term "sense" designates not only the external and internal senses but also discursive reason which cannot function without the help of the imagination and the sense memory. P. Chrysogono: Summa. asc. et myst., 215.

47 P. Chrysogono, op. cit., 222, 283; P. Gabriel: *St. John of the Cross, Mystical Doctor,* 82. (French Edition).

48 H.A., IX, 159; M.C., f. 7 v. No doubt the spiritual dryness which Therese experienced in her mental prayer was partly due to her physical exhaustion; but even this was permitted by God, for it was in line with His plan for the purification and sanctification of her soul.

49 H.A., IX, 158; M.C., f. 6. She said on another occasion that she was then suffering for a soul which the devil did not wish to release from his grip. H.A., XII, 239.

50 H.A., IX, 158-161; M.C., f. 7

51 Doc. Lis.

52 H.A., X, 188; M.C., f. 25 v.; Ag., Sept., 1890; Cel., July 18, 1893.

53 Doc. Lis.; Proc. Gen.; Philip. 232.

54 Doc. Lis.; H.A., VII, 127; M.A., f. 73 v.; H.A., VIII, 146; M.A., f. 83.

55 H.A., VIII, M.A., f. 83.

56 Cel., July 7, 1894.

57 Souv. inedits.

58 H.A., VIII, 132; M.A., f. 75 v.

59 Castl., 6th Mans., c. 5.

60 N.V., July 11; H.A., XII, 226.

61 H.A., XII, 226; N.V., July 7.

62 *Life*, XXIX.

63 *Living Flame*, Str. II, 152; trad. Greg. p. 47; trad. Cyprien 997.

64 Cel., August 15, 1892; Ag., Jan. 9, 1889. The term "sentiment" is used here in the sense of "intimate awareness."

65 M.A., f. 75 v., 76.

66 H.A., VIII, 146; XI, 208; M.A., f. 83 v.; M.B. f. 1.

67 N.V., Sept. 24.

68 Ag., August, 1890.

69 Cel., Oct. 20, 1890.

70 H.A., IX, 159; M.C. f. 6 v.

71 M.S.C., Sept. 17, 1896.

72 H.A., X, 204; M.C. f. 36 v.

73 H.A., XI, 221; M.V. f. 5 v.

74 H.A., XI, 209; M.B. f. 1 v.

75 N.V., Sept. 25.

76 H.A., XII, 244.

77 However, this loving knowledge can at the same time cast its light on the concepts that are in the understanding. In such a case the soul will be enlightened simultaneously in a way that is distinct and in another that is not distinct. Cf. *Riviste di vita spirituale;* P. Benjamin de la Ste Trinité: "The action of God in St. Therese of the Child Jesus." Cf. also: P. Gabriel de Ste M.-Mad.: The contemplative Prayer of St. Therese of the Child Jesus. *Etudes et Documents de Lisieux,* April and July, 1953.

78 H.A., V, 81; M.A., f. 48 v.

79 H.A., VIII, 132, 146; M.A., f. 76; f. 83; H.A., X, 183; M.C., f. 22 v.

80 It seems that she asked for this on two occasions: at the beginning of May, 1884 and on October 23, 1887. Combes: Intr. 63-71.

81 H.A., VII, 119; M.A., f. 70.

82 H.A., VIII, 136; M.A., f. 80 v.

83 H.A., VII, 120; M.A., f. 71; Proc. ap. Gen.

84 Souv. ined. Regarding the value of spiritual direction, cf. Phil. 184, 246.

85 St. John of the Cross: *Spir. Cant.*, Str. XXVIII, Section 2-XXX; transl. of P. Cyprien, edited by P. Lucien.

86 *Int. Castle*, VII Mans., c. 2 and 3.

87 *Life*, c. XXIX.

88 H.A., XII, 227.

89 H.A., XII, 226.

90 *Cant.*, II, 9.

91 H.A., XII, 239.

92 H.A., VIII, 148; M.A., f. 84.

93 H.A., VII, 126; M.A., f. 73 v.; H.A., IX, 160; M.C., f. 7; H.A., XII, 235.

94 H.A., VIII, 146; M.A., f. 83 v.

95 H.A., IX, 152, 156; M.C., f. 2, f. 4; N.V., August 4; Sept. 30; Pet. 125.

96 *Living Flame*, Str. I, 56.

97 *Int. Cast.*, VII Mans., c. 2, 348; C., 3, 359.

98 Ibid., c. 4, 365.

99 Ibid., c. 4.

100 *Cast.*, VII Mans., c. 4.

101 *Spir. Cant.*, Chevalier, Str. 29; Cyprien-Lucien, Str. 31; Gregoire, Str. 29, 30.

102 Cf. *Ephemerides Carmeliticae*, 1949. "From the Sacred Heart to the Trinity," fasc. II, by P. Gabriel de Ste Marie-Mad.

103 H.A., X, 158; M.C., f. 6.

104 *Spir. Cant.*, Str. 26, 28.

105 Doc. Lis.

106 N.V., July 7.

107 *Way of Perf.*, c. 19, 20; *Cast.*, V M., c. 3.

108 *Way of Perf.*, c. 22.

109 *Dark Night*, c. 9.

110 H.A., X, 203; M.C., f. 36.

111 D.L.

112 Testimony of M. Agnes at Apost. Proc.

113 Regarding Therese's prayer and methods of mental prayer, cf. Combes: Int. c. VII. Phil., 296, 298.

CHAPTER XIV

1 Several poems are consecrated exclusively to Jesus. They bear the titles: *Vivre d'amour; Jésus, mon Bien-Aimé, rappelle-toi; La rose effeuillée; Jésus seul* (A Life of Love; Jesus, my Beloved, Remember; Scattered Rose Petals; Jesus alone). Note the use of the familiar "toi."

2 H.A., I, 7; M.A., f. 3 v.

3 H.A., IV, 59-61; M.A., f. 35, 36.

4 Cel., Oct. 15, 1889.

5 H.A., IV, 65; M.A., f. 39 v.; Ag., Jan. 9, 1889.

6 *A Lily among Thorns.*

7 Cel., Oct. 20, 1888.

8 Cel., Oct. 13, 1889.

9 H.A., VIII, 146; M.A., f. 83 v.

10 Cel., July 6, 1893.

11 H.A., VIII, 132, 146; M.A., f. 76, 83 v.

12 M. Trin.

13 Leon., July 16, 1897.

14 Cel., Apr. 26, 1892.

15 H.A., VIII, 134; M.A., f. 76 bis.

16 *To the Sacred Heart.*

17 M.G., July, 1890.

18 H.A., IX, 165-173; M.C., f. 11 v.

19 H.A., XII, 244.

20 Ag., May, 1889; Cel., Sept. 23, 1890; H.A., XI, 213; M.B., f. 3 v.

21 I Cor., III, 23.

22 *Life of Love*, 1895.

23 Cel., July, 1894.

24 H.A., VII, 121; M.A., f. 71.

25 Lettres, 106.

26 Isaias, 53, 1-5; Cel., July 18.

27 N.V., August 5.

28 Cel., Apr. 4, 1889.

29 Cel., Oct. 19, 1892.

30 Ag., Sept. 4 or 5, 1890.

31 H.A., VII, 121; M.A., f. 71.

32 Ag., May, 1890; Cel., July 7, 1894; M.V., August 5.

33 Cel., July 18, 1890; H.A., VII, 121; M.A., f. 71.

34 Ag., May, 1890.

35 Therese had chosen the name of Mary of the Holy Face for Celine. The latter, after her entrance into Carmel bore this name until she received the habit.

36 Cel., Oct. 22, 1889.

37 H.A., VII, 120; M.A., f. 71.

38 Ag., Sept. 1890.

39 H.A., VIII, 140; M.A., f. 79 v.

40 Pet., 44; Lav., 256; It seems that the Saint would have liked to preserve the Sacred Species within herself. At least, it was in this sense that her sisters interpreted her words in the Act of Offering: "Remain in me as in the Tabernacle."

41 H.A., X, 201, 305; M.C., f. 34 v. Act of Offering.

42 H.A., XI, 216-219; M.B., f. 3 v., 4 v.
43 C.S., 241.
44 Souv. ined.
45 C.S., 270; N.V., July 15.
46 H.A., XII, 243.
47 I. Cor., I, 23.
48 John, XIV, 26.
49 I. Cor., I, 30.
50 John, XIV, 16.

CHAPTER XV

1 J. H. Nicolas: *Connaitre Dieu*, 217.
2 Doc. Lis.
3 P. Louis de St. Thérèse, O.C.D. in: *La Vie Mariale de Ste. Thérèse de l'Enfant Jésus*, and Abbé Henri Martin.
4 H.A., VI, 95; M.A., f. 56 v.-57.
5 H.A., VI, 100; M.A., f. 59 v.-60.
6 H.A., VII, 134; M.A., f. 77.
7 N.V., August 23.
8 N.V., August 20 and 23.
9 *Why I love you, O Mary.*
10 H.A., VI, 95; M.A., f. 56 v.-57.
11 Souv. ined., Espr., 74.
12 M.C., f. 26.
13 N.V., June 4.
14 N.V., August 29.
15 C.S., 295; Sum.
16 N.V., Sept. 5; Sum.; M. Trin.
17 N.V., June 4.
18 N.V., August 19.
19 N.V., August 15.
20 N.V., June 4; July 29.
21 Doc. Lis.
22 N.V., July 8.
23 H.A., XII, 431.
24 H.A., XII, 238.
25 Sum. M. Trin.
26 Cel., Oct. 19, 1892; N.V., August 23.
27 N.V., July 11.
28 Rom., VIII, 9.

CHAPTER XVI

1 Pet., 169.
2 Ps. 118, 100.
3 H.A., X, 155, 156; M.C., f. 4.
4 Lav., 276; Esp., 99.
5 H.A., X, 185; M.C., f. 23 v.
6 C.S., 298.
7 C.S., 298.
8 H.A., X, 181; M.C., f. 21.
9 Pet., 232.
10 H.A., X, 184; M.C., f. 23.
11 D.C.L.; Combes, Cont. et Apost.—For an account of the manner in which Therese directed her novices, cf. Chapter X of *The Story of a Soul*. Also p. 298 of *Conseils et Souvenirs*. There is also a Letter to Celine, July 18, 1894. Cf. Mgr. Laveille, Chapt. X. Cf. also, P. Victor de la Vierge, O.C.D. *Réalisme spirituel de Sainte Thérèse de Lisieux.*

12 C.S., 283, 263.
13 Pet., 224.
14 H.A., XII, 232.
15 H.A., X, 180; M.C., f. 21; Pet. 226.
16 A.N., 375; Pet. 232.
17 Pet., 231; N.V., August 9 and 19.
18 Poem: *Mes armes.*
19 Pet., 233.—Therese had both prudence and discretion; these are essential for the rare occasions on which a religious would be justified in intervening in a similar manner.
20 Pet., 167.

RESUME

1 Pius XI, Disc., Febr. 11, 1923; Homily of the Mass of Canon.; Benedict XV, Disc., August 14, 1921.
2 Stanislas Fumet: "Une Sainte parmi Nous."
3 I Cor., 15, 28; Eph., 2, 7.
4 This does not exclude the fact that Therese also offered herself to repay God for the ingratitude of those who refuse to love Him. Cf. Ch. X, Act of Oblation.
5 Ag., March 1888.
6 Cel., October 20, 1888.
7 M.A., f., 76; 83 v.
8 Cel., July 6, 1893.
9 M.A., f. 32; M. C., f. 2-3.
10 Cel., April 1892.
11 S. M. du S. C., September 14, 1896.
12 M.A., f. 32.
13 Cel., April 1892.
14 C. S., 290.

Bibliography

Readers who desire to examine the original French texts quoted in the present work will find the necessary references in the work from which the present translation has been made, namely,

FRANCOIS DE L' IMMACULEE CONCEPTION, O. C. D., *Mieux connaitre Sainte Thérèse de Lisieux,* Librairie Saint-Paul, 6, rue Cassette, Paris VI. 1958.

SOURCES:

ANDRE NOCHE, S. J. La Petite Sainte de Max. Vandermeersch devant la critique et devant les textes. Edittions St. Paul, 1950.

CIRCULAIRE NECROLOGIQUE de Sr. Marie de la Trinité.

COMBES, Amour de Jésus chez sainte Thérèse de Lisieux.

COMBES, Contemplation et apostolat.

COMBES, Introduction à la spiritualité de S. Thérèse de l' Enfant -Jésus. 2nd ed. Paris. Vrin, 1948.

COMBES, Le Probléme de l' Histoire d' une ame et des oeuvres complètes de sainte Thèrése de Lisieux. Paris, Edit. St. Paul, 1950.

CONSEILS ET SOUVENRIS dans l' Histoire d' une ame.

CONSEIL SET SOUVENIRS publiés par Sr. Geneviève. Edit. St. Paul.

DESPOSITION de Mère Agnès

DESPOSITION de Sr. Geneviève

DESPOSTION de Sr. Marie du S. Coeur

DESPOSITION de Sr. Marie de la Trinité.

DOCUMENTATION du Carmel de Lisieux.

ESPRIT DE SAINTE THERESE DE L' ENFANT JESUS.

SAINT JOHN OF THE CROSS, Works.

LAVEILLE MGR., Sainte Thérèse de l' Enfant-Jésus.

LETTERS TO : 1. Sr. Agnès
              2. Abbé Bellière

3. Sr. Céline
4. Sr. Geneviéve
5. Madame Guérin
6. Marie Guérin
7. Sr. Marie du S. Coeur
8. Sr. Léonie
9. Pére Rouland

LETTERS DE SAINTE THERESE DE L' ENFANT JESUS

MANUSCRIPTS : 1. Addressed to Mother Agnes: Chapter 1 to 8 of Histoire d' une ame.
2. Addressed to Sr. Marie du S. of Coeur : Chapter 11 of Hist. d. a.
3. Addressed to Mother Marie de Gonzague: Chapter 9 and 10 of H. d. a.

MARTIN MGR., La Petite voie d' enfance spirituelle.

NOVISSIMA VERBA

PETITOT, O. P. Sainte Thérèse de Lisieux. Une renaissance spirituelle.

PHILIPON, O. P., Sainte Thérèse de Lisieux. Une voie toute nouvelle.

SOUVENIRS INEDITS.